Books by Ronald Gross and Paul Osterman

High School

Individualism

The New Professionals

Books by Ronald Gross

Radical School Reform
(with Beatrice Gross)

The Arts and the Poor
(with Judith Murphy)

Learning by Television
(with Judith Murphy)

Pop Poems

The Teacher and the Taught: Education
in Theory and Practice from Plato to
Conant

The Revolution in the Schools
(with Judith Murphy)

The New Professionals

EDITED BY

Ronald Gross

AND

Paul Osterman

Simon and Schuster

New York

First printing
SBN 671–21313–X
Library of Congress Catalog Card Number: 72–83901
Designed by Irving Perkins
Manufactured in the United States of America

The editors would like to acknowledge the invaluable editorial counsel and assistance of the following people: Judith Alexander, Carol Florio, Richard L. Grossman, and Gloria Steinem.

Our greatest debt, however, is to Beatrice Gross, for her imagination and wisdom throughout.

This book grew out of the work of The Free Learning Project, an exploration of how adults can take command of their lives within and outside of institutions.

Contents

Introduction

All professions are conspiracies against the laity.
                              —GEORGE BERNARD SHAW

*I had the idea that one could find work to do and that
being able to work was what was needed. Well, we
have disagreed, America and I, about the nature of
the work one ought to do, yet on the whole I think I
was right back then. You must find work to do in your
country. . . .*

                              —JAMES HERNDON

SHAW'S CYNICISM crackles, and Herndon's
hopefulness is dark and cautious, but together their observa-
tions bracket a range of impulses, aspirations and passions
constituting a new experience for people in the professions today—especially for young people just starting their working
lives. Virtually every one of the major professions is deeply
troubled, and most are in the process of renewal, reconstruction, reform and, occasionally, revolution. Regularly, professional meetings are disrupted, pecking orders challenged, elite
leadership confronted. In hospitals, schools, churches, corporations, universities, political parties, law offices, laboratories
and newspapers widening cracks appear in the solid front
which used to be all the public saw. Dissident groups will not
be squelched. Colleague confronts colleague over issues which
transcend the heretofore inviolable ethos of professional solidarity.

9

The failure of the professions has become increasingly apparent in the last decade, as we have been forced to recognize the inequities and hypocrisies at the center of our social and political life. The professions justify themselves as organized efforts to assure that society's vital needs are met: the need for justice, for health, for knowledge, for spiritual guidance, for communication, for governance, for the creation and maintenance of a physical environment, for the socially responsible provision of goods and services.

But over the past ten years we have been forced to recognize that something is amiss. Vital needs are unmet, and the organized professions seem perversely or arrogantly opposed to change. Vast increases in funding for medicine, education, law and welfare have been accompanied by declines in service to those most in need.

The young have learned this lesson almost too well. Paul Goodman, five years ago, taught a course on "Professionalism" at the New School for Social Research in New York City. Goodman brought in professionals to explain "the obstacles that stood in the way of honest practice, and their own life experiences in circumventing them." These professionals were rejected by the students, who called them "liars, finks, mystifiers, or deluded." * Goodman realized that the students "did not believe in the existence of real professions at all; professions were concepts of repressive society and 'linear thinking.' I asked them to envisage any social order they pleased . . . and wouldn't there be engineers who know about materials and stresses and strains? Wouldn't people get sick and need to be treated? Wouldn't there be problems of communication? No, they insisted; it was important only to be human, and all else would follow." Goodman believes that these students had so well learned that "physical and sociological research is sub-

* "The New Reformation," *New York Times Magazine,* September 14, 1969.

sidized and conducted for the benefit of the ruling class that they did not believe that there was such a thing as simple truth." Thus these students had taken the starting assumption of the New Professionals about the nature of professionalism as currently practiced, and had extended it to include all professional practice, old or new. Without doubt these suspicions are shared by many students in college and high school today.

What has gone wrong? Why this drastic loss of faith in those associations of people which are supposed to meet our deepest societal needs and assure fulfillment for individuals?

People usually enter a profession to serve ideals such as teaching, healing and justice. But you do not simply heal, teach or serve justice—you become a doctor, teacher, or lawyer. The professions have become established, institutionalized and rigid. Each profession has developed its own complex of training schools, licensing procedures, professional associations and regulations.

Because of these institutional relationships, the professions, and professionals, have become deeply concerned with values —like prestige and high income—not directly related to the ideals of the profession. And in order to protect these, and fend off criticism and outside scrutiny, the professions have developed a mystique which defines their work as extremely complex, requiring extended education, great intelligence and skill, and highly sophisticated judgment.

This ideology implies that only other professionals (in the same field) are qualified to judge each others' work—either the purpose or the quality—and that outsiders must remain respectful of professional judgments and decisions. Professionals are responsible only to their colleagues and not to the people they serve. As Eliot Freidson says,

The crux of the matter is that expertise is not mere knowledge. It is the practice of knowledge, organized socially and serving as the focus for the practitioner's commitment. The worker develops around his work and ideology, and with the best of intentions, an "imperialism" that stresses the technical superiority of his work and his capacity to perform it.*

What does all this mean in terms of the quality of service? Aren't people healed and taught, aren't cities planned and justice served?

To begin with, only certain people get adequate health care, schooling and legal assistance. These people are almost always white and upper middle class or rich. The professions simply have not served the poor people, whether by accident or design. It may be by accident because poor people generally can't afford the services of professionals who charge high fees. It may also be design, because professionals have been trained by other white middle-class people who naturally orient the education toward how to serve their own breed.

In medicine, for example, great sums are spent on research of rare diseases. The beneficiaries of this research can only be the researchers, who get rich and gain a reputation, and the well-off patients who can find a doctor with the time and interest to diagnose the illness, and who can afford the treatment. At the same time that this research is taking place, poor people are suffering from lead poisoning, tuberculosis, and numerous other defects which have been solved years ago. The Chinese "barefoot doctors," who work alongside their patients and can treat a wide variety of common ailments through their minimal expertise, have no counterparts here. Money isn't spent and interest isn't generated among professionals to deliver the services. And, of course, it is the professional associations which help determine how the money is spent, and what are the reward structures and the education which determine professional interests.†

Another example of the consequences of professionalism is in education, where rigid certification rules and long and tedious teacher education programs have combined to exclude

---

* *Professional Dominance: The Social Structure of Medical Care.* New York: Atherton Press, 1970.

† See *The American Health Empire.* Health-Pac, Random House, 1971.

minority groups, writers, poets, scientists, and new ideas from the schools.

All the professions are pervaded by essentially the same pathologies of this sort, and require the same kind of reform, as Joseph Featherstone points out:

The bureaucratic sickness of the education profession is only an extreme instance of a more general disease afflicting other professions as well, notably medicine and law. The cure is the same for all: to replace the unresponsive hierarchies that now exist to serve entrenched interests with new, humane professions that really serve their clients, particularly poor clients.*

But in a period of escalating social crises, it was inevitable that these professional practices would be exposed and attacked. In the early 1960's, simultaneously with the growing realization that the professions weren't doing their job, the federal government, responding to demands of minority groups and the poor, passed legislation which encouraged and underwrote the activity of professionals who wished to act as advocates for the dispossessed. This support helped transform a nascent movement into one with substantial support and viability.

The best example is the OEO legislation which mandated "maximum feasible participation" of the poor, but other bills, from juvenile delinquency legislation in 1961 to model cities legislation in 1968, have served the same purpose. In each case the poor were given the wherewithal to hire and direct professionals committed primarily to serve their interests. Planners, such as ARCH in New York, have worked with community groups to develop alternatives to urban renewal which improve, not eliminate, neighborhoods and homes for the poor. Social workers have worked with the National Welfare Rights Movement and other organizations to attack the welfare bureaucracy and make it responsive to the real needs of the people.

The best example of the impact of federal legislation on the

* *Schools Where Children Learn.* New York: Liveright, 1971, p. x.

professions, however, is in the legal field. Traditional legal aid was intended to fit the poor to the system, to lessen the pain perhaps, but essentially to enable the courts and police to deal speedily and efficiently with the poor. Federal-supported programs such as OEO legal services, Mobilization for Youth legal services, and VISTA lawyers changed that. These lawyers have taken vigorous activist roles, and have not limited themselves to litigating individual actions dealing with criminal law, divorce, housing, etc. They have initiated class action suits designed to force the system to respond to real needs. These actions can be painfully effective—OEO legal services, for example, forced the state of California to rescind massive medicare cutbacks. The result of this success is also instructive; Governor Reagan launched a campaign against the California Rural Legal Assistance program which in turn sparked a national campaign among "new lawyers" in support of the program.

The progress which has been made in humanizing the professions is highly disparate as one moves from one field to another. Perhaps the most advanced is teaching. The "free school" movement and the well-articulated philosophy of radical school reform in the works of John Holt, Paul Goodman, Jonathan Kozol, Edgar Friedenberg and others, have generated a critical mass of "new teachers." They work within the system as well as outside, ranging from those who start or work in their own schools, exemplified by Peter Marin, George Dennison and Joel Denker, to those who foment change within the system, like Herbert Kohl, James Herndon and Neil Postman. The important point is that a corps of new teachers does exist, has gotten it together in solving some of the problems of getting training and certification, has created institutions to permit them to teach as they want and need and must, and has had an increasingly pronounced effect on the rest of their profession—as Neil Postman's essay notes.

At the other extreme, perhaps, would be the profession of engineering. The essay by Ullmann and Melman reveals that in this field "a change—a renewal—is badly needed and yet it shows little sign of happening." For this reason the essay is of particular interest. It shows how the economics, politics, sociology and psychology of a profession can constrain its practitioners from acting upon their best impulses and adhering to their highest standards.

In every field the new professionals must contest the control exercised by the established conservative old guard. Neither the American Medical Association, the National Education Association, the United States Chamber of Commerce, the Democratic Party, nor the American Society of Newspaper Editors is willing or able to welcome the kind of changes which are needed. They must be changed, through alliances between their most progressive older members and the fresh young professionals entering the field with new commitments.

Because professionals have it made—only their brethren can judge them, and they enjoy high prestige and fat fees— they have resisted attempts to make them more responsible or to alleviate some of the consequences of their behavior. In virtually every service profession—medicine, social work, teaching—there is a serious shortage of trained manpower with interest and ability in working with poor people on problems caused by the urban squalor. One of the most important recent developments has been the use of individuals from local neighborhoods who are trained in a skill (health assistant, legal assistant, etc.) and put to work. Professionals and professional associations sometimes resisted this development out of a fear that the new careerists were endangering their prestige and power. The outcome, of course, is deficient service to the people who need it most. Fortunately, as the essay by Frank Riessman and Alan Gartner indicates, the human service professional associations have now come to include paraprofessionals, and increasingly welcome them into their fields.

Every movement needs troops, and the troops for the new professions come from young college graduates who are rejecting the traditional ideas of careers focused on money, status and power. These young people have been shaped by the experience of the sixties—the war, the racial crises, and campus strife. In normal times, the established professions could expect to pick and choose from among each new crop of graduates and shape these young people to their values. There would be little rebellion against established ideas. Now, the young graduates are insisting on working on behalf of social change, adding new momentum to the movement to reshape the professions.

Hence each June another group of graduates confronts the critical decision about career and each June more and more choose against the old answers. Education majors teach in free schools, lawyers enter public interest work, social workers eschew case work and take up community organizing, and writers either free-lance or work for independent journals. All of this has happened before, but today it is occurring on an unprecedented scale.

Richard Flacks* has characterized these young graduates as an emerging new class in America—the intelligentsia. Raised by socially progressive parents who emphasized human values and de-emphasized money and status, and educated during a period of widespread social upheaval, these young people first came together in the early 1960's around civil rights and student politics. The youth movement grew rapidly during the escalation of the Vietnam War and is now widening its net throughout the college-age generation and down to the high schools.

These people will not, and are not, settling easily into established career patterns. As Flacks notes:

Their impulses to autonomy and individuality, their relative freedom from economic anxiety and their own parents' ambivalence toward the occupational structure would make it difficult for them to decide easily on a fixed vocational goal or life style, would make them aspire to construct their lives outside conventional career lines, would make them

* Richard Flacks, "Young Intelligentsia in Revolt," *Transaction*, June 1970.

deeply critical of the compromise, corruption and unfreedom inherent in the occupations of their fathers—the very occupations for which they were being trained.

What is their alternative? "Service for Change" is the way Paul Lauter and Florence Howe define these youngsters' ideal in *The Conspiracy of the Young*. They distinguish this new concept from the essentially Victorian Kennedy idea of service (Peace Corps, VISTA, or the proposed National Service Corps) by its twin aims: first, to transform the institutions of society (rather than merely augment or support their work), and, secondly, to liberate, rather than merely to help, the oppressed and poor.

"Social reconstruction and immediately meaningful work" is another way they express these dual goals. And they note an interesting relationship between them. Not only does the creation of socially relevant and useful jobs provide meaningful career opportunities for those who want them—it also works the other way. "Society is already being transformed," they write, "when men and women create jobs that are extensions of their hopes and ideals, or when many of us as workers begin to see in our work our 'reason for being.'"

The new professions movement is an answer to that perennial question which parents pose to their activist youngsters: "But what will you do when you grow up?" The question derives from the "moratorium" theory of adolescent protest and activism: that college age youngsters "deserve" to have a period of their lives when they question the prevailing mores of society, before they inevitably "settle down" and become "solid citizens." The new professionals are models that answer: You *can* shape for yourself an adult life-style, a way of making your way, which does not deny the idealism and energy you now have for social change and human relationships. The new professionals are the "solid citizens" of the counter-culture, the answer to those who see our youth slipping into laziness, ennui, and doped somnolence.

Indeed, one striking indication of the scale of the movement is the communications network which has sprung up among new professionals. This network is essential because it provides a national communications base, permits sharing of ideas, experiences and resources, and rejects the rigid specialization, pecking order, and value systems which characterize most professional journals.

One of the oldest links in the new profession movement is the magazine *Vocations for Social Change. VSC* has defined the movement's objectives much as we do above, in terms of both social reform and individual fulfillment:

Vocations for Social Change is based on two great hopes. We feel that there is a great need for institutional change in this country so that ordinary citizens can have greater control over the forces that limit their lives. We believe that it is possible for far-reaching change to occur in this country if enough human energy is devoted to the task. At the same time, we are greatly concerned about the quality of our lives and the lives of our fellow citizens. We want our work to produce change in the society and we also want it to provide meaning for us. Similarly we hope that others can work towards and achieve this kind of confluence.

This means that we view a job as a focus for individual involvement, not as a way to earn some money to do things with.

Another broadly interdisciplinary magazine is *Social Policy*, edited by Frank Riessman, co-founder of the New Careers Movement. Concerned primarily with the service professions —education, social work, planning, medicine, etc.—the magazine provides scholarly criticism of the old ideas about professionalism and is a rich source of information about new ideas and developments.

Individual fields have their own magazines and newsletters. In education, for example, there are *The New Schools Exchange Letter, The Teacher Paper, No More Teachers' Dirty*

Looks, This Magazine Is About Schools, and *Edcentric.* In law there is *Juris Doctor,* in medicine there are the Health-Pac Publications. It is virtually impossible to develop a complete list or make an accurate estimate of how many people are affected by the network. It is obvious, however, that the network is growing, that increasing numbers of professionals and pre-professionals are getting involved.

What ideas are espoused by new professionals active in this network? The first principle or underlying assumption, has to do with purpose.* In each profession the new practitioner is primarily concerned with the well-being of people, and with the social change necessary to achieve it. This, rather than loyalty to the profession, to money, or to status, is the prime motivator. For example, in architecture and planning, there is "a growing band of 'advocate' architects and planners, working closely with ghetto residents both to build anew and to fight city and state planning agencies with 'counterplans' of their own, giving the poor, in effect, a professional voice." †

In law, too, more and more young lawyers are turning away from offers from well-heeled firms and are taking up pro-bono law or poverty law. The success of the California Rural Legal Assistance program is illustrative. The work of Ralph Nader, the mentor of pro-bono lawyers, is another example. Successful legal fights have been fought across the country on behalf of welfare reform, ecology, consumerism, prison reform, and numerous other public issues. As significant as the issues themselves is the fact that the lawyers are often full-time public service lawyers, not established lawyers dabbling out of a sense of *noblesse oblige.*

The second major principle of new professionalism is accountability or client control. Traditionally the professions,

---

* The following discussion of the principles of new professionalism owes much to Matthew Dumont's fine essay "The Changing Face of Professionalism" in *Social Policy,* May–June 1970.

† *Newsweek,* April 19, 1971, p. 79.

relying on a complex vocabulary and a mystique of expertise, have refused to enter into any kind of dialogue with clients. This refusal has served to protect the professions from annoying questions and from any attempts to hold them accountable for their actions. Most doctors refuse to disclose the facts and options to patients, teachers pose as the omnipotent fount of professional wisdom and learning, and resist attempts of parents and communities to involve themselves and direct the educational process. This kind of separation has pernicious consequences. The distance between professional and client means that the client has no way of determining what is in his best interest, what his options are, and what the consequences of different actions will be.

Hence, public schools can continue a policy of channeling, subjugating, and socializing the young without fear of reaction. Planners can proceed with renewal plans which may displace families, reroute traffic through residential neighborhoods, or lead to urban decay—again without fear of consequence. Hospitals can emphasize expensive and esoteric research at the expense of preventive medicine, without challenge.

The new professional puts his expertise at the service of the client, of the poor. Dispossessed groups which lack the expertise or technical knowledge to evaluate what is happening to them and what they can do about it, now find professionals who are willing both to advise them and to take their directions. Hence community education groups work with teachers to challenge the oppressive omnipotence of the public schools and to create alternative institutions. Neighborhoods now enjoy the assistance of planners who analyze the implications of plans created by city bureaucracies, and who prepare alternatives to the official plans. As a result, people are beginning to gain a measure of control over their destiny; they are ceasing to be at the mercy of experts who speak an impenetrable language and who claim a monopoly on wisdom.

This impulse has emerged even in professions seemingly unamenable to such an approach. For example, George I. Miller devoted his presidential address to the American Psychological Association in 1969 to the theme "Turning Psychology Over to the Unwashed."

Our responsibility is less to assume the role of experts and try to apply psychology ourselves than to give it away to the people who really need it—and that includes everyone. . . . The practice of valid psychology by non-psychologists will inevitably change people's conception of themselves and what they can do. When we have accomplished that we will really have caused a psychological revolution. Psychology must be practiced by non-psychologists. We are not physicians; the secrets of our trade need not be reserved for highly trained specialists. . . . I can imagine nothing we could do that would be more relevant to human welfare, and nothing that could pose a greater challenge to the next generation of psychologists, than to discover how best to give psychology away.*

The third major principle of new professionals in an attack on the credential system. In most professions a credential—the degree, the license, the certification—serves to maintain a monopoly on the practice of skills. A man can't argue in court even if he knows the law—he must have a law degree and have passed the bar. He can't teach simply because he knows his field and is good with children—he must have passed some education courses and a certification test. He can't preach on Sunday because he has wisdom and a way with words—he must have a degree and be ordained. In short, the credential enables the profession to determine who can practice and who can't; it creates an artificial monopoly.

The worship of the credential is part and parcel of the mystique of complexity and natural superiority that professions perpetuate about themselves. It serves an economic purpose—when the supply of needed skills is kept artificially short, the return is higher—and it permits the professionals to remain

* *Psychology Today,* December 1969, pp. 70–74.

comfortable as the all-knowing experts by virtue of possession of a rare or difficult-to-obtain credential. In some cases, notably in teaching, the credential also serves as a mechanism for racial discrimination; it seems that not too many blacks obtain the elementary school principal's credential in New York City.

Of course, the credential system may help keep some quacks out of the profession (though the failure of our schools, inadequate health care service, urban renewal blight, and collapse of the churches don't give one confidence in once-in-a-lifetime certificate health). But essentially it maintains the myth of professional invincibility, and keeps skilled people from working. In psychiatry, for instance, as Matthew Dumont notes:

Psychiatrists who work with low-income communities, particularly Black and Spanish-American ones, have learned how irrelevant much of their training is. They have also begun to learn that carefully selected, trained and supervised non-professionals from the target community can be extraordinarily effective intervention agents, perhaps more effective than the professionals themselves. The implications of these experiences has yet to be accepted by most mental health professionals—but is obvious to some. There are natural resources within the communities that transcend the credentialed abilities of the professionals to meet the mental health needs of the nation. *

Much the same statement can be made about professionals in many other fields. Paraprofessionals in education, medical assistants, and lay clergy can frequently, given the proper selection, training, and supervision, perform some "professional" tasks with high competence—yet they are resisted by the old professional.

Another thrust of the attack on credentials is aimed at professional education itself. Graduate training in most fields is long and drawn out, narrow in focus, and largely irrelevant to real life situations. A psychiatrist doesn't need to know the

* Matthew Dumont, *op. cit.*

bones in the feet. Teacher education programs require a thicket of methods and philosophy courses which could be supplanted by a semester in the field. Not only is professional education short on practical experience, it is long on rigid specialization. As Garrett de Bell notes in his article, the effective biologist (ecologist) needs to learn politics, sociology, and law. Try to find a graduate program which encompasses these fields. These problems—length, limited field work, and over-specialization—characterize most professional education and fuel further attacks on credentialitis.

In short, a national movement of new professionals is growing, united by a network of publications and new organizations. This movement, devoted to social change, client control, and anti-credentialism, has already performed important services and is growing with each graduating class.

None the less, not everyone sympathetic with the goals of the movement supports all of its manifestations. For example, Frances Fox Pivin, a professor of social policy at the Columbia School of Social Work, argues that

advocate planners involve community groups in endless discussion of technical alternatives which serves to blunt and channel the only effective approach to social change, militant action. It is into . . . intellectual exercises that advocate planners are leading community groups who are aroused by bad housing or the threat of redevelopment, and the planners generally lack even the virtue of radical outlook. Study and analysis, of course, are only the first step, a step to be followed by endless meetings and lengthy negotiations with innumerable bureaucrats. Later, there may be a plan but, as sad experience shows, one that will probably never be implemented. Meanwhile, no housing is built and no mass transit facilities are added, and with leaders absorbed in bureaucratic minuets there may be no force left in the community to press for them.*

* Frances Fox Pivin, "Whom Does the Advocate Planner Serve?", *Social Policy*, May–June 1970.

One of our contributors, Jack Geiger, has argued elsewhere, using his own field as an example, that the new radical professionals sometimes carry their justified critique of professionals and professional roles to the absurd point of denying the usefulness of knowledge and the value of expertise. Summarizing the views of the radical doctors, which exemplify those of new professionals in most fields, Geiger comments sharply:

My point is not that these viewpoints are without foundation; indeed, such comments frequently are painfully close to the truth. However, they invariably fail to distinguish between technical training (the specific acquisition of specific knowledge and skills) and the reactionary socialization that often accompanies this training. They fail to distinguish between technical knowledge or expertise, itself quite neutral, and its misuse for status and elitist purposes. And they fail to distinguish between technical competence in a professional and that professional's sociopolitical morality, his views of the social order and the way he structures the settings (hospitals, etc.) and relationships (with patients, with the power structure) in which he uses that expertise. They are both important, but they are different. Furthermore, the criticisms grossly misrepresent the real (or at least the original) purposes of accreditation and licensure, which were reformed 60 years ago not as elitist devices, but as mechanisms to attempt to assure competence. They also grossly distort the reasons for the appearance of specialization and the disappearance of the general practitioner, who started to disappear not because he could not "provide a full range of comprehensive services"—specialists don't do that either—but because one man could no longer possibly learn what it was necessary to learn, and do what it was necessary to do. Whatever its consequences in monopoly control, specialization developed out of a concern for technical quality. It is extraordinarily important to separate that base and that concern from the other issues of misuse, prestige, profit, and the like.

Though demystification of specialized knowledge is a desirable social goal, all knowledge is not instantly transferable in the name of demystification. Technical knowledge has value in its own right; it is not just a "monopolistic weapon." Agreed, it is not the only kind of knowledge; perhaps it should not be the only criterion of competence. It most certainly is now locked into a system that differentially exploits trainee, practitioner, and patient. But the critics I cite argue as if we did not have hard, solid, and consistent data on the technical quality of medical performance by generalists as opposed to internists, or on the justifications for (and outcomes of) surgery by generalists as opposed to surgeons, or on the comparative performance of health-care systems in which technical competence is rigorously reviewed and those in which it is not. I am not arguing for a moment that in our own existing system, technical competence is rigorously used to protect the poor, the Black, the Chicano, or others to anything like the same extent that it may protect the wealthier, or those with more choices; nor will I argue that our current system provides anything like adequate technical protection for anybody (except perhaps the professional). But we will not change that by attacking technical professionalism or knowledge per se on the grounds that it has been misused.*

Other complaints about new professionalism deal with nuts-and-bolts issues of efficiency and competency. One legal services lawyer† has complained that service is poor for the client and uncomfortable for the lawyer because working conditions are inadequate, the attorneys are overworked, clients are uncooperative, the lawyers lack experience, the judges and juries sometimes resent the young lawyers' long hair and modish dress.

All of these criticisms—that new professionals retain many of the vices of the old ones, that they may divert the energies of the poor into technical and nonproductive activities, and that the working conditions and quality of service may leave something to be desired—are valid in part.

Though these criticisms are important, they are negligible compared to the strong reasons why the new professionals movement should be encouraged and nurtured. Social change in America will not come easily. As Richard Flacks has pointed out, it may be the most important insight of recent

* H. Jack Geiger, "Hidden Professional Roles The Physician as Reactionary, Reformer, Revolutionary," *Social Policy*, March–April 1971.

† Gerald McLaughlin, "The Legal Services Merry-Go-Round," *Juris Doctor*, February 1971.

years that political organization is not enough, that civil society and culture must be reconstructed. If this is true, then the new professionals have an important role to play as they undertake a "long march through the institutions" and transform the shape of the bureaucracies and professions which control power. By working from within they are forcing the professions and bureaucracies to become responsive to real needs. By working from without they are creating alternate institutions. In both ways, the new professionals will make a big difference. Furthermore, as Flacks notes, "struggle by communities for control of their own development and services prepares the basis for a decentralized and democratized civil society. It is obvious that all such developments have profound need for the services of professional, intellectual, cultural and scientific workers."

Equally important is the hope that the new professionals movement holds out for the young. Growing up in high school and college today isn't easy. These young people, having been exposed to and participating in the growing protest movement, must go through deep agony wondering what will become of them after graduation. As Paul Goodman noted some years ago, it's hard to grow up when there is not enough man's work to do. By that he meant that there were few jobs which combine meaningful and important work and self-fulfillment. The traditional American response to this problem has been materialism; workers who can't find self-respect and dignity in their work search for it through material possessions—the two cars, the color TV, the house in suburbia. Yet this is precisely the road most young people have rejected.

Staughton Lynd has observed that the desperation young people feel when faced with their life before them is one of the causes of nihilistic violence. "If there is some sense in which we are all supposed to be teachers, if only in having been students longer, for God's sake let us not present young people a definition of the choices open to them which is more grim and confined than that of reality itself." The new professionals movement offers another choice.

The import of the new professions is even deeper than providing humanly satisfying work for practitioners, deeper even than attacking some of our most pervasive social problems. It has to do with the way we define our human problems, and therefore the way we work toward becoming more fully human, individually and collectively.

By organizing into professions our collective effort to make the world and ourselves more fully human, we have bureaucratized our most existential concerns. "The deepest of our collective responsibilities is taken out of our hands," writes the British educator and poet Edwin Mason. "But the problems that matter most are those least often discussed which are common to us all, not those which can be earmarked as belonging to any profession."

Thus the net of the professions, while seeming to strengthen our capability to deal with our problems, actually lets life slip through its huge interstices. Those problems or conditions which cannot be defined in the terms developed for jurisprudence, pedagogy, politics, or one of the other disciplines, lose their claim on our attention, and even their reality. We cannot name them: Attorneys talk law but are embarrassed to speak about justice; doctors know all the labels for diseases but cannot define health or fight for it; journalists hide behind the concept of objectivity when what is needed desperately is to write the truth.

Ivan Illich has indicted our entire system of service institutions for reducing their clients to dependency, usurping our right to autonomy and authenticity, and monopolizing resources which should be made directly available to consumers. In short, Illich would reorganize society to enable every man, to the maximum feasible degree, to see to his own education, health, housing and sustenance, governance, and general welfare.

Clearly, the mere improvement in professional *technics* is not adequate to today's problems. Improvements in the efficiency of services in a profession, without commensurate improvements in the authenticity of relationship with clients, leads to technocracy.

The editors hope that this volume will be concretely useful to young people looking ahead to their work lives, as well as to established professionals seeking a new orientation. In this sense it tries to answer to a challenge presented to the editors by John Holt. Holt tells about asking numerous groups of college kids what they want to do after they graduate. Usually, the answer is an "ist"—I want to be an internist, an anthropologist, a physicist, or one of the other professions.

All right, Holt answers, let's assume you've got the diploma or the credential or the license: You *are* what you say you want to become. What do you want *to do?* The students mostly envisage working in some organization or institution: a university, a hospital, a school. Holt presses further: Suppose you were in that job, then what do you want to *do?* At this point the discussion breaks down, all too often, because the students just don't know what it is that a professional in the field really does, or could do, or should do.

Holt concludes that it is highly regrettable—often tragic— that young people do not have the option of associating themselves with a person who is doing what they think they would like to do, in order to find out what it is really like.

This book is a modest attempt to meet that need, through the vicarious experience of reading about people pursuing, in a humane and authentic way, the major professions.

This book is, of course, incomplete. Important fields are missing, either because we consciously drew the line or because it was simply unfeasible to obtain the kind of statement we wanted. Most notable are broadcast communications (including advertising), the several arts, social work, psychiatry, law enforcement and penology, civil service, architecture and planning, the military. We believe, however, that this collection provides enough guidance and reflects a wide enough range of experience, to help readers find their way toward a life's work which is worth doing.

Moreover, this book's focus on the professions leaves out those other areas of work which are equally in need of re-examination and reform. The blue-collar worker has no less a need than his college-educated brother for work that is personally satisfying and socially useful. Widespread recognition of this fact, through the writings of people like Harvey Swados, Paul Goodman, George Friedmann, Erich Fromm, Patricia Sexton, Daniel Bell, and Eli Ginzburg, has brought the matter increasingly to the fore. And recent concern over the alienation and anguish of the lower middle class in America has given it added urgency. Democracy at the work place is an ideal only dimly envisaged even today by those who represent the working man—but movement toward it will certainly accelerate in the next few years. And an integral part of democracy is a concern for the individual worker's need for those same kinds of fulfillment sought by the new professionals.

Readers will not, we hope, read only those essays which bear most closely on their own interests and aspirations. There is highly useful advice in each of them, relevant to all of the other fields. The reader most interested in Staughton Lynd's piece on "The New Intellectual" will also find quite useful Garrett de Bell's advice on how to put together for yourself a socially relevant and humane graduate degree program. And Lynd's piece, in turn, gives some unexpected and very knowledgeable counsel on political organizing during the seventies.

Our authors have, quite naturally, bolted their ostensible topics. For each of them, the real subject is man and society— what is wrong and what must be done. For this reason the editors think it not merely rhetorical to affirm that the book as a whole, in the picture it provides of the New Professionals, and in the guidance it offers to becoming one, adds up to more than the mere sum of the individual essays. But it does this only because of the quality of each individual contributor's work, vision, and commitment.

Making
Ideas
Relevant

The New Intellectual

by STAUGHTON LYND

Staughton Lynd is the son of Robert and Helen Lynd, who wrote *Middletown* and *Middletown in Transition*. For the past ten years he has attempted to combine historical scholarship with political activity in the New Left.

In 1946, Lynd directed the Freedom Schools part of the Mississippi Summer Project. In December 1965-January 1966, Lynd, Thomas Hayden, and Herbert Aptheker made one of the first forbidden trips to the capital of the "other side," Hanoi.

As a result of this trip Lynd, who was then teaching at Yale, has been blackballed in his profession and has held no full-time teaching job since 1966. Since 1969 he has done labor history and community organizing in the Gary, Indiana area. In December 1969 he was the Radical Caucus nominee for president of the American Historical Association.

Lynd's books include a collection of essays on the period of the American Revolution, *Class Conflict, Slavery, and the United States Constitution,* and (together with Michael Ferber) *The Resistance,* a history of draft resistance to the Vietnam War. He is a member of the collective which puts out *Liberation* magazine.

THE RADICAL academic is a more and more common figure. Like the radical lawyer, the radical engineer, or the radical doctor, the radical academic feels driven to improvise new ways of practicing old crafts.

But there are additional pressures peculiar to the university. About 1969, uncannily coinciding with the disintegration of SDS and the general disorientation of the American New

33

Left, recipients of advanced degrees began to find it much
more difficult to get jobs. The radical academic was doubly
disadvantaged: Already subject to discrimination because of
his views and actions, he was more than ever last hired and
first fired as the job market tightened. The class one used to
read about in studies of prerevolutionary France or Third
World societies with strong socialist movements, namely, intellectuals out of work, has begun to materialize in the United
States.

Only a few years ago radical intellectuals were few and far
between. At a professional convention in those days, a person
slunk from pillar to pillar of the inevitable plush hotel lobby
worrying about things like: Am I dressed acceptably? Is there
too much radicalism in the paper I am going to read? Why do
I feel so miserable in the community of my colleagues?

In those days the alternatives seemed few. The choice was
between pursuing an academic or professional career in a
manner long ago defined by others, or cataclysmically dropping out, and becoming a nonintellectual activist or organizer.
It was hard to remember how many intellectuals in world history, and more particularly in the history of socialism, were
not teachers. Lost sight of, too, was the fact that in Europe
intellectuals at the top of their profession often taught at the
high-school level.

One new possibility which emerged in the second half of
the 1960's was the "socialist scholar." The first Socialist Scholars Conference took place in 1965. Marxism again became
mentionable over sherry. But socialist scholarship revealed itself to most intellectuals influenced by the New Left as a half-
way house. Socialist scholars' conferences turned out to resemble other conventions: the same plush hotels, the same
panel format of a few speakers and a multitude of listeners
and, above all, the same remoteness from action. Controversy
was moving onto the campus in those same years, and a different sort of radical academic began to sit-in with his students.

The socialist scholar resembled his nonsocialist counterpart in the way he looked at his profession. Both thought the elite schools the best schools, and when the socialist scholar found himself teaching at Podunk Normal he emanated missionary vibrations which John McDermott characterized as "the laying on of culture."

The socialist scholar also shared the common academic tendency to define oneself as an onlooking eye rather than a making, creative hand. Intellectual life remained a spectator sport. This was variously justified, for instance, by the argument that radical intellectual victories of any kind were significant in establishing "hegemony" over bourgeois culture.

Meanwhile a growing number of radical intellectuals harken to a drummer of other tunes. They want to be radical in every aspect of their lives. They insist on redefining the form as well as the content of their intellectual disciplines. They want to marry thought and action, and they want to serve both truth and the people.

These comments are for them.

INTELLECTUALS IN THE MASS MOVEMENTS OF THE 1970's

The movement of the 1970's will be characterized by the formation of large radical organizations (toward the beginning of the decade) and by the explicit affirmation of socialism (by the end of it).

The large organizations will be made up of those hundreds of thousands of persons whose "minds were blown" by the movement of the 1960's and its continuing vibrations. To begin with, they will often be organizations of intellectuals or professionals, such as a new national student union to replace SDS, the New University Conference of radical graduate students and junior professors, caucuses in the various academic disciplines, unions of teaching assistants and other campus employees, and so on. In these the intellectual can participate without self-consciousness as one member among many.

As the decade goes on there will be more and more radical organizations among off-campus constituencies. To these the radical intellectual, whether or not he is still teaching in a university, will want to relate. Experience suggests this will not be easy.

Leninism and the movement of the 1960's offer models which are equally unsatisfactory. In the Leninist scenario one would begin with the handful of middle-class intellectuals already in possession of "correct theory." Working-class initiates would be added, but never in a manner that would cause the originating group to lose its hold on the party apparatus. This small vanguard party would in turn seek to act as board of directors for larger and more working-class organizations which spring up in the course of struggle, like the soviets in the Russian Revolution.

There is a liberal equivalent of this model in movement politics in the United States. A directing center of intellectuals reproduces itself in cadres of intellectuals and professionals in communities across the country. After the Great Renunciation of letting one presidential election year go by, these busy technicians have sufficient local standing to launch a national political campaign in the next-election-but-one.

Whether Leninist or liberal, this model is elitist. Whatever revolution or reform resulted the mass of people would have been only superficially involved in making it. The twentieth century is one long testimony that a movement built in concentric circles around a core of intellectuals cannot create a democratic society.

The Movement of the 1960's went to the opposite extreme. "Let the people decide" meant that the organizer-intellectual made himself so far as possible invisible. He was not up front with his politics; for all practical purposes he had no politics;

he was only there to serve. In this spirit SNCC organizers, for instance, built a Mississippi Freedom Democratic Party held together by a memory of common struggle and a vague ideology of "democracy." Not surprisingly, before long its members were Democrats with a capital "D."

In the movement of the 1970's the radical intellectual and the not-quite-so-radical worker, housewife and GI, are going to have to learn how to be equals. Each must be able to respect himself or herself, and speak in the idiom that is most natural, assured that his or her contribution is desired. This must happen both in the microcosms of small staffs of co-workers and in the coalition politics of a mighty radical mass movement.

We have to find ways for a radical intellectual or professional who moves into a strange community to build, person by person, a nucleus group which prefigures in composition and character the regional socialist movement-party which is his goal.

It will be a great deal easier for all concerned if some of the nucleus group have or obtain straight jobs in the community. The full-time organizer or professional revolutionary comes across to Middle America as an idler with a hustle. Rank-and-file working-class leaders who are located in the organizing process will understandably come to want a piece of the action. If all the organizers make it "without working," the organizees will imitate that model.

There may or may not be an existing working-class organization with some claim to speak for the community, like Citizens for a Better Lynn (Massachusetts). If there is not, it is important that the strange intellectual have some kind of invitation from someone. A weak invitation is better than none.

"Identity" and "invitation," then, are essential elements in the credentials which a person must be able to offer in the first two or three sentences after he knocks on someone's door. "Good afternoon. I am a teacher at the (local community col-

lege). I have been asked by (organization X, or Reverend Y)
to make a survey of so-and-so." Or again (my own case):
"How do you do? I am an historian, working on the history of
the CIO in the Calumet Area. I am also working as a volunteer with the Calumet Community Congress."

Credentials provide the intellectual a context for his work.
The next step is to sharpen the definition of that work.

Noam Chomsky has written devastating things about the
modern "mandarins" who go from Harvard and Yale to Washington, and work on the implementation of genocide as a
merely technical problem. And yet, a case can be made that
radical academics need more than anything to become more
technically effective. Intellectuals who accept the premises of
the system have plenty of opportunity to practice within those
limits. *Their* need is to step back, to raise questions about
their starting point, to ask "What for?" Radical intellectuals,
on the other hand, are long on fundamental criticism and desperately short on detailed analysis of particular institutions
together with recommendations for specific next steps.

Hence, despite the relative abundance of Left academics,
still no solid Left argumentation exists for a socialist health
plan, a socialist vision of the city, a socialist conception of
courts and punishments, and so on. As academics, we find it
easy to locate the relevant books on a subject; harder to find
the relevant people; and hardest of all to work out practical
suggestions. The beginning of wisdom for the intellectual who
wants to be useful to social change is to be willing to do things
he had formerly thought "technical" rather than "intellectual,"
and in the broadest sense "outside his field."

The pervasive concept of "advocacy" begins to get at this.
We hear of advocate city planners and advocate attorneys.
Could there be an advocate academic? What would he do? If
an advocate is one who takes sides, does not pretend to be
objective, declares for his client, how can there be advocates
in a profession whose task is, simply, to tell the truth?

I think it helps to remember that the mass radical movement of the 1970's will grow from small radical movements in particular places, among specific constituencies. It may be ludicrous for an intellectual to be an advocate for something so vast as a national movement. At a local level, however, the available academic, the intellectual jack-of-all-trades, can be a very useful person. For a number of years Jack Minnis was almost a one-man research office for the entire Southern civil rights movement. The person who, in effect, says that the distribution of his time, his choice of research topics, the mix of intellectual activities he selects will be to some extent guided by the practical political needs of a mass organization as its work unfolds, is not necessarily a hack, an intellectual prostitute. No one condemns the "Movement lawyer" because he gives priority to cases in which Movement people are involved. Why should the Movement economist, or Movement historian, be condemned for the same kind of choice?

One reason mass organizations become opportunist, in the precise sense of restricting themselves to the most obvious immediate interests of their present members, is that so few intellectuals condescend to dirty their hands with work that might help them. Opportunism can be combated by research which brings out many sides of an issue, by analysis which links issues together in a wider frame. But this work must be done from the inside, by persons who are there when you need them, who become known to their co-workers as whole persons, who sell papers as well as write them and get their hands inky in the process.

The work of the radical intellectual begins, then, with doing the same sorts of things (research and writing) that he was doing previously; but doing, perhaps, a more empirical, policy-oriented kind of research, and a more popular kind of writing.

This is only a beginning, however. There remains "teaching," or better, learning together: the impact of personality on personality; the quicksilver things which happen when people make themselves vulnerable to each other; the realm, not of "proposition," "experiment," "demonstration," and "truth," but of "commitment," "risk," "consensus," and "trust." If the intellectual is to be something more than an instrument, he must enter this realm. It is the domain of pain and rejection, as well as solidarity. A good deal of the history of the movement of the 1960's could be written as cycles of projection into this experience (going South, for instance) and withdrawal from it to a more familiar world (the campus). In the movement of the 1970's, we need a steadier balance. We need organizers and intellectuals who will root themselves in particular settings for a period of years. We need people capable of standing up for their own needs, and at the same time able to help others stand up for their needs, too.

It is possible, without becoming a mouthpiece or a ghost writer, to assist people in articulating what they feel. Among Left historians much good work has been done in the past fifteen years in recreating the history of "the inarticulate." Inevitably, though, the thoughts and feelings of dead people remain elusive. What evidence remains is mainly indirect: court records and the like. Even were the inarticulate alive and in front of us the task would not be so simple. My dominant impression in talking to living working people is that their ideas are often inconsistent, like any one else's ideas, but without the self-conscious effort to seem consistent one would find in a university. The assumption that somewhere among the dead leaves of the past, or the green growth of the present, there is *a* working-class philosophy waiting to be articulated, is romantic and false.

What there are, however, are men and women whom the schools and factories and armies of this society have taught from childhood not to take their own ideas seriously. In every class, but especially in the more economically vulnerable working class, a young person's groping efforts to be articulate and, more important, to take his articulateness seriously and act on it, is countered by parental warnings that the person who dares to be different will become a failure, losing what security parents had painfully achieved. Upon reaching maturity there is the job. The defining characteristic of factory and factorylike jobs is that the worker makes no real decisions. There is no improvisation, no creative new response to an unprecedented situation, hence no building of confidence through mastering the unexpected. The institutionalized dependence of the adult work situation is overlaid upon the institutionalized fear of youth.

This smothering of subjectivity is Public Enemy No. 1 in the working-class communities of Middle America. Compassionate solidarity with the struggle to overcome it is the most important contribution that an intellectual can make. This is a far more delicate task than the production of "objective" inputs: economic analysis, power structure research, technical aid in all those skills having to do with words on paper. The intellectual cannot hide his own beliefs. He must recognize that, for better or worse, he will teach by his own example; hopefully, an example of independent-mindedness. At the same time the intellectual should recognize that the independent-mindedness of others may express itself in forms quite different than those natural to himself. For instance, in the area where I have been working the most interesting group of teachers are devotees of Ayn Rand. They have a union, indeed half of the teachers in their school system were fired for joining it. I try to convince them that a union implies the recognition that the solitary individual needs help, and that this contradicts Rand's titanic individualism. They answer that the kind of teachers' union in which they believe will put the development of individual children (and teachers) ahead of wage gains. For them, Rand signifies the assertion that a person who insists on his own reality can win through to live the life he or she chooses. From the heights of Marxism one can dismiss that as a petty-bourgeois illusion. In

Lake County, Indiana, however, it has kept a number of individuals going.

Not the assumption of a sculpture waiting ready-made inside the block of marble, nor the assumption of a blank tablet waiting to be written on by middle-class intellectuals: instead something in between, more human, more natural, but difficult to define in a formula. I will try to talk about some parts of a definition I have personally experienced.

Most important is that the working class itself has produced young radical intellectuals, touched by the same ideas as their middle-class counterparts. When the concept of "new working class" was first advanced in SDS in 1966–1968, it tended to be assumed that the term applied to young persons from middle-class families who were being trained for new white-collar jobs in an automated economy. The Mario Savios and Mark Rudds of the student protest were assumed to be persons who came from a background of professional independence and at first imagined that a university degree would make this possible for them as well, only to discover (so the theory went) that they were being bent, folded, spindled and mutilated to become a new kind of proletarian.

There is another and perhaps more significant kind of "new worker," however. Their parents are steel workers or oil workers, and never made it out of the factory. They themselves have often worked in the mills, during summers, or part-time in the winter while attending a commuter college in the community. Having been sent to college by parents who hoped that their children would thereby be enabled to escape blue-collar work, this group of young persons nevertheless became radicalized. What does radicalism mean to them? Like their middle-class fellow students, they wear their hair long, smoke pot, display the peace sign and read *The National Guardian*. (Inland Steel in East Chicago, Indiana, has given up trying to prohibit long hair: hair down to the shoulders under a hard hat is a common sight now.) But they have no illusions about factories. I have yet to meet one who intends to spend his life in a steel mill. The existential question for these new workers of working-class origin is whether, as teachers or social workers or health technicians, they will stay in the community where they grew up and function as radicals. This choice involves the child deciding to be proud of blue-collar parents, and the parents finding it in them to accept the fact that (especially in a time of high unemployment) a college degree may not work economic miracles.

These young working-class intellectuals, not the middle-class agitator from the outside, are the persons who if possible should found a newspaper, manage a forum series, research the power structure—in short, do those things which intellectuals can do to assist a mass movement.

At the same time, if things fall out right, they will act as interpreters between older working-class people and middle-class radicals from the outside.

A second, tentative proposition about the way of the intellectual who seeks to be part of a popular movement without either dominating it or abasing himself before it:

The thing will happen in the best and most natural way if an intellectual's practice of his craft reinforces political conviction in defining a new role. Consider the radical cameraman who finds a way to put movie cameras in the hands of workers on strike so that, using half-inch video-tape at $17 a half hour, *they* can be the recorders of their own struggle, so that they can transmit their experience to other working people in a visual form they have created themselves. This cameraman will not find it a sacrifice to leave a lucrative conventional job, because his politics take him in the same direction as his redefinition of the film medium. The doctor who, in becoming part of a people's health clinic, discovers new things about disease and its prevention in the process will last longer at the health clinic. Radical attorneys who have found aesthetic delight as well as political satisfaction in inventing ways for citizens to initiate litigation and for juries to recover their ancient power to define law as well as fact—these attorneys will be around for a while. For myself, as an historian, I am convinced that how I try to do history now is closer to what history was meant to be, to what history would be as a spontaneous human function in the absence of historians, than the professional way I practiced history as a university teacher.

What all these redefinitions of craft have in common is something more than "advocacy." The attorney becomes a people's attorney, the doctor becomes a doctor for the poor—so far so good. The more radical and important process is that the people (the jury à la Kunstler, for instance) take to themselves a portion of the work of the professional, while at the same time the professional (such as Bill Kunstler charged for contempt along with his defendants) experiences some of the burden of life for those he used to "serve." That breaking down of the distinction between workers of hand and workers of brain which Marx spoke of as a goal of revolution becomes part of the revolutionary process. And it does so not sentimentally, as something pasted-on, but as an organic product. Thus in history it now seems to me that the full and accurate recording of an historical episode of popular struggle requires the participation of so-called amateurs who took part in the many-sided, geographically decentralized, and diversely particular battles of the campaign.

The most attractive twentieth century revolutions are those which undertook a reconstruction of education and of the relation of intellectuals to working people soon after the seizure of power (China, Cuba). Would it not make for a still more democratic and egalitarian transformation if intellectuals could begin to become workers, and workers intellectuals, at every stage of struggle?

This goal is very empirical, not at all esoteric. It is an army private documenting the My Lai massacre by seeking out and talking with participants. (He should have had the Pulitzer Prize.) It is workers in the coke oven department of U.S. Steel Gary Works testifying about the doors that don't fit and the use of chemicals judged unfit to be put into Lake Michigan to douse (quench) the coke and so enter the air. For every step we as intellectuals take toward the people there must be a corresponding step whereby people who have thought themselves incapable of being historians, speaking in court, and more broadly articulating the meaning of their life situation and putting into words their neglected desires, discover that they are intellectuals, too.

IN SCHOOL OR OUT OF IT?

It used to be much debated (for instance, at the founding convention of the New University Conference in spring 1968) whether the true radical intellectual should stay in the university or leave it.

That is no longer an especially useful discussion. It assumed (1) that staying in the university was an easy, safe and conventional thing to do; (2) that leaving the university meant ceasing to be an intellectual. Neither assumption has much substance now. As with other dichotomous propositions in Movement debate of the 1960's—electoral politics or direct action? Marxism or anarchism? above ground or underground? exile or jail?—this one needs to be transcended. The point is to be a radical, whether in a university or out of it. The radical in the university must be prepared to be fired. The radical out of the university must be prepared to defend his work in the most rigorous intellectual terms. Neither course is easy, safe or conventional; neither is inherently more intellectual than the other.

Most of these remarks have been directed to the intellectual outside the university, for the very good reason that the author has not been a full-time academic for five years. In closing, something will be said about the character of work now being done by radical academics.

The New University Conference represents the most important thrust. Founded by some of the same persons who built SDS—Richard Flacks, Bob Ross, Richard Rothstein, Paul Lauter, John McDermott, among others—NUC has more and more emphasized the community and junior colleges where SDS was weak. Many of its demands are summed up in the programmatic perspective "Open up the Schools." This means, among other things: (1) Equal pay for all workers in the education industry, from the janitor at a public elementary school to the full professor at an Ivy League university; (2) the abolition of all "tracking," and of grades as an instrument of tracking; (3) day care centers; (4) open admissions; (5) remuneration for part-time work at full-time rates. The last is as important to radical men as to radical women, for the present university system institutionalizes the separation of brain work and manual (or non-university) work by making it as hard as possible for a person to do both at the same time.

Other radical thrusts in the academic world are the movement toward trade unions of campus workers, and the formation of radical caucuses in the professions.

The most important aspect of the movement toward trade unions is the recognition that academic life in our society shares with the surrounding economy the myth that ability wins out, and that the sufficiently capable competitor needs no help from his fellows, indeed is justified in climbing upward on their necks. From kindergarten to graduate seminar, learners in the educational institutions of our society are set similar or identical tasks in competition with each other. Who can remember a teacher who began the year by saying, "Here is a problem for us to solve together"? Competition and grading give future employers clues about whom to hire; they do nothing but damage to teachers and students. When a student, a graduate teaching assistant, a teacher, and especially a professor at a prestige university, joins a union, he or she is saying with action that the Horatio Alger model of learning is both inhuman and untrue.

For the radical, the possibility of collective direct action is his only real job security. Students, of course, have learned to rely on the potential for disruption by their fellow students. The radical teacher is in the same position. Ostensibly he is protected by the American Association of University Professors. No doubt the threat of AAUP sanction has a certain deterring effect on university administrations. But: (1) As Jesse Lemisch has demonstrated, academic freedom is violated by senior professors, not only by college presidents and boards of regents, and an organization of senior professors like the AAUP is hardly an effective instrument against such action; (2) AAUP process is directed to chastising the institution rather than safeguarding the aggrieved teacher, so that when and if sanction materializes the radical who initiated the complaint is usually long since gone; (3) like the grievance procedure in industrial situations, the time-consuming and legalistic AAUP procedure functions to deter immediate direct action which might be much more effective; (4) formally and informally, the AAUP still leans toward the propositions that the college professor has a special responsibility to be truthful and decorous in his citizenly actions, and that any disruptive action in a university is wrong. Both off and on the campus, that is to say, AAUP custom and use makes the teacher a second-class citizen.

There can be no effective union without the right to strike and no effective strike which is not disruptive. Accordingly, the union movement on campus runs head-on into the current orthodoxy that interference with the rights of others to learn and teach is proper cause for expulsion (of students) and dismissal (of teachers). It is not surprising that President Nixon's commission on campus unrest came to this Neanderthal conclusion. What is distressing is to find organizations like the AAUP and ACLU seconding it. Radicals must insist that this doctrine embodies a series of premises that are simply false. It is *not* true that the university is a kind of institutionalized Socratic dialogue in which all participants have equal power and in which, therefore, no group of participants need combine together to protect their common interests. It is *not* true that employment at a university presupposes assent to an invisible body of rules over and above what employers can justly demand of employees in other wage contracts. Evidently we must expect a period in which university presidents will formally escort scabs through campus picket lines so that they may exercise their right to work, their right to learn and teach. Radicals should respond that they will consider the appropriateness of such rules when and only when all members of the university community (including students and secretaries) take part in decisions about tuition (or abolition of same), promotion (or abolition of same), defense research (or abolition of same), and every other kind of decision in the university on a one person = one vote basis.

This is not to say that all forms of disruption are equivalent. On the contrary, it is precisely a protest against lumping sit-ins and mass picketing indiscriminately with bomb-throwing and the destruction of research materials.

Radical caucuses in the various disciplines are less important than unions, I have come to think, because they have no power. A union could conceivably do something about the overproduction of Ph.D.s and the underpromotion of radicals. A radical caucus can't. What a radical caucus can do is to act out the possibility of a radical way of being, say, an historian or an English teacher under the very noses of the senior professionals who preside when the community of that discipline gathers. This may mean counter-sessions in which radicals discuss topics of interest to them, or give a platform to persons not ordinarily listened to by the profession; it may mean challeng-

ing the doctrine that the profession can pass a resolution supporting World War I but not a resolution condemning the war
in Indochina; it may mean doing what can be done through
publicity and exposure to monitor the behavior of departments toward women, radicals and other minorities.

Radicals have had a confused and inconsistent image of
what the university should be. Sometimes it is envisioned as
an ivory tower of pure research, which should not contami-
nate itself by defense contracts and counter-insurgency programs. However, when the outsiders are SNCC recruiters
rather than recruiters for the Dow Chemical Company, or
when the institution seeking assistance is a Black Panther
clinic rather than the United States Army, rhetoric has had a
tendency to adjust, and the image of the university as a kind
of service center for a people's movement has come to the fore.
All that this means, I have come to feel, is that loyalty to the
university is not a radical's highest loyalty, and there is hardly
more reason to have a consistent position on university neu-
trality than to be consistent on the (rather analogous) issue of
states' rights.

Loyalty to truth and universal norms is something else. In
or out of the university, the radical intellectual has a special
responsibility to truth-telling and (I would argue) to the application of consistent standards in decision-making. Every
radical movement struggles between a narrow and parochial
understanding of its goals and a wider consciousness which
reaches out to all those who are oppressed. Every radical
movement experiences moments when deception or conceal-
ment of differences seems a better course than full debate.
Even the weakest radical movement knows the temptation to
misuse the helpless adversary, including those within the
movement itself. Radical intellectuals have no special claim to
competence in such matters but they do have a special responsibility, it seems to me.

The radical calling of Socrates involved an integrity more

three-dimensional than simple truth-telling. To face political decisions, not as a separate world of compromise and Realpolitik, but as a realm which claims the very best of which one is capable, and in any case all of oneself, is what it means to be both a radical and a disciple of the life of the mind.

Sources of Further Information

In almost every academic field there is a "radical caucus" which can best be encountered by attending a professional convention and looking for it. The New University Conference, 622 W. Diversey, Chicago, Illinois is the closest thing to an organization uniting these groups nationally. Regional groupings of radical intellectuals include the Peoples Appalachia Research Collective, Route 8, Box 292 K, Morgantown, West Virginia. Among the journals in which the dilemmas of radical intellectuals are regularly discussed are *Radical America*, 1237 Spaight Street, Madison, Wisconsin and *Liberation*, 339 Lafayette Street, New York City.

The New Professor

by PAUL LAUTER

What Paul Lauter writes about the problems of socially concerned academics grows out of his own experiences as an activist and a teacher.

In 1963 he temporarily left teaching English to work full time in the Peace Education Section of the American Friends Service Committee. The following summer he worked in Freedom Schools in Mississippi, to which he also returned in 1965. After a year back teaching at Smith, and getting arrested in Montgomery, Alabama, Lauter returned to the Quakers as Peace Education Secretary in Chicago. There he worked with the SDS anti-draft program, helped organize Clergy and Laymen Concerned About Vietnam, and helped to put together one of the first large meetings of trade unionists against the war. He also taught in the Roosevelt University Upward Bound program.

In 1967, he became the project director of the Adams-Morgan Community School in Washington, D.C., one of the first experiments with community control of public schools in the country. That year, he was among the organizers of Resist, the organization whose activities led to the Boston trial of Dr. Spock, William Sloane Coffin, Mitchell Goodman and others. He has been national director of Resist ever since. The following year he helped start the New University Conference, and remained one of its executive committee members for two years.

In 1970, he and Florence Howe (to whom he is married) published *The Conspiracy of the Young*, an extensive and carefully documented survey of the youth movement of the sixties and an analysis of the institutions which control young people in the United States. At about the same time, Lauter was fired from the University of Maryland, allegedly for "subversion of the grading system." The American Civil Liberties Union is helping him fight that firing in court. Currently, he is working for the United States Servicemen's Fund, an organization that supports work in the G.I. movement.

How CAN one aim toward doing the kind of teaching which so many young students would like to do today? How can one build a career which includes the kinds of off-campus commitments which Staughton Lynd talks about in his essay? How can one prepare to work with the sorts of students one hopes to have more and more of?

The answers to all of these questions involve changing the nature of academic work and the roles we play in colleges. Perhaps the best way of explaining why I emphasize changing our roles and, therefore, changing the institutions of higher education, is to lay out in some detail my understanding of certain conflicts which I believe define conventional professors.

Academics seem to vibrate between self-hatred and self-interest. That's a psychological reality anyone thinking of becoming a college teacher must encounter. A social reality is this: Decent and humane as they may be, teachers more often end by doing what their institutional roles demand than what their liberal or radical instincts propose. These may seem depressing, if abstract, propositions. But I want to state them at the outset, both because of the illusions people still seem to carry about academic life, and also because the first step toward changing the university is to understand the sources of these psychological and social contradictions.

People become college or university teachers for a variety of reasons. Some like the security offered by tenure and decent pay scales. For some, it's a means of climbing socially: It wasn't so long ago—when I entered college in the forties, as a matter of fact—that the phrase "Jewish professor" was all but a contradiction in terms. None of my undergraduate teachers, even at New York University, was a Jew; one, *rara avis*, was black, one female. We had Jewish doctors and lawyers, court reporters and municipal bureaucrats. But professors . . . ? In graduate school, where many of the rising students were Jews, we sometimes smiled among ourselves at the odd joke academic growth, scholarship funds, and intellectual competition were playing on the WASP gentlemen who set the tone of the profession. Well—not quite a "profession" yet, more a "calling," a diminuendo priesthood after Matthew Arnold and Brander Matthews. It was to be a profession soon enough, to be sure, and we learned the techniques of professional advancement: Publish—in legitimate fields and established journals; be an interesting teacher, if possible—but don't call attention to yourself; accept committee assignments gracefully —but don't get too involved. It was all very clear: Those who published got prestigious jobs, less teaching, more advanced students, fellowships and years off. There was no place, I was once told by our director of graduate studies, "that one couldn't publish one's way out of."

I emphasize these professional considerations—and there are others, like the long vacations and often comfortable campus locations—not because I think they are primary, but because most of us would be dishonest to disclaim them altogether. Nor do I mention them out of cynicism about the educational or civilizing functions of college professors. There are a few benighted souls, indeed, who utterly disdain the enlightenment of students as a function of university faculties. It might be easier for most college teachers if they did. For the guilt and anger so characteristic of college faculties grow first from the sharp tension between what we tell ourselves we should be doing as educators and our commitments to professional advancement. It is not a criticism of individual college teachers but a statement of institutional fact that considerations of career almost invariably have triumphed over the ideals posed for bringers of culture and learning.

Not surprisingly. Consider the record since students' complaints over bureaucratization and giantism in education were first made vivid at Sproul Hall in 1965. Paeans to teaching have been pronounced, "good teacher" awards begun, and innumerable reports, like that of the "Muscatine Committee" at

Berkeley, presented. But the Muscatine Report is pretty much a dead letter at Cal and so are most of the other proposals for the modest reconstruction of undergraduate—and graduate—instruction. Class size, under pressure of fiscal tightening, is once more on the rise, and it remains as clear as ever that those who publish get prestigious jobs, less teaching, etc. College teachers, whatever else they may be, aren't fools—they know lip service when they see it. And they know how scarce jobs of any kind are getting.

This is not to say that *no* changes have been instituted. A few universities, including some notorious for the pedantry of their graduate programs, have now instituted something called a Doctor of Arts program—a kind of Ph.D. without dissertation, designed in theory to produce more competent teachers. At one level, the D.A. program seems a useful response to the criticism that a competent scholar or bureaucrat who might emerge from a Ph.D. program isn't very likely to be trained in, fond of, or committed to teaching. For that reason, among others, community colleges, where many of the available jobs now are, have been reluctant to hire Ph.D.s. But given the culture of the academic world, and its system of rewards, the D.A. cannot appear to oncoming graduate students as anything but a second-rate Ph.D., one that will leave its holders less mobile, less competitive in the job market, and more locked into teaching jobs in two-year institutions and in limited geographical areas, in high schools, or in the persistent Podunks. In short, what "tracking" is for high schools—channeling students from the "right" social and economic backgrounds into college, others into the army or the secretarial pool; what "cooling out" is to the four-year/two-year college system; the Ph.D./D.A. is to graduate work. It is not by any means that teaching in community colleges, for example, is either less rewarding or desirable in pedagogical or political terms—though the politics of "cooling out" make it harder. But the rewards of status, comfort, money, leisure, and the rest still accrue to the professors at Johns Hopkins and not to those at Essex Community College. There are those of us, misguided socialists no doubt, who believe that the work done by the man feeding the furnaces at the Bethlehem Steel Plant is more valuable to the society than that of the corporation's president. But who believes that, given a choice in this capitalist society, a person would select standing in front of the fire at eighty-five hundred a year instead of rolling over the golf course at eighty-five thousand, plus stock options. Admittedly, academic contrasts are not quite so sharp, but they are clear enough. In Maryland, for example, English teachers at community colleges teach four or five classes a term for two or three thousand less than their brethren at the state university, where the teaching load is three courses, none of the onerous freshman composition variety. That's aside from differences in sabbatical policy, library resources, the usual professorial perquisites. And at Johns Hopkins University, the Princeton of Maryland, I suppose, most of the senior English faculty is still being alternately coaxed and threatened to expose themselves to undergraduates, for whom they have not previously been expected to assume more responsibility than a single course a year. There are lots of good, young academics with ideals about equality of educational opportunity and ideologies that call them to non-elite institutions; some community colleges, and high schools, and low-prestige institutions still need faculty. And, if current expansion rates of two-year colleges and open admissions policies persist, they will continue to need faculty. "Well, then, young lady, the D.A. is just for you: no tedious dissertation, teacher training—or whatever they call it—by our own faculty, and a job after your own ideals—instructing those less fortunate students who do not come here." What is not said, never alluded to, is that the graduate student channeled, perhaps by her own idealism, into the D.A. is, ideals or no, in fact being channeled into the lower echelon of the academy, just as effectively, and as permanently, as the community college student, aspiring to be a doctor, is "cooled out" into becoming a medical technician. Nor that from the student's point of view, nothing in the D.A. program cannot be encompassed within almost any Ph.D. routine: The special courses for pedagogy are available to anyone, and even the dissertation can generally be organized by anyone with sufficient commitment and persistence around writers or movements or concerns that should enter a good teacher's classes—forgotten women or black or Wobbly poets, popular culture, people's science and health. I'm not making a case for academic careerism; quite the contrary. But it requires more than a shift in rhetoric and, in our society, appeals to social virtue, to persuade furnace men to keep stoking rather than moving into the air conditioning. The disillusionment of young teachers who discover how their idealism has been used and their teaching aspirations unfulfilled is terrible to behold.

My point here is not so much to attack the D.A., but to underline its implications. It says that within the present institutional framework, the clash between serving students through teaching and serving self through professional advancement cannot be reconciled. So what must be produced is a class of second-rate academic citizens, D.A.s, whose task it will be to teach; while the Ph.D.s continue their now less crowded course of scholarship and knowledge-production. Most of us, up to now, have found this tension *within* us, feeling, on the one hand, the strength of obligation to our students and our subjects, and knowing, on the other, what it was that career and promotion and even keeping a job required of us. Thus the self-hatred and the self-interest with which we began.

It is paradoxical, no doubt, that the demands of professionalism in the academic world have in serious measure contradicted the interests of students. That paradox is but one dimension of the tension between the social functions colleges do, in fact, perform and our persistent conceptions of their role. People in this country continue to agree about the virtues of formal education—the more the better. Education: the means to social mobility, the key to unlock the poverty cycle, investment in human capital. In fact, there is a good deal of evidence to suggest that schools, colleges and universities included, do rather little by way of job training, imparting useful information, or developing important intellectual skills. If one considers, for example, the millions of students who have passed through required elementary biology and chemistry classes, how few became scientists, especially on the basis of that experience, and how little whatever is learned affects the students' lives, one must conclude that such courses have very little to do either with pre-professional training or, despite the rubric under which they are taught, the general education of students. Certainly, the minuscule return from such courses on the investments of professorial and student time and energy, laboratory facilities, and administrative structure could be justified in a business only if it were devoted to the production of waste. The same argument can be made about "culture courses," from sophomore literature to the French requirement to elementary logic to Western civilization. The theory is that such requirements and their subsequent majors produce more cultivated, humane people. But has anyone shown how the English major who reads *Time* is more cultivated than the garment worker who reads the ILGWU *Bulletin,* or how the political science student who learns to drop napalm on Vietnam after graduation is more humane than the enlisted men who slog through the mud, kill or be killed? Just what did Calley study?

I don't want to pursue arguments I have made elsewhere in detail.* The point is not that schools don't educate at all, but

* See Florence Howe and Paul Lauter, *The Conspiracy of the Young.* New York: World Publishing, 1970, especially chapters 4, 8, 9, and 10; and Louis Kampf and Paul Lauter, "Introduction" to a forthcoming "Anti-Text" (*The Politics of Literature*) to be issued by Pantheon, spring 1972.

that mainly they perform other, more basic functions for the society. They socialize the work force, for example, helping to instill in people the bureaucratic habits of unquestioning performance of alienated work imposed by external authority.° Through grading, among other means, they help develop competitive attitudes and expectations.† They separate—the technical jargon is "differentiate"—the work force, channeling those with the requisite cultural attributes—like passivity, middle-class speech, financial security—toward corporate management and institutional bureaucracy, others to technology, others to the infantry, the assembly line, and the kitchen.

What all this means is that, regardless of private intent, college teachers perform institutional roles having to do with such socialization processes. If you don't believe it, try, for example, to institute a grading system that does not, like the curve, produce competition and isn't merely neutral, but encourages collective work; or one even that asks not what people "get out" of a class but what they contributed to the learning of others. I got fired from my last job ostensibly for doing that sort of thing. Or consider how sacrosanct the divisions of "knowledge" are—English here, history there, sociology yet elsewhere—when it might be shown that such division prevents students from developing a comprehensive, let alone a radical or Marxist, understanding of how their society operates, in whose interests, and how to change it.

I have gone on at such length to try to illustrate why sensitive or radical teachers are caught in two fundamental contradictions: one between their own career needs and their students' desires for teachers, for co-participants in learning; the other between the functions imposed upon them by the social roles colleges perform, and their desire increasingly shared by young people to create a society more devoted to

° See Michael Katz, *The Irony of Early School Reform*. Cambridge, 1968, pp. 87–92.
† See Jules Henry, "Golden Rule Days," *Culture Against Man*. New York: Random House, 1963.

collective and humane goals, or even to ending the war, racism and sexism. These contradictions provide the context in which all college faculty, however radical, must work. And they produce many defectors, drop-outs, casualties. For some, the resolution of such tensions lies along the lines Staughton Lynd has described—essentially off campus; for all of us, I think, some continuing relationship to struggling communities oppressed by U.S. society is vital. For others, such tensions produce guilt, contempt for teaching as a meaningful activity for a "radical," disillusionment with their subjects, with ideas, with themselves. And even if they remain in teaching, such people often regard it as a rip-off, the place where you get the money to do elsewhere what you define as important. For others, the tensions define the terms of the struggle on campus; it comes down to this: Organizing for change is the necessity imposed on us by those conditions.

II

To define our jobs as organizing for change is, in itself, to begin altering the roles we play on campus. It suggests a differing approach to what we do with our time: what we teach, how we focus our research, the campus concerns we engage. I want to suggest what seem to me some of the critical areas around which organizing and consciousness-raising might go on: these involve the constitution of student bodies, the nature of academic standards, as well as curriculum development and scholarship.

Within the near future, somewhat over 50 per cent of young Americans in each age cadre will have some exposure to higher education. That presents an enormous opportunity for radical faculty to affect the thinking and lives of half our youth. To be sure, as things now stand, much of college education appears to these students, the bulk of them from relatively privileged backgrounds, as a bore forced on them by parents, social norms, job pressures, the marriage mart or the draft. I want to return below to the remarkable incapacity of college curricula to challenge students' imaginations, let alone their values or lives. But here I want to turn to the half of our youth excluded from higher education, mainly the children of working-class people, of ethnic and racial minorities.

For with all its failings, and worse, with all its successes in tracking, controlling, and finally limiting the opportunities of such young people, higher education will still remain a goal for them. There is no way to follow Vice President Agnew's suggestion of turning the clock back and limiting college admissions to a "natural aristocracy." It is no doubt true that most personnel demands for a B.A. are spurious, simply an "upgrading" of job requirements without any comparable increase in needed skills. It is true, too, that the educational system has tended to detach individuals from their class or racial origins, setting them adrift in the culture of capitalist competition—make it on your own or sink. But the pattern of increasing exposure of Americans to formal education seems to me too well established, and asserted by too many social forces to be reversed either by Left paternalism—"most education is damaging, for them"—or Right elitism—"most education is unnecessary, for them"—however much truth there might be in each case. For us, then, the problem is opening up the educational system and changing it to serve rather than to control the new students coming in.

From our own points of view, there are some very good reasons to concentrate on changing the elitist character of student bodies. (I'm obviously not talking here of the still relatively *few* urban community colleges that have heterogeneous and largely under-class student bodies.) "Open admissions" programs or other efforts to change the campus population have seldom been successful without strong pressures from poor and usually black or Latin communities. Campaigns for open admissions, for "community control," or for integrating the largely white and middle-class campuses of big state university systems provide one legitimate basis for radical faculty to begin relating to off-campus communities of the sort Staughton Lynd has described. Simply from the point of view of more valuable and interesting classrooms, too, many of us have found that—in the humanities and social sciences, at any rate—our middle-class white students learn more from those blacks willing to come to class and speak up than vice versa. A paradox, perhaps, for those befuddled by theories of "cultural deprivation," but not really surprising if one thinks of the books written by people like Eldridge Cleaver, Bobby Seale and George Jackson, and the experience from which such writing emerges.

Moreover, one of the major sources of pressure for needed changes in academic standards and curriculum has been students—blacks, Chicanos, women—heretofore largely excluded from or ignored by normal academic processes. To understand why, we might glance at some problems faced by the Chinese educational system as their revolution was consolidated. Schools presented two particular problems. Their traditions and their teachers were highly authoritarian and geared to the culture of the classes that had ruled China for millennia. In practice, that meant that schools were not oriented to solving the social and technical problems of a society undergoing the most thorough change; they tended to look backward to authorities, to known ways, even to issues of little importance to peasants or workers. Moreover, for such people —those in whose name and by whose sacrifices the revolution was being made—now entering the educational system in significant numbers for the first time, the traditional practices put them at a serious disadvantage. They had no heritage of Confucian culture, not even a tradition of literacy. The educational system, instead of overcoming their disadvantages *vis à vis* the children of bourgeois or ex-landowning families, simply reinforced the lower status of those conceived by the professoriat as—to borrow an American term—"culturally deprived." The Great Proletarian Cultural Revolution was, among other things, an attempt to overthrow traditional education and the control of bourgeois intellectuals over it. And to substitute a system more responsive to the needs of the mass of Chinese people—peasants, workers and soldiers—and to the needs of the society to direct its energies to solving concrete problems of production, health, housing, and so forth. Among the major ways of accomplishing such goals were the destruction of old structures of academic authority, the breaking down of barriers between intellectual and practical work, and the insistence on "putting politics in command," especially in the form of the thought and inspiration of Mao Tsetung.

The problems of education in the United States are not precisely the same, most of all, of course, because we have not yet created a socialist revolution. But there are analogies. Here the educational system does not so much disable people from solving technical problems as it inhibits the solution of fundamental social conflicts. It does so in part by conceiving these in technical rather than in political terms (how do you design models for police-community relations, rather than how do you change who controls the police), in part by separating the study of technical and of social problems (my job is to learn how to change chromosomes; someone else will decide what we do with what I find). To put it another way, the central tradition of American education is to produce proficient technicians who do not, however, ask *why* problems like getting to the moon or building highways or electing a President should be solved, or in whose interest it is to solve them in a particular way. When the main objective of the society was developing its productive forces, such an educational system had some real advantages. But when the main problem of a society is the breakdown of all its social institutions, the kind of educational tradition that discourages asking fundamental, radical questions about them becomes a liability—just as the Chinese tradition was, in its way, for them.

It is a liability for the whole society, but especially for the underclasses, those heretofore largely excluded from higher education. And, in part, for reasons precisely analogous to those in China. Not only do institutional breakdowns—as of urban transit, health care, welfare or justice—bear more heavily on them, but the educational system itself is used not to solve their problems, to provide changed lives for whole classes and groups, but to maintain the current class structure. Here's one way that works: Socially accepted norms of language, for example, or of "correct" writing are determined by what is the ordinary usage of a society's dominant class or caste. In school, such class norms are translated into immutable "standards." Teachers simply assume that the linguistic norms to which they have been bred or trained are "correct," and the usage of students from differing backgrounds is just "wrong." I can recall, when I taught as a graduate student at a big Midwestern university, flunking black students—precious few there were—for leaving "d's" off past participles, and Indiana farm boys for using run-on sentences in their themes. I felt very righteous: They had to learn *English,* didn't they? And that was that. Now one can make an argument for the value to people from subordinated cultures of learning fluency in the dominant forms. But the effect of the usual imposition of standards of "correct" speaking or writing has not, on the whole, been to teach people to cope with the dominant culture, but to flunk them and remove them from the race, at best to "cool them out," direct them away from upper-echelon jobs for which a cultural veneer is a primary requisite. And to persuade them that the problem lay in their own inadequacy or inferiority, their or their family's lack of culture or knowledge. This practice of class-based standards being used, consciously or not, to keep people in their place has been a serious problem in China and in this country—as it is likely to be in any society with a formal education system, one of whose main functions is to transmit dominant norms that help maintain class or racial hegemony.

Another example of the political and class nature of "academic standards" is provided by a recent issue of the *Yale Alumni Magazine* (July, 1971). In its news section the magazine reported that Paul M. Sweezey, a Marxist and former Harvard professor, had "turned down the invitation to teach a course in Marxian economics" at Yale because, he said, "while increasing numbers of students are requesting instruction in Marxism . . . teachers capable of such courses are dropped from the academic world before acquiring tenure." In reply, the chairman of the Economics Department claimed a shortage of Marxian economists, adding, "We've been reluctant to waive normal academic standards to have them on the faculty." This is an academic Catch-22. "Normal academic standards" means a Ph.D., preferably from a prestigious institution, a string of articles and books, some consulting for government agencies or industry. But certainly *not* active participation in movements for social change. But Marxism emphasizes a unity of theory and practice, "that theory is based on practice and in turn serves practice," * that one studies a society or its economy in order to change it—not to write articles about it. For many Marxists that means working in movements for change rather than piling up "normal academic" credentials. And not just as a matter of personal choice between two equally reasonable alternatives—academic or activist—but rather because dialectical materialists see that we understand the nature of social reality *only* in the process of trying to change it. In Mao Tse-tung's words: "If you want knowledge, you must take part in the practice of changing reality. If you want to know the taste of a pear, you must change the pear by eating it yourself." Without commenting on the validity of

* Mao Tse-tung, "On Practice," *Selected Works.* Peking, 1946, I: 297.

Mao's epistemology, one can see readily that a practicing Marxist in this tradition would effectively be excluded from Yale's faculty, as from the faculties of most American institutions, by the simple logic of "normal academic standards." Marx himself would have been excluded. For who wants a "journalist," a "rabble-rouser," a revolutionary? A practitioner of change?

My own experience in teaching a course in revolutionary literature made this academic Catch vivid for me. It was just after the first term I gave the course that I was fired from my last job, ostensibly for "subversion of the grading system"—interesting language considering the context. One of the major problems I had with student and faculty reaction to the course was the question of what works like Che Guevara's *Reflections of the Cuban Revolutionary War* or Hinton's *Fanshen* were doing in a "literature" course—what literary purpose could be served by teaching such works? What literary purpose, indeed? For I began to realize the absurdity of such a phrase as applied to such a course. Were we to trace the metaphors and symbols? discover the "tragic nature of human experience," or some other pat literary phrase, in the plots? evaluate the place of *Man's Fate* in the hierarchy of French fiction? Was "Revolutionary Literature 101" to become another consumer product in the university catalogue? Could the duty, I got to think, of the teacher of revolutionary literature be other than creating at least revolutionary consciousness if not revolutionaries? But what, then, of that other academic shibboleth, my "objectivity"? Should I be presenting the Kuomintang side of the 1927 massacre of Communists and worker cadre in Shanghai? Or the feelings of the Gusanos who fled revolutionary Cuba? Clearly I was partisan. But I knew that it was my own experience as an activist that enabled me to relate to the books we were reading, and to many others in more "normal" courses, in immediate, substantial ways, to understand something of political struggle, of mass move-

ments, of social conflict and revolutionary optimism. And thus
to make the course a living experience for some of the students. For all that, one didn't accumulate "normal academic"
credits at a demonstration. One got fired. The thing was that
my partisanship violated "normal academic standards,"
whereas the teacher who glorified Hemingway's sexist, individualistic ideology, or commended Eliot's reactionary piety,
or who restricted Victorian prose to the works of Cardinal
Newman, Carlyle, Arnold, Ruskin and Pater—their partisanship, falling within the boundaries of bourgeois politics, was
not "partisanship" at all but critical judgment!

Similarly with respect to grading. I was fired for trying to
overcome some of the effects of grading detrimental to learning: like competition, cheating, "learning" just to pass tests,
grinding out meaningless papers. Some of my colleagues who
presided over giant required courses in the social and physical
sciences boasted of their curves, which insured that some fixed
percentage determined by them would flunk. *They* were
maintaining "normal academic standards"—and not so incidentally producing panic, cribbing, cramming, hatred, and
other aberrations in student behavior. Whereas I was "sub-
verting the grading system."

The long and the short of all this is that "normal academic
standards" are largely a blind to conceal academic privilege,
political conservatism and intellectual rigidity. To keep things
as they are. It was no accident that that same issue of the *Yale
Alumni Magazine,* focusing on the 1971 commencement, presented as the major controversy of that event a continuing
strike by Yale's nonacademic employees, some of whom were
paid so little that they were on food stamps or welfare. No
doubt they had some valuable economic lessons to teach Yale
undergraduates—or Yale professors, for that matter. But—
was it a matter of "normal academic standards"?—the commencement parade went on, more or less its usual way, while
New Haven cops clubbed the strikers and their comrades
away from its route.

In China, the official approach to the problem of academic standards has been to examine, challenge, and often force changes in them—and in the professoriat itself. And to seek the means to insure that "standards" would not be used to keep peasants and workers from educational advancement— and professors in positions of comfort and control. Here, the pressure developed by "open admissions" demands and the entrance of new groups of students has only begun to generate the needed revaluations of academic practices and norms. Most often, open admissions students have been tracked— "sidetracked" might be the more appropriate term—into compensatory or preparatory programs designed, in theory, to "bring them up" to existing standards (but from which most never emerge). Rather seldom have those standards themselves been reviewed. But for that 50 per cent of young Americans excluded from higher education—and for the large percentage of those who now never make it through—only serious alterations of standards will open the gates for them or make sense of what they find once in. For such reasons, they are likely to remain a key source of pressure for academic change.

We are obviously not confined simply to awaiting such change or to the emergence of a mass movement to act. In our own work we can alter grading practices, curriculum, and research tactics and priorities. And as graduate students, we can begin preparing ourselves for these changes. In the process, I think we will find classroom experience less a chore for our students and more of a creative influence on their sensibilities, their ideas, and even their values. For if a substantial proportion of students now in school are "turned off," it may not be simply that they're "spoiled" by affluence or disabled by poverty. It may be, rather, that they have little at stake in the traditional curriculum, apart from getting through it, and do really feel oppressed by the reactionary pressures of "normal academic" practices. Without elaborating the argument here, I'd simply suggest that significant departures from academic norms and the new curricular developments—like those in hundreds of women's studies courses—can have the effect of recharging classrooms.

Take grading once again. It is an issue which I've never thought very useful for organizing. In the first place, neither individual instructors nor small groups can bring about substantial changes in the impact of the grading system by unilateral action. Nor is the effort to institute a credit/no credit system—which would be considerably superior to what most places now use—an issue around which campuses rise up. At the same time, departures from grading norms are often used by administrators as excuses for firing dissenting faculty. Nevertheless, within classrooms, discussions of grading, as of other academic procedures, are among the most useful ways of getting at what is actually learned. For example, one issue in my Revolutionary Literature course was always the distinction between bourgeois, individualistic values and working-class, collective values. A number of the books we read touch on this contradiction and on the difficulties people have in altering their own conduct even during social revolutions. We read and discussed works like Desnoes' *Inconsolable Memories*, Senders' *Seven Red Sundays*, and Mao's "Talks at the Yenan Forum on Art and Literature." We even talked about the way in which students were socialized, partly by grading, to accept competitive norms and how threatening it would be for them to be graded on the basis of how much they contributed to the learning of others. But the issue remained abstract for them until some people in one class proposed, in the spirit generated by the May Day, 1971, demonstrations in Washington, that a group of them join in writing a collective final— rather than the exam I'd worked up—and in demanding a collective grade. Sentimentally, a number of the students were all for collective work—"down with capitalist individualism"— but when it came to practice . . . Well, couldn't they do better on their own? why bother with all the hours of discussion?

what if Lauter won't accept our exam? since he was already fired for giving a collective grade? or thinks it worth only a lousy mark? The debates and the personal agonies evidently extended over many days—and some, intellectually radical, would not finally join. Others discovered what peer pressure toward unifying theory and practice was. Those who did join, however, came to a sharp, internalized realization of what competitive norms, enforced by grading, meant and how difficult it was for them, youthful products of bourgeois culture, to enter into collective work. In other words, one of the central themes in the books they'd read suddenly came alive in their own experience. I can report analogous results with experiments in using criticism and self-criticism sessions in class and in basing campus organizing in classroom projects.

With respect to curriculum, colleges which have in other ways changed very little assert much less control than in the past over an instructor's initiative. And even in standard literature or social science courses significant new material can at least be added. The problems in developing new curricula lie less, I would suggest, in external constraints on our teaching than in our own heads, our subjection to the holy divisions of knowledge and to the separation of politics from subject matter, our ignorance about what's omitted from our own education.

I can recall in my own case apologizing to myself and developing elaborate rationalizations for including slave narratives and Margaret Fuller's essays in American literature, or the "nonfiction" I mentioned before in the "Issues in Modern Literature" course that I eventually transformed into Revolutionary Literature. Such things, my graduate school prejudices told me, weren't as "good," but they were "interesting." I found, too, that I knew of no contemporary Cuban writers— hardly any Latin Americans—and no Chinese or Vietnamese. Closer to home, I knew very few black artists, and those mainly contemporary; nothing of women like Fuller, Kate

Chopin, Rebecca Harding Davis and Charlotte Perkins Gilman, among others; and little of radicals like Jack London, Upton Sinclair and Big Bill Haywood. But the necessary processes of self-education and of rethinking my own standards could begin, I realized, only after I'd made the initial decision to try unifying my politics and my teaching in my classrooms. If combating racism or sexism was vital in my life, should not that struggle go on in as well as out of the classroom? Didn't such "political" considerations help legitimately to establish priorities in what we read or talked about? Didn't they affect what we conceived of as "good" or "interesting"? I'd never apologized for teaching Henry James, though I found his presentation of people's political and economic lives more than slightly absurd. Why should I apologize for Frederick Douglass' *Narrative* of his life or for Jack London's *The Iron Heel*, which didn't elaborate as James did the nuances of upper-class consciousness but which portrayed certain realities of social conflict in the U.S.? What ideology had I accepted that made Emerson's "The Over-Soul" or *Nature* standard texts, but Margaret Fuller's *Woman in the Nineteenth Century* peripheral? Was Henry Adams' autobiography more legitimate in a literature course because he elaborated fuller metaphors than Big Bill Haywood did in his book? Or was it Adams' substitution of aestheticism and world-weariness for political struggle? Was I more concerned with aesthetic criteria, the artfulness of art, or with the ability of a work to stir and shape my students' sensibilities and my own, to develop our capacities to understand, respond to, and change our world? Clearly the latter; that's what made classroom work serious for me. The only thing stopping me from putting politics in command, that is, from emphasizing social and political engagement with the books as well as aesthetic discussion in the classroom was . . . me.

By which I do not mean to discount the external pressures, the firings, the rejuvenated blacklist of radical faculty. But only to point out that if we are to stay in teaching at all as committed people, we cannot allow our major point of contact with our students, our classrooms, to be emptied of political content; or, rather, to be filled with "end of ideology" politics or similar deceptions, or with the absurd notion that curriculum is isolated from politics. It isn't that we want to cram socialism down the gullets of our students—though bourgeois ideologies are, in fact, what's crammed into them now—but that we shouldn't evade the political content of our subjects, the class, racial, and sexual standards implicit in choices of subject matter, emphasis, analysis. On the contrary, choosing works or projects or areas of interest precisely because of their political importance to us and to our students is one way of overcoming the sterility and abstractness of most college curricula. And if the need to clarify or deepen political or social understanding arises, as it will, we should be prepared to break down the current divisions of knowledge, to introduce Engels' *The Condition of the Working Class in England* into a novel course including Dickens and George Eliot; or Conrad's *Nostromo* and Auh Duc's *Hon Dat* into a foreign policy course; or Ho Chi Minh's poems into the stock curriculum on Communist ideology. Or to insist on pursuing the social implications of genetic control into the microbiology curriculum.

The point is that academics who call themselves radicals have often abandoned the field without struggle, turning their backs on the classroom or the curriculum as inevitably oppressive or "bourgeois." Now I would not argue that political, social, or educational miracles will emerge from changed curricula. More than half the sections of Revolutionary Literature I taught were failures—unchallenging to my students and boring to me. The class worked when, one way or another, political action intersected with the discussion of books and theory in the classroom. And for some students, the class was always a significant learning experience. Which isn't bad in anybody's terms. It seems to me that if we approach classrooms without *exaggerated* ideas about their function as educational or political experiences, and if we get over the ideology that separates our politics from our teaching, we can in fact do exciting and useful work in college teaching.

III

It is very hard to do the sort of work I've been describing alone. And so in the last part of this essay I want to comment on a few of the new institutional supports that have emerged among people like the audience for this book. There aren't many such "institutions." But such as they are, they seem to me of more importance to those concerned for the kind of work and values I've been describing than, say, choice of a graduate school. As a matter of fact, one of the best ways of choosing a graduate school is probably to seek out people active in such organizations or others whose political and professional work you admire and to figure out with them where it seems useful to go and what to do there.

I emphasize "counter" *institutions*, rather than individual arrangements, for a number of reasons. In the first place, individual arrangements are *individual;* they aren't transferable, nor are they often the results of or entrances to organizing for change. A friend of mine teaches part-time at an experimental college, which pays him; he has helped organize a radical school, to which students do pay some tuition; he writes a column for a muckraking magazine; and he does a monthly program for a listener-supported station. The work he does is very useful and fulfilling, but no one else could put it together that way. And the opportunities for doing so aren't yet available to many of us. More academics committed to change will in the coming years evolve work-patterns like this friend's—one foot in a college, the other in Movement institutions. But their— our—ability to do so will depend upon creating such opportunities by generating new institutions. I'm referring here to research-action groups like the North American Committee on Latin America (NACLA) and the Africa Research Group, Movement "think tanks" like the Pacific Studies Center and the Institute for Policy Studies, publishing efforts like The Feminist Press and Times Change Press, new schools, film collectives, radical magazines.* Such institutions help define people's academic work in relation to movements for social change as well as providing work for people committed to social change.

Within the framework of academe, many organizations of "radical" or politically involved teachers flourish for rather short periods of time, fizzing out as crises that provoke participation subside. The Sociology Liberation Movement (SLM) dominated at least the consciousness of those at the 1968 American Sociological Association convention in Boston with its slogans of "No Chicago" and "Knowledge for Whom?" By the end of the 1969 convention it was dead. Similarly, what became the Modern Language Caucus (MLC) of the New University Conference was a major force in the 1968 convention of the Modern Language Association, forcing significant changes on the Association and electing one of its organizers, Louis Kampf, as vice president. During 1969, people in the MLC produced some significant papers in cultural and political criticism of literature, organized exciting panels and workshops at the NUC and Modern Language Association conventions, and began to reinvigorate the idea of criticism as a tool for social change. But by 1970, the group had pretty much fallen apart, living—and then only fitfully—at the MLA meeting.

This is not the place to analyze the failures of such groups —both objective conditions and leadership are involved. But

* A very useful guide to these and other organizations devoted to radical social change is available in *Vocations for Social Change*, Box 13, Canyon, California 94516.

it seems true that organizations of "new academics" seem most successful either when they provide a vehicle for changing one's professional work, especially one's scholarship, or when they group people in similar objective circumstances. Of the former, I think that the Union of Radical Political Economists (URPE) and the Committee of Concerned Asian Scholars provide good examples. Even in name, URPE challenges the prevalent separation of "Political Science" and "Economics." The name, and the work people in URPE have done, argues for a unity, suggested by Marxist practice, in the disciplines concerned with studying social, political, economic and cultural forces. That unity grows from the political commitment, implicit in the word *Radical* in URPE's name, to changing, rather than simply describing or maintaining, social institutions. Similarly, the Committee of Concerned Asian Scholars came into being precisely because so many of the established professors in the field were involved in formulating and otherwise supporting or apologizing for the United States' war policy in Vietnam. In a sense, the Committee first amounted to a form of anti-war protest. But in making its opposition to the war increasingly substantial, it initiated projects that helped change the professional work of the young scholars drawn into it. These have come increasingly to reflect a sense of collective responsibility for developing anti-imperialist policies in Asia. And so it was natural that one of the first groups of Americans to enter China after the U.S. ping-pong team was a substantial representation of the Committee.

The other kinds of groups that seem to be successfully developing, those that draw together people in similar situations, are most evident among women. Where the SLM and MLC have faltered, the Women's Caucuses of the American Sociological Association and the MLA have continued and grown. Among psychologists, where radical groups have not had much success, the Association for Women Psychologists has had increasing impact on the profession. These groups, and even official bodies like the MLA Commission on the Status of Women, have challenged male hegemony over the profession, and have begun forcing admission of women into higher professional echelons, attacked sexist stereotyping, and, perhaps most usefully, have helped in a remarkably short time to develop new curricula and research areas concerned with women. To be sure, there is no guarantee that the pressure generated by the women's groups will not end simply with the elevation of more female professionals into traditional slots and with the establishment of some newly legitimized professional areas—like the Sociology of Sex Roles or Women's History—not bad developments by themselves. That's already begun to happen. But considering the incredibly heavy male domination of the academic world and the way in which male-oriented thinking is built into the curriculum as well as into academic structures (like part-time employment and nepotism policies), it seems likely that groups of radical, activist women will continue to play significant roles in changing the academic world for the foreseeable future. In any case, the women's movement and the academic women's groups that have developed from it have generated more excitement in scholarship and teaching—mainly among women—than I've ever observed.

In underlining the work of groups like these, I do not mean to dismiss significant developments within the existing structures of some professional organizations. The Social Responsibility Round Table of the American Library Association has been a most progressive force in its field, while *College English,* a magazine of the National Council of Teachers of English, has published what I think is the best radical literary and cultural criticism within the last few years, as well as some of the most stimulating articles on teaching. Nor would I wish to ignore the more established Marxist or black centers of scholarship, like the American Institute for Marxist Studies and the Institute for the Black World. But the groups I have been describing, however short their lives may finally prove to be, suggest an important departure from academic norms in their attempts to unify activism and scholarship, political commitment and professional competence. That may be a pattern for the future.

On the other hand, maintaining a viable unity of activism and scholarship, political engagement and teaching does not seem easy, either personally or organizationally. When some of us, mostly activists, organized the New University Conference (NUC), we thought the organization could maintain that unity. But we were wrong. The failure of NUC—and it has, I'm afraid, failed to sustain its momentum or to establish a significant campus presence—needs much more extensive analysis than I can give it here. As an organization, NUC has responded less and less to the needs of people committed to teaching. In fact, a certain culture hostile to continuing academic work has developed. And that has helped exacerbate the kinds of internal tensions I described at the beginning. At the same time, political firings—often connected with NUC activities—have taken a significant toll of young academics. And the radical movement has developed no adequate responses to such repression. As a result of these and other factors, especially the contraction of the job market, the expected broadening of the membership of NUC has not happened. Rather, membership and politics have, if anything, narrowed so that the organization remains viable at perhaps a score of campuses, mainly as a political reference group for younger activists with reasonably well-developed socialist politics.

The problems of NUC illustrate what is, I think, a fundamental difficulty which must be faced by anyone who takes these pages seriously. Namely, that to maintain a political, let alone socialist practice in this society, we need to be involved in the day to day efforts to change it, in the sort of work described by Staughton Lynd, for example. Yet the thrust of academic life, its professionalism and its privilege, draws us away. There are plenty of problems *on* the campus, some of those seductive inner voices keep telling us, why get too involved with welfare rights, or the Brown Berets, or the steel workers' wildcat strike? Insensibly, perhaps, with increasing guilt, we slip into privacy, doing "what we can" in classrooms or committees, but always more distant from the sources of energy for change. These are not in our heads, but in the struggles of oppressed or exploited people to alter the conditions of their lives. Drawn into their struggles, it is often hard to remain on campus, with the stuffy academic flaps, the jockeying for status and position, the often trivial research concerns. And it is true, after all, that campuses will not be fundamentally changed until the society itself is. Why then not leave it for the work of the free-lance revolutionary?

Some of us do. And some of us fade into privacy. And yet it seems to me that a creative dialectic in our lives, and a coherent political perspective can be maintained only at the cost of maintaining these contrary pulls. For radically changing the United States is not, I think, so much a matter of taking to the hills and caves—whether with guns or macrobiotic diets. It is rather a process of struggling to gather power over and to alter the structure and functions of institutions like the education, health and legal systems. That work is long, and it will not be casual nor, often, spectacular. But it is, I assume, the struggle to which we are together committed.

The New Scientist

by GARRETT DE BELL

Garrett de Bell is one of a new breed of scientist trying to turn us from the path of eco-catastrophe, toward an ecologically sane individual and national life-style.

De Bell received a B.S. in Biology from Stanford University in 1966. He was a candidate for the doctorate degree in zoology at the University of California at Berkeley, when he came to the conviction that the detachment of most academic scientists is one important cause of the environmental crisis.

De Bell dropped out to devote full time to ecological problems. He was the first Washington lobbyist for Zero Population Growth, and edited and contributed to *The Environmental Handbook* and *The Voter's Guide to Environmental Politics*.

Currently, de Bell is developing and living "a life-style low on consumption and high on nature." He is also working on a project to clearly outline and effectively advocate some ecologically sound alternatives to our present priorities.

THE NEW SCIENTIST must practice his calling with full concern for its relevance to the problems and needs of our time. Scientists, like most other professionals, will have to adopt radically new ways of training, research, and even life-styles to make their work relevant in this way. The New Scientist will bear little resemblance to the pursuer of pure fact, unrelated to other aspects of life, that we have grown accustomed to in the past.

What does "relevance" mean in this context? I operate on the assumption that science is *not* "objective," that its studies, its findings, and its applications have social and political consequences. Those consequences can be good or bad, and science is often as much an adversary system as our courts of law. Scientific research can be used to rake in huge profits for corporations, or it can be used for the general welfare. Any scientist who imagines his work to be ethically neutral is kidding himself.

The very choice of what to study, and what not to study, can be a political decision. Say you are a plant ecologist; you can study plant communities in the crannies high up in alpine mountain regions, a subject of undoubted theoretical interest. Or you can study the conditions of plant growth along highways and power lines with the intention of figuring out ways to control them without using herbicides. If you are convinced by the evidence that some herbicides may cause birth defects, then your efforts—far from being neutral and value-free— should be aimed at getting rid of them.

Relevant research deals with all the important aspects of broad social problems, and it is intended not simply to understand them but to *solve* them.

I am going to focus on the science of ecology in this article, because that is my field, because it is the foremost available example of how scientists can make their work socially relevant, and because in talking with people in other disciplines I have become convinced that the factors which have made most professional ecologists useless in the current environmental crisis plague other sciences as well. Hopefully, the parallels with other fields will be easily perceived.

One important difference between the "old ecology" and the "new ecology" lies in the distinction between the interdisciplinary approach and the approach which studies isolated phenomena. The flaw in most ecology programs and teaching up to now has been the attempt to mimic the physicist, to narrow every investigation down to some microscopic question that could be engraved on the head of a pin. An appropriate Ph.D. thesis for the "old ecology" might study two subspecies of white crowned sparrows' clutch size in order to test Lack's theories of population dynamics.

As a rule, any problem broad enough so that an understanding of it might be useful in solving a difficulty in the "real" world was—and often still is—considered inappropriate for a Ph.D. thesis. If you doubt this, go to your university library and look up the Ph.D. theses for the past five years in the biological sciences. Among all the studies that deal with the relationships between organisms and their environment, you will find few about humans and their environment, and fewer still about the complex biological and social causes of environmental deterioration.

The new ecology, in its interdisciplinary approach, would make it possible to write a thesis taking into account material not only from several biological fields, but from social, psychological, economic, and political sciences as well. A thesis of that sort might study and evaluate changes in farming practice brought about by corporate ownership of large farms, increased mechanization, monoculture of single crops, and the use of pesticides and herbicides. Is this really progress, producing more food cheaper, or does it just shunt costs off onto society instead of the farmer? What is the effect of corporate farming on wildlife? On the "small farmer" who is bought out and must move to the city, increasing urban overcrowding? All of these implications would traditionally be considered too vague or irrelevant to be included in a thesis.

It is difficult to give many examples of ecologists who are doing the kind of broad-perspective, interdisciplinary work that is needed; there aren't many. Of those that I know, most came through the traditional academic machine but expanded beyond the usual tunnel vision that such a background tends to induce.

Paul Ehrlich, author of *The Population Bomb* and *Population, Resources, Environment*, is undoubtedly the best known. He started out studying the population dynamics of the checkerspot butterfly.

Robert Stebbins' films, popular field guides, and curriculum guides for elementary school teachers are the work of a one-time specialist who has gone beyond normal, accepted academic faculty routines to spread environmental awareness.

Professor Arnold Schultz of the University of California has tried to get interdisciplinary programs established at both graduate and undergraduate levels. He and Stebbins have experienced strong pressure from numerous ordinary ecologists who worry about proper professional behavior and maintaining established distinctions between fields.

Truly interdisciplinary study and teaching are keynotes of the new scientist. Students must be free to ask questions about any ecological issue that concerns them, even such "nonacademic" questions as whether automating agriculture is really a good thing or not.

My own training, at Stanford, was in biology. Fortunately, it allowed me enough latitude to spend a lot of time on ecology, environmental problems and social sciences.

My graduate experience at Berkeley, though, was largely a frustrating attempt to deal with a mindless university. I did learn a few things in applied courses like forestry and wildlife management, and enjoyed natural history courses. But it was clear that any meaningful thesis I might have wanted to do was out of the question.

I finally settled on a thesis on the population dynamics and bioenergetics of a species of wolf spider. At the time I started on my project I really liked the spiders I was working on; but as I became increasingly aware of what man was doing to the world's ecosystems and the irrelevance of my going through the motions of getting a Ph.D., I figured I would wind up hating the spiders by the time I got my doctorate. One day I just walked off the campus and never came back as a student. For a few months after that I taught ecology at the Berkeley Ecology Center, which seemed a lot more important than academic games.

The trouble with the academic approach is that it rarely is directed toward *solving* the problems. It is not enough to understand that mercury concentrates in food chains, and that that is an interesting example of the cycling of materials in nature. *Why* is the mercury there? Its sources have to be found, and its discharge into the system has to be stopped. This will involve studying the industries that use mercury (as a fungicide in paper manufacturing, as an electrode in chlorine production, in the manufacture of many plastics). It will be necessary to find out what can be done to eliminate mercury loss into the environment in all of these processes, and furthermore, to look for ways of doing without materials whose production releases mercury into the environment.

Nor would the thesis stop there. It might also be necessary to look into the advertising that stimulates the use of products that result in mercury pollution, as well as the lobbying tactics and expenditures of industries to prevent the lowering of acceptable mercury levels in food.

Many similar research projects in the fields of pesticides, industrial chemicals and so on could be formulated. As things stand, they would almost certainly be rejected as Ph.D. theses, for their common characteristic is that they bridge many disciplines, and not only study what is but what should be. And they include an open-eyed recognition that change will be fought by powerful interests, and that whatever results the studies produce must be brought to public attention, not left to gather cobwebs in the university library.

Even specialized researchers, however, can contribute in ways that specifically relate to the environmental crisis. Dr. Robert Risebrough of the University of California's Institute of Marine Resources chose to study the brown pelican to show

how DDT concentrations were making them produce eggs that wouldn't hatch. The threat of the birds' extinction became a notable *cause célèbre* among conservationists and added fuel to the movement to ban DDT. Dr. Robert Payne studies humpback whales, and recently produced a popular record of their eerily beautiful songs as part of a campaign to save whales from extinction. Dr. Robert Rudd, who wrote the definitive *Pesticides and the Living Landscape,* and Dr. Donald Dahlsten and other ecologists have worked to develop biological control as an alternative to pesticides.

What sort of college curricula are needed? Generally, the curriculum would include a solid grounding in biology and chemistry, along with statistics. Ecology is a statistical field, often dealing with large numbers, probabilities, small variable samples, etc. It is often helpful to be familiar with computers, if only to be able to head off the charlatans who will try to use them to their advantage.

For those who incline toward an interdisciplinary approach, it is a good idea to spend a lot of time on political science, economics and sociology. Read books on your own, which are often more unorthodox and stimulating than assigned textbooks.

Whenever possible, talk with people who have worked in government, industry, or independently rather than those who have spent their working hours in lecture halls. Six months involvement in politics is worth more than a Ph.D. in political science. A year with the farmworkers will teach you more about "agri-business" than a graduate program in agricultural economics.

Ecology, even in its narrow sense, has many differing schools, and it is best to get some exposure to each. Some consider problems of energy flow and nutrient cycling through ecosystems. Phillips' book *Ecological Energetics* and part of Odum's *Fundamentals of Ecology* stem from this approach. Practical applications include dealing with concentrations of harmful substances in food chains (mercury, DDT, strontium-90), analysis of nitrogen and phosphorus cycles in nature, and ecologically sound agriculture. Properly applied, the ecosystems approach could lead to alternate kinds of agriculture that wouldn't spread DDT and organophosphates around the planet or drain phosphorus into lakes to support the growth of undesirable algae (eutrophication). Unfortunately, many professors would be horrified if a Ph.D. thesis contained a chapter on the agricultural chemical lobby or necessary legislation to get agriculture back on a sound ecological basis.

Another school deals with physiological ecology, the effect of variation in the environment on organisms. Here again, if the full implications were brought out, a study of the variation in oxygen or silt content in water on survival rates of trout might serve as a powerful argument to stop an Army Corps of Engineers' channelization project that might increase silt and decrease oxygen.

The traditional course of graduate training to a Ph.D. can be productive, under the right circumstances. You have to be very careful, though, not to get caught up in the maze of academic irrelevance which constitutes so many programs.

The first thing to check out is whether the program you are considering will allow you to spend your time training for the research you really want to do, and whether the problems *you* think are important would be acceptable Ph.D. proposals. Many schools have caught on to all the vogue phrases—"interdisciplinary," "problem-oriented," "relevant to the needs of our time," in order to draw in more money for the time-yellowed programs they've been offering for years. In my own experience at Berkeley, I found that the rhetoric about stimulating environments and freedom to follow your own interests was not matched by the practice. Graduate school at Berkeley differed in no significant way from the service schools I attended in the army, except that the pretense of freedom just led to more frustration.

One test you can make is to see if this year's "interdisciplinary, problem-oriented" program differs in any concrete way from those of previous years. Look in old catalogs and try and find people who were in the programs previously.

One red warning flag should pop up immediately when you run across what seem to be pointless requirements, which your advisor justifies with arguments like: "Well, this is a pet subject of the department chairman's—you might as well just do it, it'll be less trouble than to try to get it changed." Rigid course requirements which have no direct bearing on your interests, such as language exams, are usually a harbinger of narrow standards for thesis acceptability.

The best bet, if you can find one, is a school that allows a Ph.D. to be awarded upon the satisfaction of requirements by *any* three professors from any departments. Some schools have Ph.D. programs run out of the graduate dean's office or out of an interdisciplinary committee that are often quite free.*

So let's say you've gone through the mill and gotten your Ph.D. What can you do now?

Well, there are possibilities as a college professor. They depend largely on having the guts to do what you think is worthwhile in teaching and research without regard to your promotion, tenure, or being asked to serve on government advisory committees. Even if you think these things aren't important to you, the pressure is still tremendous. Even basically honest faculty members I know are always pulling back from doing research they really want to do, or from letting their students

---

* Graduate students who find it hard to fit their wide interests into the Procrustean bed of ordinary Ph.D. programs might want to investigate an experimental program called the Union Graduate School, sponsored by the Union for Experimenting Colleges and Universities at Antioch College (Yellow Springs, Ohio 45387). Says the Union's brochure: "The degree is not dependent on any total of course credits or period of time. It is dependent rather on the quality of the student's thinking; the breadth and depth of his knowledge; the rigor with which he holds to standards of excellence for himself and others; his demonstrated and potential creativity; the achievement of genuine integration among physical, mental, and emotional aspects of living; and the fusion of individual goals with social values."

do a valuable thesis, for fear of subtle reprisals. It even inhibits full professors who couldn't be fired for anything less than raping a coed.

You can also work within the establishment in other ways. There is a crying need for ecologists who can write. So much of what appears in the popular press about the environment is superficial, quoting or misquoting "experts" or citing conflicting authorities. Paul Ehrlich is an excellent example of an ecologist who has exerted a strong force on public opinion through his writing, which is scientific yet colorful and polished.

Many organizations that *should* be applying ecology, but often aren't, are being "infiltrated" by people working to adopt more sound policies. The Forest Service and National Park Service come to mind. There is a lot that you can do, even at the lower levels, within the bounds of existing policy in such organizations.

Even in the Atomic Energy Commission, which is diametrically opposed to ecologically sound policy, Drs. Arthur Tamplin and John Gofman have shown what can be done. From their positions of expertise within the AEC's Lawrence Radiation Lab, they have exposed that standards for permissible radiation are at least ten times too high. Ralph Nader is setting up a new organization to encourage people who observe harmful practices where they work to reveal them through his group. Hopefully, this will encourage many more like Gofman and Tamplin to speak out.

But suppose you don't want to work for the establishment. What then?

You might as well accept one thing at the start. To do anything really constructive without being under the wing of some giant organization, you will have to live simply and inexpensively. Not just to use up fewer resources (although that will be one benefit), but because to make a lot of money dealing with the environment you will have to be a whore. The enemy will pay you well to come up with good public relations and shallow window-dressing advertisements which make it appear that they're doing their part.

There are many people who feel that it's worthwhile to try to work within the corporate system. I personally doubt it. For all their concern with image, I don't see any evidence that major industries are willing to make any fundamental changes in direction. Coca-Cola is unlikely to hire anyone who is going to tell them that they must market only returnable bottles, as well as support legislation to force all manufacturers to do the same.

I have written to the major container manufacturers and some beverage firms, asking their support for a disposal tax which would force the no-deposit, no-return container off the market. They were horrified. Oh, yes, they want to "clean up" the environment, but on the voluntary recycling, please-don't-litter approach they've been pushing. The trouble with that is it ignores the waste of resources, depends on human nature which is not always conscientious, and doesn't have a chance of solving the litter and solid-waste problems.

If you want to change the direction of major industries, you are not going to do it by getting jobs with them. You will have to work independently with a group representing the public interest. Most are very poor, which is why I mentioned the necessity of living cheaply if you plan to look for a job with one of them.

(There are occasional exceptions, environmental groups that are well-heeled. My own inclination is to distrust them. They tend to be public-relations minded, always on the make for grants from foundations or the government and hence rigidly apolitical, or a cop-out for wealthy conservationists concerned about African endangered species while they make their money from oil, real estate, or the stock market.)

By now, there are literally hundreds of environmental groups. Zero Population Growth, Sierra Club, The Wilderness

Society, The Environmental Defense Fund, Friends of the Earth, and Ralph Nader's Center for the Study of Responsive Law all work for the cause of stopping man's destruction of his environment. They all deserve support for their efforts. The larger they get, the more jobs they will have available to scientists and others who want to work for a quality environment in ways that would not be possible in universities or government. Each citizen should consider it a duty to help support one or more of these groups that work for the public interest and have no product to sell or profit to make.

And it's better to throw as much support as possible to one group than to spread it around. Instead of giving five dollars each to groups A, B, C, D and E, give twenty-five dollars to one of them. The reason for this is that much of each group's income goes for overhead: of the five dollars you send to group A, half of it may go to sending you their newsletter, future contribution pitches, etc. But the overhead costs are the same for the organization you donate twenty-five dollars to, and a larger percentage of your money goes for useful work.

Working through organizations like these, scientists can turn their expertise to the benefit of the environment in many ways. They can analyze government and corporate planning proposals and nail any flaws that might have bad consequences for the environment. They can testify at public hearings against such atrocities as the supersonic transport. The respectability that attaches in the public mind to scientists enables them to speak as one having authority, enabling the audience, perhaps, to more readily accept the idea that building more freeways does not solve transportation problems.

Incidentally, while I am all for academics using whatever influence they have for the good of the environment, I strongly discourage reverence for degrees per se. Having a Ph.D. may be an indication of profound knowledge in one's field, or it may reflect a glibness with words and the ability to hit it off well with faculty committees. And knowledge is not necessarily synonymous with wisdom, imagination and breadth of vision.

Most importantly, the scientist with imagination can offer plans for a future in which the world's ecosystem and human warmth and contact are preserved, as an alternative to the dehumanized megalopolises now being planned for us by the technology-firsters.

Still, there *are* more scientists who want to work for the environment than there are jobs in the field, even at minimal salaries. Can anything be done to help the situation?

There is a lot of money floating around that could be used to fund ecologically relevant jobs, and luckily not all of it is in the hands of foundations. Take, for instance, the so-called "youth market." According to the Youth Research Institute, young people spent a record high of $22.3 billion in 1969, with a good percentage of that by college students. Supposedly young people are rejecting the materialism of their elders, putting down the conspicuous consumption-planned obsolescence economy. Maybe some of them are, but in many cases the products have just changed; instead of cigarettes, Corvettes, fancy suits and expensive dates, young people now shell out for stereos, records, leather boots, marijuana and electrically heated water beds.

So there is a lot of money on every college campus that could be used to fund socially relevant jobs, and a little organizing ability can pry it loose.

Routine pitches for contributions are relatively futile because there are too many competing causes looking for handouts. Let's take a lesson from the labor movement, add a little brashness, and try to come up with a scheme for an automatic, compulsory collection mechanism.

Say you have a campus of 20,000 students. Organize a campaign for an initiative in student elections to impose a one-dollar increase in the student fee (or more if you can get away with it). One dollar per quarter would raise $80,000, enough to fund sixteen jobs at $5,000 a year. A student committee could determine what jobs needed most to be funded, and choose recent graduates or other qualified applicants to fill them.

Some might object to the compulsory nature of the system. But it would be instituted only by a campuswide vote. Student fees now go to support the school band and football team, which many students couldn't care less about. If it was necessary to pass the proposal, a proviso could be added giving students the option of not paying by checking a box on the fee card. The necessity for making an active gesture to avoid the payment should be part of the system.

Ralph Nader is pushing this approach. Last year, he gave a pitch to students at nine campuses in Oregon to kick in three dollars per year for a statewide public service fund with its own board of directors and goals. Fifty per cent of the enrollment of the nine colleges signed up, and out of this was formed the Oregon Students Public Interest Research Group. This organization's particular emphasis is on public service law as practiced by Nader's Washington organization, but the funding mechanism is appropriate for any environmental concern.

Local control of money raised locally to support important jobs now going undone can give more strength and a better balance to the environmental movement. First, the potential number of jobs that could be created this way is enormous. The membership of all the organizations listed above is less than the student body of the University of California. Second, this should get more people directly involved instead of just paying their dues to a group or two and sitting by their TV waiting for their group's charismatic leader to solve all their problems for them. It is very important to have strong national groups that can wage battles to stop the SST, Save the Grand Canyon, get a Redwood National Park and so forth. But many important decisions are decided at a state and local level where the big national groups only have rare opportunities to be of help. I am now giving top priority to stimulating this sort of direct involvement by the people, as it is the only way to solve environmental problems permanently. Standard Oil, Shell, Dow, General Motors and the freeway builders are all working full time to pave the earth and cover it with an oily coat. Environmentalists need thousands of full-time workers watching their activities, exposing problems, developing sound alternatives and pushing for ecologically sound policy in legislative bodies, administrative agencies and the courts.

The widespread interest in ecology of the last few years has been more than just a reaction against the wreckage we have been inflicting on our planet. It is part of an intellectual trend and a new world view which may yet be as important as any turning point in the history of western thought. We are discovering, or rediscovering, the necessity of looking at things in their relationships with everything else, not as isolated phenomena.

This attitude may be more important in science than anywhere else. Science is not "neutral"; its techniques and discoveries can make existence safer and happier for all forms of life, or they can be bent to destruction, manipulation and selfish interests by political or corporate groups.

Which way science is applied depends in large part on whether the scientist chooses to study problems of social importance and is willing to seek solutions that go beyond the traditional, narrow limits of his discipline. He must recognize the connection between the specific problem to which he is applying himself and the rest of life. We are learning to recognize the interconnectedness of everything, and it is in this way that the New Scientist must approach his work today.

Transforming
the
Traditional
Professions

The New Doctor

by H. JACK GEIGER

H. Jack Geiger made his first impact on medicine and social change in 1947, when—as an undergraduate at a university in Chicago—he organized and led a strike of more than 5,000 students and faculty members in a successful effort to crack racially discriminatory admission policies in the university's medical school and teaching hospitals. The action was atypical in the sense that it occurred nearly two decades before such issue-oriented strikes and confrontations became a common and effective technique in American educational change. Geiger has been pioneering ever since.

Today he is known as a leading proponent—and explicator—of the thesis that the major task of the health professions is to accomplish change in a social order that produces poverty and ill health; as an originator and developer of the neighborhood health center movement in American medicine; and as a pioneer in the use of health services as a base for community organization and community control.

Geiger was one of the founding members of the Medical Committee for Human Rights, originally organized to protect civil rights workers in Mississippi and later the major radical health organization opposing the American Medical Association. During the next seven years he simultaneously organized, developed, and served as project director of the first urban and the first rural community health centers funded by OEO —the Tufts–Columbia Point Health Center in Boston and the Tufts–Delta Health Center in Bolivar County, Mississippi—which became models for a nationwide network of such new health institutions. The Mississippi center pioneered in the development of a community corporation of the poor which now owns and manages the program; the organization of a 600-acre cooperative farm; the development of a low-cost rural housing cooperative; and the inclusion of environmental health services, youth programs, a transportation network, and a black cultural center.

A former merchant seaman, newspaper reporter, and union organizer, Geiger entered medical school at thirty and trained in internal medicine, epidemiology, and the social sciences, with studies of international health and social change in Africa. Currently he is professor and chairman of the Department of Community Medicine, School of Medicine, State University of New York at Stony Brook, New York.

ANYONE WHO is thinking now about beginning the long process of becoming a physician will, in fact, spend most of his active professional career between the years 1980 and 2020—and so he or she needs to be thinking about what it will mean to be a doctor *then*. In a time of enormously rapid social and technological change, when prediction for the next year or two is a difficult and baffling task, can we hope to look that far into the future? Yes, in a general way, because the major forces that seem likely to shape American medical care for at least the next decade are already identifiable, and the social and professional changes that will affect being a doctor *then* have already begun. We can get some clues, at least, by looking not so much at what *all* doctors today are doing as at what some of the youngest and newest physicians today are doing.

In one month recently, the interns and residents on the house staff of a big-city municipal teaching hospital were organizing to protest the abysmal treatment of low-income patients—the indignities, poor or non-existent nursing care, long waits, overcrowding, and fragmentation of care—and to help patients assert their own rights. At the same time, other young physicians and students were working in new health centers, free clinics, pregnancy counseling services, welfare rights offices and other community programs in a hundred different locations across the nation. A "conservative" medical student organization was planning a year-round project for health care for isolated whites in rural Appalachia; a more radical group was working with black and Puerto Rican community organizations in Chicago to help them establish their own health centers. Some physicians and students were carrying out research to demonstrate to a skeptical or indifferent public that serious malnutrition and hunger do exist, on a large scale, in this country. Thousands, in one way or another, were working against the war in Vietnam, the draft, the pursuit of chemical and biological warfare. In short, it was possible to find young physicians and medical students on picket lines as well as in laboratories, and in community programs as well as in the teaching-hospital wards or private offices. And these new physicians and physicians-in-training regard their time on the picket line, or in the community, as a legitimate part of their careers as doctors.

Even in the generation a few years older, and a few years more established in medical careers, substantial numbers of physicians were trying to learn something about the economics of medical care, trying to organize group practices for whole neighborhoods or areas, trying to bring new kinds of medical care services into being instead of perpetuating the old.

It would be grossly misleading to suggest that this is the whole picture, or even the dominant aspect, of contemporary American medicine, for this is simply not so. The overwhelming majority of American physicians are doing what they have always done in the last half-century: seeing their patients in their offices and in the hospital; examining, testing, listening, diagnosing and treating sick and anxious human beings; working in the operating theater and the research laboratory; teaching; studying. These are important and rewarding tasks; they are the very basis of what "doctor" means to us. At the core of what the new young physicians do, too, is the task of caring for sick people.

Yet these other activities of young health professionals today are symptomatic of a new set of realizations and beliefs that is already changing medical practice and health care in the country. These activities give explicit recognition to the beliefs that (1) there is something seriously wrong with the health-care system in this country, something that blocks adequate, available, high-quality, reasonable-cost care both to the poor and minority groups and to the middle class; (2) it is part of the physician's job to help deal with those problems and help change that system; (3) there is something wrong with the social order in this country to the extent that it makes large numbers of people sick by condemning them to miserable housing, hunger, joblessness, social and biological and environmental stress; and (4) it is part of the physician's job to help change that, too.

First, the question of health and poverty. The health of the poor in the United States is an ongoing national disaster. We have known about the general dimensions of this disaster for a long time, just as we have known about the relationships between poverty and health, without fully facing up to either of them. The poor are likelier to be sick. The sick are likelier to be poor. Without intervention, the poor get sicker and the sick get poorer. And that is just what has been happening, and is happening today, in the central cities and ghettos of the urban North, the sharecroppers' shacks of the rural South, in the migrant farm workers' hovels that can be found an hour's drive from New York City, or Los Angeles, in the poor-white coalfield slag of Appalachia, among the Mexican-Americans of the Southwest, and on Indian reservations. Thirty-five years ago we heard of one-third of a nation ill-housed, ill-fed and ill-clothed. Today it is estimated that about one-fifth of all the people in this affluent country live in poverty. The apparent improvement conceals the growing health gap between the poor and the rest of the population: In 1940, for example, the infant mortality rate of nonwhites was 70 per cent greater than that for whites and in 1962, twenty-two years later, it was 90 per cent greater. A few years ago, Dr. George James estimated that the annual excess mortality among the poor in New York City alone was 13,000 lives, and he added, "It is no exaggeration to state that these deaths are caused by poverty." In short, the poor are likelier to die—sooner and younger than others.

Second, health and race—a topic almost but not quite co-terminous with the question of poverty. It is hardly startling that the association between race and poor health is even stronger, for here the crushing burden of racial discrimination is superimposed on the effects of economic deprivation and social deprivation. There is a phrase in the Book of Common Prayer that is tragically precise in describing our national per-formance with respect to the health of the Negro population. It reads: "We have left undone those things which we ought to have done; and we have done those things which we ought not to have done; and there is no health in us."

The undeniable fact is: Infant or adult, man or woman, northerner or southerner, the Negro is substantially less healthy than the white. He gets less medical care, less ade-quate medical care, and less assistance in meeting its cost.

The effects of racial discrimination and economic disadvan-tage begin before birth—and never stop. Most Negro expect-ant mothers simply do not get the basic prenatal care that most white expectant mothers take for granted. Fewer Negro mothers have their babies in hospitals than do white mothers. The national Negro infant mortality rate is almost twice the white rate. And women without prenatal care are about three times more likely to give birth to premature babies than those who do receive proper care. Very small premature infants are ten times more likely to be mentally retarded than full-term children. And some of the infants who do survive beyond a year, particularly in the rural Southeast, are likely to be syste-matically and chronically malnourished, and we are just beginning to explore the contribution of malnutrition to men-tal retardation.

The figures go on and on. A white baby boy born today can

expect to live long enough to celebrate his sixty-eighth birth-day. For a Negro baby, the chances are that his life will be cut short seven years sooner. Or again: Of every one thousand white Americans in their late forties, five will die in the coming year. Of every one thousand Negroes, ten will die. And what of the survivors? In comparison with the white, the American Negro has one-third more days when he is unable to function at full physical capacity, is sick enough to require bed rest on twice as many days, and loses one and one-half times more days from work because of disease and disability.

Finally, and briefly, urban growth. The demographers tell us that within thirty years most of the population of the United States will be living in huge urban megalopolises. One of them, with more than 50 million residents, will be Bos-Wash —a continuous urban belt from Boston to Washington. Another, with more than 30 million people, will be Chi-Pitts—Chicago to Pittsburgh; and a third, with 20 million, will be San-San—San Francisco to San Diego. The prospects are as distasteful as the names—but they are real, and we will have to start to deal with them now and recognize their magnitude. In health care and in other areas, it is just no use to build a better mousetrap—when the problem is elephants.

And so, in summary, we have a whole segment of our population—the poor, the Negro, the rural migrant, the central city-dweller—sinking into the lower depths, isolated more and more from the mainstreams of American life. They are aliens within our own country, with a powerful and despairing conviction that the major institutions of American life do not serve them, are not intended to serve them. And the consequences are apparent in their health.

But how can this be, we ask? Look at our magnificent teaching hospitals, our medical centers, our medical schools, our networks of community hospitals, our public health departments and their vast networks of clinics, our great array of social service agencies and voluntary organizations. The poor, the Negro, the in-migrant, regardless of ability to pay, can get medical care of the very highest technical quality! It must be the fault of the poor themselves—they are apathetic and uncooperative.

This convenient fiction has been called the Mt. Everest fallacy, and it runs like this: I have constructed a wonderful medical center, complete with a trained professional staff, the latest equipment, open to rich and poor alike, with a huge outpatient department. And I have put it on top of Mt. Everest. If my only regular patients are Tenzing Sherpa and Sir Edmund Hillary, obviously the rest of the world is apathetic and uncooperative.

I am saying that many of our health services for the poor, while they are of high technical quality, are characterized by a series of nearly insuperable barriers. For poverty populations, these include the barriers of time and distance—the simple physical remoteness of many health facilities, the inadequacies of public transportation in slum areas, the long hours of travel and waiting time. In Watts, it was a two-hour bus trip (when you could find a bus) or a ten-dollar cab ride to Los Angeles County Hospital's outpatient department; if you were sick, the question was whether or not you were "ten dollars sick." If you lost half a day's pay—for after all, the outpatient department is only open during working hours, and the jobs available to most poor people are not characterized by sick-leave provisions—that's your problem. If there are four other children at home, and no one to care for them, that's your problem. Add to these the barriers of cost and of confusing, complex and contradictory eligibility requirements. Add the barriers of discontinuity, irrelevance and impersonality—what Dr. Alonzo Yerby has called "the pervasive stigma of charity," and the ignominious bargain under which, in his words, the poor are forced to barter their dignity for their health. And then add the barrier of fragmentation of the health-care system: well-child care in one place—but some place else for the same child when he's sick; adult care somewhere else, ambulatory care at another locus, in-hospital care unconnected with these, social work and visiting nurse resources at still other locations. One of the reasons for the great rise in the use of the hospital emergency room at night is simply that the so-called apathetic poor are making highly intelligent use of the health-care system: They have discovered that you can get the same piecemeal, episodic, discontinuous, uncoordinated medical care cheaper and faster in the emergency room at night than in the outpatient department in the daytime.

It is within the usual outpatient department, however, that the system really becomes absurd. Consider, for example, the following case description of Dr. James. It is only a little extreme.

"Let me give an actual case of a man of seventy-six. He lives in a housing project in Queens. He has the following medical problems: cancer of the larynx; his throat was operated upon and his larynx removed. He has a tracheotomy, and speaks through the use of his esophagus with special equipment. If he would go to one of our good teaching hospitals, he would go to the ear, nose, and throat clinic and the cancer clinic. He has cataract of his left eye, so he'd go to the eye clinic. He has chronic bronchitis, so he'd go to the chest clinic. He has a hypertrophied prostate, so he'd go to the genitourinary clinic. He has varicose veins, so he'd go to the vascular clinic. He has arteriosclerotic heart disease and an old coronary thrombosis, but he'd be followed in the heart clinic. He has marked constipation, a diverticulosis sigmoid colon, a hiatus hernia, a diaphragmatic hernia—and so he'd go to the medical clinic. He also has diabetes mellitus—so he'd go to the metabolism clinic.

"Here's a man of seventy-six who happens to live four miles from the nearest available hospital, who would have to go to ten different clinics."

Now this may be a wonderfully efficient system for the

training of interns and residents in the medical specialties. It may be an efficient way to run a hospital, from the point of view of the hospital. It may be a wonderful system for the diagnosis and treatment of diseased organs—but it doesn't work for *sick people,* and most diseased organs come in that kind of package. It doesn't work for sick families, and most people are part of a family. It has nothing to do with communities, yet most families live in communities—and family and community (the biological, social and physical environment) are powerful determinants of health and illness.

How did this happen? It didn't come into being because most health professionals, physicians, nurses, social workers, hospital administrators and others just didn't care, or haven't tried hard, or aren't concerned and trying hard now. It happened because, for the past fifty years, we have been experiencing the revolution of scientific medicine: accurate diagnosis, powerful therapy, the real ability to save lives. We have made the hospital the center of this revolution, and more and more of medical care, the complex equipment, the multiple diagnostic procedures and the concentration of specialist resources has been pulled centripetally into the hospital and medical center. In medical care, the hospital is the hub of the universe. This has had an enormous and important effect on the quality of medical care. But it has left the community, the people, and a whole set of deeper social needs behind.

And so, on the upper floors of the hospital, we have the very best that American medicine can offer. And down on the street floor—or in the basement—we have that great medical soup kitchen, that cafeteria of clinics, that Siberia of medical care, the old-fashioned outpatient department.

Sir Geoffrey Vickers has defined the history of public health as a series of "successive redefinitions of the unacceptable." If the old outpatient department is unacceptable, then innovation is needed.

We have an example of such innovation, I believe, in the

Tufts Comprehensive Community Health Action Program and its two component health centers in Columbia Point, Boston, and in Bolivar County, Mississippi, and I think it is important briefly to describe this effort and some of its results.

The comprehensive neighborhood health center, in our view, is a new kind of social institution. It is not a mere outpatient clinic, nor even just a group practice, that happens to be in the community; it is much more than either of these more familiar models. For example, the Columbia Point Health Center was designed as a resource that provides or definitively arranges for total, family-centered, ambulatory care for an entire community of some 6,000 persons. It is *in* the community it serves, thus breaking the distance barrier. Its doors are open to every resident of the community—there is no confusing barrier of cost or eligibility for access. It has been open and staffed by physicians and other health professionals twenty-four hours a day, seven days a week, thus breaking the barriers of time and convenience. Its staff—full-time faculty and staff of Tufts Medical School—includes internists, pediatricians, community health nurses, social workers, community organizers, technicians and others—and a substantial number of community residents both in traditional jobs and in new career roles. In addition to physicians' examining and consulting rooms, it includes a well-equipped emergency room, a complete laboratory and pharmacy, a modest X-ray facility, medical record library and other resources. A variety of frequently used specialists, such as obstetrician-gynecologists, are there on a part-time but regular basis, fully integrated into the center's pattern of service. When other specialist resources or services that we cannot provide ourselves are needed, we definitively arrange for these at a whole network of related hospitals and consultants, including the Tufts teaching hospitals and Boston City Hospital. To "arrange definitively" means, to us, to *take responsibility*—not just to hand out a referral slip to some other part of a soup kitchen—and so we see to it that appointments are made, that patients are transported to other facilities and back to Columbia Point where necessary, and that the resulting medical and social data from other sources are incorporated into Columbia Point Health Center records, so that continuity of care is preserved. Often we follow our patients into hospital, and often we are able to shorten their hospitalization and facilitate their early return to the community, because we are prepared to resume their care without interruption and to provide medical service at home and in the health center during convalescence.

We do more. All our care is family-centered care. Our basic unit is the family health-care group of internist, pediatrician, community health nurse, social worker and family health aide. If the adults in the Jones family see the internist from a family health-care group, then the Jones children see the pediatrician from that group, and the nurse, social worker and family health worker may see any of the Joneses—and the Joneses have their own "regular" doctors *and* nurses and others, with continuity over time. This enables us to look for—and try to deal with—*family* problems, not just individual problems.

But we try to do still more than this. What we call "community health action" represents our attempt to become truly a part of the community—not merely to provide health service but also to promote broader social change—change in education, in jobs, in income, in self-image, and in the ability of a community to organize, to mobilize itself, even if necessary to agitate effectively—an honorable democratic concept—for necessary reforms. Thus the health center and the community —through the autonomous, voluntary and freely elected Columbia Point Health Association—try to reflect and respond to community concerns. Our Department of Psychiatry, for example, does more than see individuals—or participate in the care of families; together with the Department of Community Health Action, it is deeply involved in a series of group sessions on child behavior and problems with the teachers in the local elementary schools—and with groups of mothers who organized spontaneously outside of the official parent-teachers' organization to try to achieve a better school, *and* to help bring teachers and parents together. This is a far cry from the usual outpatient department activity—or from its usual philosophy: We'll run the services and we'll let you provide the illnesses. The Columbia Point Health Association is slowly but increasingly a participant in the design and evaluation of the center's programs and work, the construction and review of its budget, the hiring and training of personnel, and the resolution of conflicts and problems.

Even after the first two years (we have been open for nearly six), we could report some results, chiefly on a few key indices of health and medical care. We managed more than 72,000 patient visits during the first two years, sometimes at a rate of more than 200 patients per day—or 3 per cent of the population every twenty-four hours—and for real and evident problems. So much for the so-called apathy of the poor toward health care! The rate of ambulatory health-care utilization by this community has more than doubled. Before we opened, only 72 per cent of the community identified itself as having *any* regular source of medical care; today that figure is over 90 per cent—and overwhelmingly represents the health center. Two years ago, only 15 per cent of the population felt it had a good source of advice about health problems; today the figure is 44 per cent. Two years ago, 23 per cent of Columbia Point families stated they had put off medical care during the preceding months; the comparable figure is now 5 per cent. Two years ago, 28 per cent of the residents had had a physical examination for preventive purposes—that is, when no known illness was present; today it is 55 per cent.

Before the health center opened, 70 per cent of the Columbia Point population reported that it took from two to five hours (and 14 per cent said it took from five to nine hours) to leave home, get medical care, and return home. Today, 89 per cent of the community reports that the door-to-door time for medical care is one hour or less—a figure much more consistent with the needs of large families, working mothers, many young children, limited transportation.

And finally, and most strikingly, we have just conducted a study of hospitalizations in a sample of 54 Columbia Point families in the year before the health center opened and in the two years since. For these 54 families, a random selection of those continuously on public assistance, there were 200 hospital days (with an average length of 8.3 days) in 1965, the year before the health center opened. In 1966, the first year of health center operations, these same families required 110 hospitalization days (with an average stay of 5.5 days); in 1967, a total of 40 days (with an average length of 5.0 days).

In this sample of families, then, the health center has reduced hospitalization by *80 per cent* in just two years.

This is a major accomplishment. If it is supported by the additional before-and-after data we are accumulating, including data on the health center's impact on the objective health state of the community, then we will, I believe, be justified in taking a long and serious look at the thesis that this new kind of institution, with this new kind of program, should replace the traditional outpatient department. I am seriously suggesting that the hospital as we now know it is an obsolete and ineffective institution for ambulatory care, and that hospitals for the future should be vastly different—in effect, intensive care units for patients with critical and complex illness, and a mixed, more modest section (*not* an OPD) for ambulatory patients requiring bed care and for completely ambulatory patients requiring complex specialty resources. The hub of the medical care universe would be a network of comprehensive community health centers. I believe this model is just as appropriate for middle-income groups as for the disadvantaged, and should not be restricted to the poor—but, in these initial efforts, the poor, with their greater need, should have first priority.

If we assume that the new trends exemplified in this project, and others like it throughout the country, will grow and broaden, if we guess that such changes will accelerate, and if we make some educated guesses about the impact of new technologies, we *can* make some predictions about the world of the physician in 1980. Here are some of the likeliest:

1. The new physician in 1980 will be serving a public that sees decent health care for everyone as a right of citizenship and an expression of American social purpose, not as a privilege dependent on ability to pay. There will be some form of national health insurance under which the costs of everyone's medical care will be met at least in major part.

2. The new physician in 1980, in consequence, will no longer be paid directly by his patients; she or he (we'll come to that in a moment) will no longer negotiate fees with individual patients, and no longer have to weigh the patient's ability to pay in deciding on the best plan of health care of illness treatment. The doctor—and the public—will still be concerned about costs, but they will be the total costs of providing complete care to a whole population, or a whole town, not to one individual or family.

3. The new physician will rarely work alone, in solo practice, in an office by himself in what amounts to a one-man business enterprise. Instead, he will work in group practices comprising many other doctors and other health professionals, all joined as a team to provide care to a defined population; or he may work for a hospital corporation. Some of these group practices and hospitals will be owned by community corporations. Others will be owned by independent or physician-controlled corporations, but all of them will have to meet a requirement for some representation on their boards and in their management of the consumers they serve.

4. The new physician will not tend to be clustered so overwhelmingly (as at present) in affluent middle-class suburbs. He or she will, instead, have a greater chance of working in inner-city and rural or small-town areas, where group prac-

tices will enable him to have adequate facilities and give good health care.

5. In the medical school graduating classes of 1980, 20 per cent of the new physicians will be blacks, Puerto Rican Americans, Mexican Americans and representatives of other minority groups. Twenty to thirty per cent will come from working-class and lower middle-class homes (at present, approximately 90 per cent of medical students are drawn from a tiny segment of the upper middle class, largely because it is the children of this segment of the population who get the best preparatory education in the best schools, the encouragement toward professional careers, and the parental and other economic support to pay college and medical school bills). And close to 50 per cent of the 1980 physician graduates will be women.

6. The 1980 physician will spend much of his time with sick or anxious patients, like his contemporary counterpart, but he will also spend a great deal of time supervising and working with new kinds of health paraprofessionals who see his patients: family health workers, physician assistants, medical corpsmen, nurse-midwives, social work assistants, mental health assistants and counselors.

7. The 1980 physician will spend less time at technical tasks, because these will be performed by new kinds of technicians, and more time on the most complex tasks facing the most seriously ill patients. The definition of "technical tasks" to be performed by non-M.D. technicians may be pretty startling: it might include setting simple fractures, taking out appendixes, and doing all normal deliveries of babies.

8. The most important technological advance in medical practice will not come from biology, chemistry, or similar research laboratories; it is already here. By 1980, the physician's life and work will be profoundly changed by the computer. Every physician's office, every group practice, and every hospital will have computer links. It is the computer that will

help take the patient's history and serve as the physician's memory for many details. It is the computer that will help estimate the different diagnostic possibilities in any given case and list the possible kinds of drugs and treatment for the physician to choose. The computer will link any physician, no matter where his practice is located, to specialized resources and perform many technical tasks: reading electrocardiograms and brain-wave tracings, for example, or analyzing blood samples. In the hospital, the computer will monitor the vital signs of the sickest patients, analyze and warn of moment-to-moment changes during surgery, and keep track of all the diagnostic tests, their results, and all the medications that may be involved for each patient.

9. The physician of 1980 will be accountable to more people than is the case today. The quality of his or her performance will be subject to review not merely by his peers—the other doctors and professionals he works with—but by independent and impartial physicians, perhaps working for a federal quality-control agency, just as airline pilots (another group of professionals responsible for human life) today are monitored by independent professional pilots representing the Federal Aviation Agency. On the one hand, poor performance, unnecessary surgery and the like will be far easier to detect and deal with; on the other hand, the physician who needs assistance and retraining, or arranging time off for further education, will find it far easier to get. Most of all, through consumer representation, physicians and health professionals will also be accountable to those they serve.

10. The physician of 1980 will have a broader range of career choices than his 1970 forerunner. Careers in medicine today tend to be focused on clinical practice in the community, academic medicine (teaching and clinical practice at a medical school and its teaching hospital), or laboratory research. To these, by 1980, will be added full-time careers in the organization and management of medical care. While we are still likely to have specialization (the range of pediatricians and

internists and surgeons and psychiatrists and cardiologists and so on), there will be much more interest in family practice (the kind of work that used to be called general practice), but—by 1980—with much better training and preparation and much more assistance from paraprofessionals. And just as the focus of interest enlarges from individual to family, so for many physicians the interest will be still larger—in whole communities, the problems they have that are related to health, the diseases they suffer, the relationships between their health and their environment.

11. Finally, medical education will be changed: more flexible and more variable. Not only will the pool of applicants be broader, and not only will the poor, the non-white and the woman have much greater access to professional careers, but there will be multiple routes to get into, and through, medical school and hospital training. Some students will still follow a traditional route through high school and four-year college to medical school; others may move up a career ladder, starting out as a family health worker, moving on to licensed practical nurse or registered nurse and then to medicine, or from physician assistant and medical corpsman to medicine through sequential training interspersed with periods of work. Students will be able to complete medical school in three years instead of four; in some cases there will be six-year programs (after high school graduation) combining a liberal arts and an M.D. degree; and medical school itself will be much more flexible, much more like a graduate school and much less like a lockstep kindergarten in which everyone must do the same things in the same way at the same time. With greatly increased federal funding of professional education, costs will not be such a major factor in career choice.

These are neither very daring nor very novel predictions. None of them is new. Every one of them represents a trend already under way. Some of them will come true even before 1980.

Curiously, there are those who see this picture of the physician a decade hence as something fearful, dangerous, or worse. "Socialism!" they cry, or "socialized medicine!" or "The doctor will be reduced to a cog in some huge bureaucratic machine" or "You'll destroy the doctor-patient relationship" or "Nobody will really have a physician of his own any more" or "You won't be able to recruit anyone into becoming a doctor."

In my view, these ominous warnings—while they are often deeply felt and seriously believed—are, in the main, tears of lament for the passing of our present non-system of medical care, organized as a cottage industry with all its inequitable distributions and escalating costs. There are some current health professionals who honestly cannot believe that health care can be organized and provided any other way. Mixed in with the tears are some cries of rage at the prospect of some loss of the unrestricted opportunity to earn income, the end of freedom from real quality control, the passing of a defiant individualism that resisted coherent organization of health care even when it was in the patient's best interest, and the tempering of special status and privilege by accountability to that lowliest of creatures in the current system, the health-care consumer. But these losses are of central significance only to the most extreme individual entrepreneurs in medicine today, and the health-care consumer (that is, the public) may feel that the medical-care system was never the right place for that kind of entrepreneurial drive to start with.

There are others who are concerned that these new developments in medical care will dehumanize the practice of medicine, and it is this fear that I have called curious—for there is (I think) every reason to believe that they will do just the opposite: re-humanize the practice of medicine, enrich it, make it possible to return it to some of its finest traditions, and make use of technology and organization to serve *human* rather than institutional or economic needs. In simpler words, the physician of the future—working in larger organizations, freed from the patient's individual economic constraints, sur-

rounded by co-workers of all sorts, with access to his computer—will have more time and greater ability to do a *better*,
warmer, more considerate and more responsive job for his patient, the patient's family, and the community.

Even more important, to my mind, is the possibility that
medicine, liberated by these new developments, may become
what it once was: a vehicle for social change and reform, and
a career therefore open to those who passionately desire social
change. A career in medicine may be open to those who believe that traditional health services are not enough: that the
biological, social, economic and political environment of
Americans in poverty is incompatible with healthy life (the
same being increasingly true of the middle class) and that no
amount of health service as such will alter it. Open to those
who believe there is no point in treating rat bites and ignoring
the rats, treating lead poisoning and ignoring the slum tene-
ments with toxic paint on their walls, treating heroin addiction and ignoring the social disorganization that leads to
addiction. Open to those who wish to rediscover the social commitments physicians made more than a century ago when they
were leaders in the fight for sanitary reform, for an end to
slum housing, for the abolition of child labor.

Let those who think this is "radical" listen to the words of
John Simon, physician and first health officer of London, during the first great urban crisis—the explosion of the cities during the industrial revolution in the 1850's. Where Simon spoke
of "sanitary reform" we have only to substitute "social reform"
and the parallel is complete. He said:

> I feel the deepest conviction that no sanitary system can be adequate
> to the requirements of the time, or can cure those radical evils which
> infest the under-framework of society, unless the importance be dis-
> tinctly recognized . . . of improving the social condition of the poor.
> I would beg any educated person to consider what are the conditions
> (of urban life); to learn, by personal inspection, how far these condi-
> tions are realized for the masses of our population; and to form for him-

self a conscientious judgment as to the need for great, if even almost revolutionary, reform. Let any such person devote an hour to visiting some very poor neighborhood in the metropolis . . . let him breathe its air, taste its water, eat its bread. Let him think of human life struggling there for years. . . . Let him, if he have a heart . . . gravely reflect whether such sickening evils ought to be the habit of our labouring populations; whether the legislature, which his voice helps to constitute, is doing all that might be done to palliate these wrongs; whether it be not a jarring discord, in the civilization we boast, that such things continue in the midst of us, scandalously neglected. . . .

If there be citizens so destitute that they can afford to live only where they must straightaway die—renting the twentieth strawheap in some lightless feverbin, breathing from the cesspool and the sewer; so destitute that they can buy no water—that milk and bread must be impoverished to meet their means of purchase, that the drugs sold them for sickness must be rubbish or poison: surely no civilized community dare avert itself from the area of this abject orphanage. If such conditions of food or dwelling are absolutely inconsistent with healthy life, what clearer right to public succour than that the subject's means fall short of providing him other conditions than those?

And that is what many of the new young physicians are saying today.

But this opening and flowering of medicine need not and will not end its more traditional components: biology, down to the level of molecular biology and molecular genetics and back up again through tissues and organs and systems to the level of that intact, complete and wonderful mechanism, the human body; or the social and behavioral sciences that deal with what makes man unique among the mammals, his intellectual and emotional and social capacities; or the specific technologies, from surgery to engineering, that are involved in diagnosis and treatment. The skills and knowledge of the past will still apply; it is the assumptions and ideas of the past as to how that knowledge was to be put into human service as the practice of medicine that are changing.

For the young man or woman now in high school or college,

and considering medicine as a career, these changes and predictions have immediate implications. It will still be possible (even relatively easy) to prepare for medical school by taking a straight academic curriculum for eight years, by majoring in the sciences, by grinding in a highly competitive way through the standard premedical courses, by spending extracurricular time in laboratories and science projects, and it will still be enormously helpful to be the children of the relatively rich, the son or daughter of a physician. But these will not be, to anything like the present extent, the only roads into medicine.

For the premedical student, heavy concentrations in science and in traditional premedical extracurricular activities will still be useful—for those who enjoy them. And so will engineering and computer technology. And so will behavioral sciences and group work, and so will community organization and political organization, and so will writing, for that matter. Even today, most medical schools have scaled down their specific (science) entrance requirements to two years of college chemistry, a year or two of biology, and a year of physics. There is more time to do your own thing.

But within a few years, the straight college-academic route should not be the only one. At least some students should be able, after high school, to enter training for the new paraprofessional health careers, as physician assistants and technicians, for example, with the expectation of returning to school (after some years of work) for more academic training, and with credit for practical knowledge already gained.

For anyone now in high school or college who wants to explore these prospects more closely, there is a source—not very often used—for making contact: not the medical school admissions office, nor the premedical advisor (though these may both be useful) but, rather, the medical students themselves, in their official and in their extracurricular organizations. With them as allies and counselors, high schools can ask medical schools to open their doors (and laboratories) for visits;

and college students can find the projects and laboratories for summer experience. But there is an additional way: to join in the work (particularly the community work) of students and young physicians. The free clinics, the counseling services, the student health organizations and their projects are not restricted to medical students alone, and certainly the community organizations are not. To go where the students and the young professionals are is to go where the action is, and that is the best kind of preparation for the future.

There is another reason, finally, for turning to the student and the young professional for experience, for partnership, and for counsel: for these are the people who are testing, changing and redefining our current models of the physician —and, indeed, of professionalism itself. These are the people, in other words, who are creating the future of medicine, and the way to join the future is to join them.

The New Lawyer

by WENDY MOONAN
and TOM GOLDSTEIN

Wendy Moonan is editor of *Juris Doctor,* a national magazine for the "new lawyer," and Tom Goldstein, a graduate of Columbia University Law School, is a former editor of the same magazine.

Juris Doctor exemplifies many of the magazines in other fields which seek to create a network for new professionals through interviews, articles, and news from across the country; this network is not only providing needed information, but is also forging an awareness among new professionals that they have much in common with other people doing the same kind of work. This sense of community and common purpose is central to the effective growth of new professionalism.

THERE'S BEEN a great deal of mixed publicity lately about "new" lawyers—glowing reports from sources as diverse as *Fortune, Redbook, Glamour, Vogue, Evergreen Review,* the *Wall Street Journal, Forbes* and *The New York Times;* scathing attacks in the press by such legal eminences as Chief Justice Warren E. Burger, Representative Wilbur D. Mills (D. Ark.), and two past presidents of the American Bar Association, Leon Jaworski and Edward Wright.

The journals praise the committed new activist lawyers who refuse to join what they damn as a conservative, elitist and abstruse profession. The lawyers are extolled as socially conscious and selflessly committed to all those shut out from the legal system—the poor, the black, the unorganized.

Their critics call the new lawyers troublemakers who are discrediting the profession. As Chief Justice Burger told the American Law Institute in a speech last year, ". . . all too often, overzealous advocates seem to think the zeal and effectiveness of a lawyer depends on how thoroughly he can disrupt the proceedings or how loud he can shout or how close he can come to insulting all those he encounters—including the judges." Burger urged the bar to severely discipline this "tiny fragment of reckless, irresponsible lawyers."

His words were echoed by Wilbur Mills, the Chairman of the House Ways and Means Committee, at the ABA's ninety-fourth annual meeting, in July 1971. There, he attacked those lawyers he termed "unloving critics of the law." "The passion of the unloving critics appears to be to deride, denigrate, vilify, and destroy the courts and all other institutions that constitute our present legal system," said Mills, an ABA member. "They deify change. They have no substitute to offer for a lawful society, but that neither dampens their ardor nor tempers their raucous outcries and destructive acts in pursuance of their goal to bring the system to its knees."

Who is right about the new lawyer? Is he an enemy of society or of his own profession? Does he, in fact, represent a new breed of lawyer or not? Is being a new lawyer a sound professional career choice?

Legal activists are lawyers trying to use the law in aggressive new ways to change established practices and institutions for the public good. They can be divided by their principal areas of concern into *public interest, poverty* and *Movement lawyers.*

The largest, most diverse, and most traditional domain of the three is the public interest. Its most prominent advocate, consumer crusader Ralph Nader, best exemplifies the attempt to represent hitherto neglected interests common to all, such as consumer protection and environmental quality. His targets are usually large private corporations or the government. The lawyers working for him investigate corporations and pressure them to assume responsibility for the safety and reliability of their products. They hound government regulatory agencies to consider the social impact of their decisions along with the standard economic criteria. With the help of about thirty lawyers and a few hundred summer student "raiders," Nader has published scathing investigative reports on the Federal Trade Commission, The Interstate Commerce Commission and the Food and Drug Administration, among others. His staff members, however, tend to be more involved in investigation than litigation.

Environmental lawyers, on the other hand, are more often found representing specific clients—the public at large—before court or governmental hearings. When outraged fishermen on the Hudson River realized that thermal pollution from a Consolidated Edison plant was killing more than 5,000 fish each day, they sought the services of an environmental law firm, the foundation-funded Natural Resources Defense Council. Their lawyers are seeking to force Con Ed to stop the fish kills by building cooling towers on their Hudson River nuclear plants. Environmental lawyers are also involved in strip mining, oil spill, pesticide and other types of air and water pollution cases.

There are probably no more than 300 public interest lawyers in the country, two-thirds of them in Washington; most are funded by foundation grants or private contributions.

Poverty lawyers, the second group of new lawyers, are government subsidized—though only recently. There have always been lawyers representing the poor and underprivileged, but until 1963, courts could appoint lawyers only from private practice to represent indigent defendants, first in capital cases and later in federal and state felony cases. The landmark case in 1963, *Gideon* v. *Wainwright*, established the principle of government-funded court-appointed counsel for all criminal defendants. This was followed by programs such as Mobilization For Youth legal services and, in 1965, by the creation of OEO's Legal Services Program, in which 2,200 lawyers represent the poor in civil cases on a full-time basis.

Only with the establishment of coast-to-coast Legal Services offices have the poor gained access to the legal system for redress of their everyday grievances. The Legal Services lawyers give advice on welfare cases, landlord-tenant disputes, consumer credit fraud and discrimination cases—the common legal complaints of all the poor. In addition, they focus on changing "bad" laws by bringing high-impact test cases (often well-publicized class-action suits). When successful, the Legal Services lawyers have established whole new legal principles —but often at the price of alienating such powerful men as California's Governor Ronald Reagan, who almost succeeded last year in vetoing funds for the continuation of the California Rural Legal Assistance program. The lawyers also antagonize local businessmen and officials by exposing pricing as unfair or deceptive, or consumer credit practices as usurious, for example.

An additional 2,000 Legal Aid and poverty lawyers also defend the poor in criminal cases as court-appointed counsel from Legal Aid or Public Defender offices which are funded by both the government and private bar associations. While the contribution they make is outstanding, the vagaries of Congressional funding leave the future of such programs wide open, and overly dependent on the country's economic outlook. Of course, this is also the case with the privately and foundation-funded public interest law firms as well.

Movement lawyers are the most colorful, controversial and political of the new activist lawyers, representing political and cultural dissidents ranging from Black Panthers and Yippies to draft evaders and drug offenders. They include the "freaky" lawyers who join in law collectives or law communes, and who are usually the most outspoken lawyers on the deficiencies of the legal system and the most responsible for provoking the ire of the established bar. Best known for trials such as the

Chicago Seven and Panther 21 cases, they openly admit trying to change the country's legal system drastically. Their tactics in and out of court are occasionally disruptive and intentionally publicity-seeking, with the aim of educating the public about what they consider the repressive nature of the government.

Whatever their social connections, Movement lawyers are *not* revolutionaries. Revolutions are sometimes made by lawyers (Castro and Lenin are two outstanding examples), but not while they are lawyering. Movement lawyers are quick to point out that while they may believe in the radical methods their clients espouse, their *job* as Movement lawyers is to keep radicals out of jail by using the normal channels of the legal system. It is difficult to gauge how many Movement lawyers there are, but it is safe to say that most join the newly revived National Lawyers' Guild, which now numbers more than 3,000.

William Kunstler, although fifty-five, is perhaps the best known and most articulate spokesman for the Movement lawyers. On the mediation panel at Attica State Prison he was the one of few who dared to denounce Governor Rockefeller's refusal to visit the prison and his decision to send troops into the prison to quash an inmate rebellion.

Together these three groups represent perhaps 6,000 lawyers or roughly 2 per cent of the profession. As new lawyers, they bear no identifiable characteristic—not even long hair, as Nader's appearance attests. Their life styles range from the very straight and typically lawyerlike Anthony Amsterdam, a brilliant Stanford law professor whose radicalism lies mainly in his legal theories, or the monastic Nader, who, ironically, is less lawyer than crusader, to the more colorful Kunstlers, Lefcourts and other Movement lawyers. The crucial characteristic distinguishing them from the rest of the profession is their decision to devote their legal skills and efforts only to those clients or causes with which they sympathize.

This notion varies quite radically from that of the traditional lawyer, who serves whoever employs him to the best of his ability. This is a time-honored professional principle which, in this country, stretches farther back than the American Revolution, when John Adams defended British soldiers accused of murder in the Boston massacre. The adversary system rests on the belief that a lawyer defends a client, *any* client, to the best of his ability.

The new lawyer defends only those clients in whose cause he believes. Unlike a lawyer working for the American Civil Liberties Union, who will defend the political or religious beliefs of anyone, from a Panther to a Nazi, new lawyers accept clients only from among the poor or the black or on behalf of the environment or the Movement. Once, when Kunstler was asked if he would use arguments for the Minutemen which he had used to defend the Panthers, he responded, "No, I wouldn't defend them at all. I'm not a lawyer for hire. I only defend those I love."

Those interested in the "new law" face two serious obstacles: law school and the bar.

"Law schools are places where old men in their twenties go to die," laments Paul Savoy, formerly a professor at the University of California at Davis.* "There is not a single lawyer I know with whom I went to law school who feels that this legal education prepared him for the practice of law (or anything else for that matter)," he pessimistically concludes. Perhaps Savoy is overstating, but back in the 1940's the late Jerome Frank, who later was to serve as a distinguished judge, commented that students trained by reading appellate opinions, which still is the standard regimen at the nation's 124 accredited law schools, "are like future horticulturists confining their studies to cut flowers, like architects who study pictures of buildings and nothing else. They resemble prospective dog breeders who never see anything but stuffed dogs. And it is beginning to be suspected that there is some correlation be-

* *Yale Law Journal,* January 1970.

tween that kind of stuffed dog study and the overproduction of stuffed shirts in the legal profession."

Bayless Manning, former Stanford Law School dean, observes that the law schools "while qualitatively differentiated, are almost carbon copies of each other in their educational programs. Their curricula and teaching methods closely adhere to a model that crystallized at the turn of the century. Training patterns in the law have undergone less development in the last three-quarters of a century than those of almost any other discipline and certainly less than any other profession; contrast, for example, the dramatic modernizing changes that have occurred during that period in our schools for training doctors, engineers and business executives."

Since Manning wrote in 1968, there have been some significant substantive changes. At least eighty of the schools, including many so-called "local" ones, have adopted clinical courses whereby students under close supervision from an instructor handle live cases, usually in the criminal, consumer protection or environmental fields. But the future of clinical programs is jeopardized because they involve huge outlays of funds, and only a severely limited number of students can participate in a clinic if it is to be successful. Then, too, clinics are meeting resistance from the traditionalists. In 1970, Solicitor General Erwin Griswold warned at a gathering at Harvard Law School, where he had served as dean for years, that he hoped the school wouldn't "go overboard in clinical legal training." In Harvard's 1970 curriculum of more than a hundred courses, one was clinical.

A proposal currently under consideration by the American Association of Law Schools—the professional organization representing 124 of the nation's law schools—would do away with the third year of legal study. The measure was unanimously recommended in a Model Course Announcement drafted in 1970 by fourteen law professors. The implementation of this proposal would greatly expand the opportunities for legal study and eliminate the boredom usually encountered by law students in their final year.

Obtaining a juris doctor degree—almost automatic after the first year of school is completed—is but the first step in a lengthy process of admission to the bar. The established bar— the courts, the bar associations and other groups, like the American Association of Law Schools and the National Conference of Bar Examiners—effectively regulates admission to the legal fraternity by prescribing educational standards, devising bar exams and requiring the nebulous showing of "good moral character." The education process is closely monitored by the established bar. Not all law schools are accredited either by the ABA or AALS, and some states refuse to recognize graduates of unaccredited schools as lawyers. Clerking (or simply doing an apprenticeship in a law office without formal study), once the most popular way of becoming a lawyer, is now officially frowned upon by the ABA. In the ten states that still permit clerking, only seven persons who prepared by law office study were admitted to the bar in 1970. Then, too, the highest court in each state usually sets certain minimum requirements of hours spent in the classroom in order to qualify for the bar.

In foreclosing the profession to all but those who have served their time, the established bar sets up the additional barrier of the bar exam. Designed to prevent incompetents from slipping into the dignity of the law, the bar exams—two- or three-day affairs testing closely on state law—draw heavily on content borrowed from law curricula of the turn of the century when a large percentage of lawyers prepared for the law by clerking. Courses that are popular today—such as environmental law and law for the poor—are almost totally ignored on these exams. Thus, a student interested in taking a heavy load of, say, consumer-oriented courses is deterred from doing so because, unless he is thoroughly grounded in the areas of law stressed on the exam, he won't be able to practice at all.

Writing in *Juris Doctor* last year, New York University law professor Norman Dorsen comments, "There is doubt whether in their present form bar examinations do more good than harm, or any good at all; and there is no doubt they introduce a demoralizing and, on the whole, an anti-intellectual element into the process of becoming a practicing lawyer." He concludes, however, that "the public is entitled to some assurance that lawyers are equipped with the minimal tools needed to advise clients and represent the interest of others." A new one-day multi-state bar exam, devised by the Educational Testing Service at Princeton (the same people who bring you the law school admission test) and already adopted by more than twenty states, was first administered last winter. The test consists of multiple choice questions on limited areas of the law—contracts, torts, property, crimes, procedure and evidence. On the second day, the participating states test on their own law.

At this stage, another example of how the profession stultifies progress emerges. In an age of mobility, lawyers are immobile. The multi-state bar exam, likely to be adopted by most states, standardizes up to half the admission exam. Nonetheless, a lawyer who passes the test in Pennsylvania will not be able to practice in California unless he takes that state's test. Some states won't recognize lawyers of other jurisdictions at all. Other states will admit those who have practiced for three, five or more years elsewhere. Since only a few of the small states do in fact immediately accept lawyers from other states, a young lawyer is usually restricted to practicing only in the state where he is admitted; and admission is circumscribed by residency requirements of up to a year.

Another major obstacle is the character committees, composed of practicing attorneys "who presume to sit in judgment of an applicant's entire post-adolescent life, conduct, association and beliefs." [J. R. A. Theagle, *Juris Doctor*, 1971.]

How, on the basis of questions like "Were you ever a boy

scout?" can a committee of no more than a dozen gentlemen, usually established lawyers in their sixties, determine whether a young man, who has spent three years of his life in law school and has passed an antiquated bar examination, will somehow cheat his clients in the next thirty years? Usually, the inquiry into fitness of a prospective practitioner's character is a *pro forma* nuisance. Occasionally, the process can become a nightmare. Last year, a man's admission was delayed several weeks because he told the character committee he was living with his girl friend. Another was challenged because, though never convicted of any crime, he was a well-known leader of a campus disturbance. During the course of several agonizing hearings (where the rules of evidence were suspended), the prospective lawyer disavowed his past acts. But it was fourteen months before he was finally allowed to engage in trial work—his lifelong ambition.

After the character committee, a lawyer is given free rein as he enters the mystical world of Latin phrases and elaborate rituals. Dean Manning notes, "Our licensing system remains a one-shot affair, and we have no institutional means for requiring, or even encouraging, members of the profession to expose themselves to continuing education in the law."

Despite the ritualistic admission procedures, professors Vern Countryman of Harvard and Ted Finman of Wisconsin, writing in *The Lawyer in Modern Society*, the standard casebook for a course examining the legal profession—a course which so far has failed to gain general acceptance as a worthy pedagogical pursuit—find that "although there are a few instances of lawyers being disciplined for negligence, we find no record of an attorney being suspended or disbarred for ignorance or incompetence." And Jerome Carlin's thorough 1962 study of the New York City bar shows that only a minute fraction of lawyers' professional ethics violations are ever brought to the attention of bar association grievance committees and other enforcement authorities.

It is doubtful that the aggregate career profile of last year's 25,000 law graduates would instill fear in the hearts of many of the established bar. In comparatively record numbers, students are choosing legal services offices, public defender programs, environmental defense funds or public interest law firms. But in record numbers, too, students are opting for the law factories. In 1969, Erwin Smigel, author of *The Wall Street Lawyer*, observed, "For the young lawyer fresh out of law school, the large prestigious Wall Street firm is still the place to go." Three years later, his conclusion seems equally valid. One reason, perhaps, for the resiliency of the corporate law firms, which typically represent the targets of the environmentalists' and consumer advocates' attacks, is that they have yielded to the pressure of young associates, many of whom refused to join the firms unless they were assured they could spend a portion of their firms' time on public service activities.

In an unusually candid internal memorandum a few years ago, Hogan & Hartson, the third largest Washington firm, established a community services department to "take on public interest representation on a nonchargeable or, where appropriate, a discounted fee basis." The firm acknowledged that such a move "may have a favorable impact upon recruitment," and attributes "the relative disfavor into which the major law firms have fallen" in part to "the feeling among recent law school graduates that *these firms failed to respond to the larger problems of contemporary society.*" Whether their response is a sufficient one "to the larger problems of contemporary society" is problematical.

In the 1930's, lawyers who wished to do something about the under-represented groups and interests in society became New Dealers. In the 1970's, although there still is a constant flow of lawyers directly into government service, such work has lost its glamour. Those wishing to serve the public are starting out on their own. Unfortunately, frightfully few public interest jobs are available. "People can't be lured for jobs which don't exist," notes C. Delos Putz, Jr., a former dean at New York University Law School. "It's unrealistic to say that young lawyers are supposed to be more idealistic and self-sacrificing than the rest of the community. There isn't going to be any real flow of lawyers into public interest work until somebody turns on the tap to supply money to pay salaries for public interest work." And a sluggish economy has forced foundations to curtail funding of such work.

But for those who can squeeze into the public interest field, now harder to crack than Wall Street, the remuneration is handsome. Except for some of Nader's lawyers, who earn as little as $4,500 a year for long hours and little glory at his Public Interest Research Group, the salary scales of these public interest firms are competitive with the corporate law firms. The Center for Law and Social Policy, which has been nursed along by $400,000 in Ford Foundation grants since it was formed in 1969, pays its senior staff attorneys $25,000 annually and associates, $15,000. The ceiling is substantially less, but the floor is the same as the largest private Washington firms. The Natural Resources Defense Council pays its thirteen lawyers, most of whom are recent Yale law graduates, $20,000 annually.

While salaries are substantially lower than in public interest work, the numerical opportunities in the OEO-funded legal services program are superior: There are presently 2,200 neighborhood lawyers with an annual turnover rate of about 200. The frustration of working in a system designed to protect the interests of the rich rather than the impoverished, however, takes its emotional toll on the underpaid, overworked legal services staff attorneys. Few make a career of it. And the unsteady commitment of the Nixon Administration to the war on poverty has discouraged many young lawyers from entering into the service of the poor. Robert Yegge, a dean of the progressive Denver College of Law, dismally concludes that OEO "cannot possibly handle all the problems that neighborhood law offices have uncovered."

Where the same need exists, opportunities for young lawyers in legal aid or public defender programs are similarly limited. A 1967 report for the National Crime Commission found that there are not enough competent criminal lawyers available to defend even those who can afford counsel. The report concluded that at least ten times the 300 or so full-time public defenders in the country are needed to handle the criminal representation needs of the poor. But there are no funds to create these jobs.

The frustration with traditional legal structures in corporate firms and government work, and the inadequacy of job opportunities in foundation-funded public interest firms and government-funded legal services offices have contributed to the re-emergence of the radical legal movement, moribund until a few years ago. A symbol of this resurgence is the National Lawyers' Guild, which is re-establishing itself as a major conduit of radical politics in the country. Formed in 1937 as a progressive alternative to the ABA, the Guild thrived in the forties but came under sharp attack in the fifties during the Joseph McCarthy era when its membership dipped to a few hundred. With its slogan, "the legal arm of the movement," the Guild now has 3,000 members—mostly young—in its fourteen chapters. Lest its growth be taken out of perspective, however, more than a third of the ABA's 160,000 members are under thirty-six, and 1,000 more young lawyers join the establishment organization each year.

Increasingly, the typical organizational structure for the radical lawyer is the collective, which supports its political work by taking a limited number of paying cases—mostly middle-class drug arrests. All decisions are made collectively; and the lawyers, without secretaries, do their own typing. Gerry Lefcourt, an early member of the innovative New York Law Commune which specialized in criminal defense work before it disbanded, estimates that about twenty law communes now operate in major metropolitan areas across the country. Shortly after New York Commune lawyers won a stunning victory in the Panther 21 trial of 1971, the commune members split up. "It was just getting too large," Lefcourt explained. Plans are being formulated to reorganize in small groups.

Psychologically, the radical lawyer is walking a tightrope to schizophrenia. Collective members follow regular courtroom procedure. They wear suits and often clip their hair in order not to alienate the judge.

In his penetrating essay in *Law Against the People,* Kunstler notes that "the radical lawyer is in an utterly impossible position. On one hand, he is bound by the strictures of an institution, which has, after all, become an indispensable establishment bulwark. On the other, he has an equally pressing obligation to defend clients who may want to destroy or overhaul that very establishment."

More than any other group, the radical lawyers underscore the malaise that is infecting the legal profession. This influx of activist lawyers has shaken some of its basic foundations. Now, lawyers, for so long secure in the cloak of professional anonymity (the bar's hallowed canons of ethics forbid advertising or soliciting for clients), have become the focus of public scrutiny. The basic contradiction emerges: The legal profession is violating the simple rules of supply and demand. It is top-heavy with corporate lawyers, yet more young lawyers than ever are being absorbed into corporate firms. The demand for activist lawyers is high, and the supply and opportunities, low.

In view of this grim over-all picture of the new lawyer's role, is it worth the hassles for someone making a career decision to enter law? For those interested in traditional legal practice, the route is obvious. Go to the most prestigious law school you can, forget about the rest of your life in your first year of law school and grind for grades. At the beginning of the second year, firms recruit for summer jobs and all they have to look at is the first year's grades. Since most large firms are indistinguishable in the type of work they do or the salary they pay, sign up for as many interviews as possible. Once you have landed a job, conserve your energy until the summer when you should be prepared to work seventy-hour weeks and be ingratiating (but not obsequious) to the partners. Then, you'll be invited back to take a full-time job after graduation.

Law school can be much more enriching if you decide before you apply that you will not end up in a large firm. The pressure of getting into a prestige school is removed. Some of the "local" law schools, such as Denver, Detroit, Rutgers and Buffalo are more innovative, offering numerous programs of community involvement. You'll be using the same textbooks, and the basic difference in the professors at these lesser-known schools is that they are more likely to be young and attuned to your interests. Once in law school, the competitiveness is lessened if you don't care about a corporate job. Do as much volunteer work as possible—for consumer groups, for legal aid, for prisoners. Take a smorgasbord of courses—but don't actively neglect the traditional subjects, such as corporations or real estate, because if you are defending a poor client, you must know how the other side works, too. If you show a strong, early commitment to activist work, there might be a job available when you graduate.

The New Clergyman

by THOMAS R. LAWS

Thomas Laws is co-pastor of St. Mary's Church, an Episcopal church in West Harlem. A graduate of Union Theological Seminary, he first came to the Church in 1964 while working toward his Ph.D. in the history of religion. He soon left the graduate program and devoted his full time to St. Mary's.

Laws' major contribution to St. Mary's and to the Harlem community is the development of the church-supported Community Outreach, which provides assistance, advice and facilities to numerous community organizations and programs. In addition, he has been very active in a number of other community programs, notably housing and health. He also participates in New York Theological Seminary's pathbreaking program— the Urban Year—designed to introduce divinity students to the realities of the urban environment and to provide them with a basis for evaluating their purposes and the direction of the church.

ANYONE WHO has exposed himself to the nurture or persuasions of conventional religions may find the very notion of "new clergyman" an almost impossible conception. The past is part of the ministry in ways not even approached by other professions. Before there were sciences to be systematized or lawsuits to be litigated, there were priests. Like their competition for the "world's oldest profession," practitioners of the ministerial office have justified their calling through generations of experience. Not only have the practical patterns of ministry been shaped by the laying on of ancient

hands, but the essential aims and content of religious participation have been most widely understood through ancient
forms and perceptions. It must be admitted that the ministry
seems inextricably tied to the past and uniquely resistant to
reform. But there are some clergymen, convinced that religious expression is a fundamental quality of human existence,
who not only attempt to think in new ways, but who hope to
forge from the elements of modern society a new ministry that
may become a viable practice in itself and that may nourish
an ongoing religious community of those whose consciousness
is shaped by the world of our own times.

Notions of who the clergyman is have proliferated in all
ages. If St. Paul, from motives of evangelism, urged being "all
things to all men," not only did his successors fulfill the commission beyond measure, but "all men" responded with their
own tags for these servants of the word. The resultant thicket
of identifying images has all but obscured the reality of cul-
ture-bound but living and breathing humans who occupy the
role.

Practically every clergyman is imagined to carry within
himself somehow the function of cultural arbiter. But execu-
tion of a role derived from historic epitome is an intoxicating
and tantalizing experience. There is constant temptation to
see more than one really sees and to assert more than one
really knows. Pretension or pomposity in a clergyman may not
reflect immodesty or megalomania, but they may be symptoms of a man earnestly, even desperately, trying to reconcile
the exalted moral sense that he has internalized from the tradition with the realities around him. If acceptance of a conception so exalted produces an existential dilemma for the
clergyman, the act of accepting indicates a clue to his identity. He is perhaps first and foremost a person of intense moral
concern.

The clergyman is also a public man. Not only for his own
hopes—and perhaps aspirations—does the clergyman find his

way into the presence of power-wielders. The most mundane schemes may seem less so when they are condoned by a representative of the eternal. So clergymen, whose views are not shared and whose counsels are not sought, are wanted for their legitimating functions. Exploiters, slaveholders, warlords and selfish men of all stripes have given aid and comfort to clergymen whose public relations they needed. As pastor, as shepherd of his flock, the clergyman bears a kind of public responsibility for persons in his charge. If his aim to represent and protect his people, and his own unexpressed ambitions, leave him subject to misalliances and delusions, it should be understood that in most cases the clergyman is a person of ordinary limitations, called upon for extraordinary wisdom, who simply may not have the strength of his convictions. But almost certainly the clergyman is a man convinced of the worth of the lives and aspirations of his fellowmen.

In urban America most people would be more than a little surprised to see a priest in vestments moving in procession through the streets with consecrated Host from the reserved sacrament and preceded by an acolyte with tinkling bell summoning passersby to reverence. The customary gestures of other times and places have given way. But, in less elegant forms of ceremonial, observances are still made. Apartment dwellers who do not speak to their next-door neighbors will greet an unknown clergyman in the streets; barbers may announce the entry of a clergyman by commanding "All right, you guys, clean up your language. Can't you see the Reverend?" Little League ball players cross themselves; on Ash Wednesday ordinarily nonchurchgoers show up to have their foreheads spotted; even the most reprobate hope for themselves a "proper" burial. In respect to these impulses, as well as for the worship of the faithful, the clergyman is a kind of holy man.

Among ministers themselves, most are deeply, even painfully, aware of their humanity. Insofar as they are regarded as holy men, however, they are subject to strong constraints. In the realms of prayer and worship the forms and roles are most rigidly prescribed by tradition. To act out of a traditional pattern may be to step out of the role, and consequently to lose the relationship with the worshippers. The situation is schizoid. But it reveals another fundamental quality of the clergyman: He acknowledges the human inkling of suprahuman relationship.

The images of the clergyman suggested in the preceding paragraphs are related to essential elements of the ministry as it has been understood traditionally. Other images are well known to nearly everyone's experience. Older generations recall a sharp-tongued preacher whose rhetoric of hell and damnation brought nightmares to children and hypocrisy to adults. Readers of Midwestern society columns recall an amiable gentleman of gentle hands and speech urging rectitude at home and charity abroad. Budding writers, in their prep school novels, conjure up in the figure of school chaplain a boorish lout trampling adolescent sensibilities as he marches toward the headmaster's chair.

Inside these images is the clergyman himself. Without resort to stereotypes or psychometrics, even from the inside it is difficult to generalize on the person and character of those in the clerical office. A personal projection might include more than ordinary sensitivity—if also ambivalence—to authority and order, a need for continuing company of people, and yet in private a shyness, a predilection for the ineffable. A clergyman is likely to be intelligent, and in most communities will be better educated than the average citizen. He is subject to insecurities, competition, sexual interest, pressures of work or family, depression, loneliness and joy. He is generally serious in his intentions, and engaged with his people to the point of overwork. He is in constant danger of losing sight of his self and his vocation. His work is demanding and lonely. He is one who accepts it.

The predicament of the clergyman is indicated by projecting the images of the profession against the realities of the man. In his own understanding of role expectations he is enlightened largely by materials from the tradition. The functions of Prophet, Pastor and Priest, intimated above, have roots so deep that their very antiquity implies a kind of human necessity. But definition of these functions has been accomplished by use of very particular forms, language and customs in relation to historically limited associations of people. Whatever sustenance may be provided from the sense of the ineffable, mundane patterns imposed from the past undoubtedly have more effect in the determination of ministerial role model. In a rapidly changing world the clergyman's own preconceptions of his calling have obvious limitations. Equally unsatisfactory are the expectations carried by his contemporaries. The situation seems to call for either strong cultural forms to which the forms of tradition can be related, or for charismatic leaders who can produce their own forms in spite of what is given them. One temptation is to become a faceless man in a rigid society, another is to lose contact with humans in their need through an individualistic binge. For the modestly endowed men who are clergymen, this is a frustrating and awesome age in which to practice.

The clergyman is an individual human being, but probably as in no other profession he must be understood as part of his community. A doctor or lawyer who has acquired the appropriate training and credentials can "hang out his shingle" and offer himself to the world for the services he is prepared to perform. In most cases a clergyman is not even permitted to practice his profession unless he does so in connection with some segment of the religious community with which he is associated. Indeed, his prime credential, that of his ordination, is conferred only by action of the community, not by the estimate of professional peers. The religious community is the *raison d'être* and the principal realm for the work of the clergyman. Whatever are his own strengths or weaknesses, the effects of a clergyman's actions are modified by the counterweights of the community.

It is evident to any more or less objective observer that clergymen and religious communities have not functioned very effectively for the purposes of either the individual seeking edification of his spiritual needs, or the society wanting equality and justice. Considering the recalcitrance, if not Original Sin, of the humanity within which they must work, this judgment is not as bad as it may seem. General Motors, by all odds, and even the public schools, work in situations far more amenable to their presumed ends than do clergymen and their religious institutions. Both profits and productive citizens are easier made than are decent human beings. But the facts remain: Religious communities are in trouble.

Surely the greatest problem of religious communities is that of conservatism. That is not to say that religious groups have right-wing tendencies—although some of them obviously do. Rather, the almost obsessive preservation of forms, habits and doctrines from the past has produced an atmosphere that muffles all ideas and actions. The past may hold wisdom, excitement and fullness of experience that are too much unknown and untapped. To be in touch with the passions of the past through memory may be both exhilarating and strengthening. But this is not the past, and no amount of remembering can make it so. If the past is to yield wisdom and inspiration, it must be approached urgently and creatively. Religious communities have allowed their pasts to settle over them like fetid smoke over a town dump. The conservatism of default has made innocuous, shapeless hulks of communities that need to be vivid and crisp.

Problems in contemporary society harshly illumine the dilemma of religious organizations. Earthquakes do still occur. And crop failures are possible. But people normally expect—and are backed by reliable insurance tables—that they will live long lives, relatively free of hunger and disease.

Death and illness still come, but society manages both with fair dispatch. The elements around which traditional religion was molded are still problematic, but they hold by no means the same significance in the consciousness of most living persons that they held centuries ago. But the matters of population, pollution, mass relations, economic survival, and individual worth are causes of immense anxieties. Were religious organizations able to forget their institutional requirements and plumb their souls, they might reform religion for the needs of contemporary men. Or if they could overcome their perverse idealistic inefficiency, as organizations they might begin to make significant impact on the structure of society. Religious organizations have lived on their pasts too long. They must live for today, or die before tomorrow.

That a religious spirit lives even within our overstimulated society is surely indicated by aspects of the youth culture. Drug use is no doubt both faddist and escapist, but in some measure it represents a search for depth of perception and the transcendence of ordinary experience. The Jesus cults that have developed with Jesus-rock music, a simple, untheological preaching, and a self-styled ascetic life are most unexpected confirmation of the power still left in an ancient gospel. Yet these phenomena have developed largely apart from the traditional and institutionalized forms of religion. These impulses of young people need to be nourished and nurtured. From them fuller life and humanity may be possible. But as that ancient curmudgeon, St. Paul, queried, "How shall they hear without a preacher?"

The question facing any new clergyman is whether a professional role shaped by centuries of practice and exercised in the midst of a tradition-oriented community can become vibrant and authentic in an age that has lost its taste for the past. Today's generations endure the agonies of war, inequality, pollution, and mechanistic relationships. Death of body, suddenly as in Vietnam or slowly as by the heroin needle in urban slums, and death of spirit from a mean and nasty society, more skilled with electricity than with humanity, are experiences that weigh heavily in the hearts of sensitive people. People yearning for the song and the dance seem fated to cacophony and hyperkinesis. Surely if there were ever a time when humans thirsted for religious experience this is the time. The need presents an awesome challenge. The new clergyman's task is nothing short of a miraculous transformation of himself and his community.

The outlook of the new clergyman has not simply sprung up *de novo* in the recent past. It is not an attempt at novelty, nor a conscious rebellion against the past. Indeed, the saving factor in religious history has been the capacity of religious institutions to reach new accommodations with societal conditions. Such accommodations were not always made when needed, but there have continued to be imaginative religious leaders throughout the generations. The new clergy attitude does not represent a school of thought or an organized movement. The monastic movement from the Middle Ages, John Wesley's Methodism from the eighteenth century, and the Social Gospel theorists from early within our own century have all helped to shape the consciousness of the new clergyman. But the genius of the new clergy outlook is its lack of dogmatism, its lack of partisanship, and its essentially pragmatic, open attitude. New clergymen can use the past; they simply refuse to be bound by it. That sense of responsible freedom is the essence of the new clergy movement.

There has come about a kind of religion espoused by politicians and public figures that utilizes the vocabulary and images of religion without reference to their traditional or theological antecedents.* On the one hand, this phenomenon is manifested in an "establishment" outlook that probably does

---

* See Robert N. Bellah, "Civil Religion in America," *Daedalus*, 96 (1967): 1–21.

contribute to stability of the polity. But on the other, it consists of an incredible mish-mash arrived at through absolutely
no intellectual rigor and signifying nothing with respect to
fundamental human qualities. The tragedy is that neither the
public nor the various religious communities have sufficient
knowledge and discipline to appreciate the misrepresenta-
tion. There is an almost total inability to distinguish between
the use of "religious" symbols by theologically trained clergymen and rabble-rousing politicians. Leaving aside whatever
effect this may have on formation of the nation's laws and
policies, it produces a general insensitivity to authentic religious considerations that practically defies intervention by a
serious clergyman.

Mindless state religion all too frequently combines with in-
effectual theology to produce devastating effects on the mani-
fest religious communities, the denominations and congregations. Of course there are all sorts of other petty and personal
reasons why religious organizations can come to grief, but persons who engage in intentional manipulations are not touched
with poignance as are those who innocently believe they are
serving religious ends through their pharisaical strictures. Such
shallow-thinking persons are more than likely to occupy key
roles in the direction and control of religious bodies, especially so since more sensitive souls may be less capable of single-minded determination. Religious organizations so stunted
in their vision and experience settle for moralism and propri-
ety as the meaning of religion. The value-transmitting function of these institutions is not abandoned. Rather, they bear
with them sets of values that may be quite inconsistent with
their avowed purposes. The clergyman who dares to call into
question these shoddily formed attitudes may be attacked as
vehemently as an acknowledged heretic. In practice, congregations often are not the purposeful coordinates of the clergyman in nourishing true religious sentiments. But where else
can he practice his profession?

New clergymen and some of the more apt religious communities are struggling to create new forms that will meet the world on its own terms. Not all these efforts have been well conceived or well designed. Some have failed for lack of support. Some have failed for lack of leadership. Some lived long enough to inspire others before expiring. Some are still going strong, probably lacking at any given time financial support, staff, facilities or wisdom—but still trying to break through with authentic expressions of religious attitudes among today's men.

These efforts require ability to think clearly and creatively, they require work and endurance of disappointment, they require diligent examination of both tradition and contemporary life for discovery of the significant points of relationship from which intellectual and organizational structures may be built. New clergymen may err in their judgment or they may fail in their efforts. But in any success there is the joy of a new creation useful to mankind.

A prototype of the efforts by new clergymen was the East Harlem Protestant Parish. East Harlem was, and is, a slum neighborhood of Puerto Ricans, blacks and Italians. In the years after World War II, slum housing was pervasive, overcrowding was prevalent, and violence was rife. Men, now middle-aged, came out of Union Theological Seminary determined to place the Church among the people in the streets. Storefront centers were set up, liturgies and Bible-study groups were self-consciously developed, ministries to various aspects of the social need were organized. The project was long on naïveté, enthusiasm, and patronizing white liberalism. Its organizers were good fund-raisers and were not unresponsive to realities that differed from their preconceptions. So the effort was a remarkable success. East Harlem is still a slum area. Some buildings are probably worse than they were at the project's advent. Most of the project's organizers have been gone for some time, and some of them left under less than happy circumstances. But new religious communities did develop in East Harlem. Some housing improvements and neighborhood renewal did result from the work of the project. Moreover, its early successes inspired dozens of similar efforts in cities all over the country. As times and attitudes have changed, the project's shortcomings have become more obvious. It has lost the glamorous quality it held ten years ago. However, the imagination and spirit that engendered the project typify the outlook of today's new clergymen.

In other places other types of ministry have been developed. On the West Coast, the Glide Foundation in San Francisco has addressed itself to problems of students, homosexuals, and others lost in the city environment. Also, the California Migrant Ministry has worked for improvement of the despicable conditions in which farm laborers must work. In Mississippi, the Delta Ministry has mounted community organization and educational projects among deprived black residents. In Chicago, the Ecumenical Institute has created a curriculum and a community in relationship with a poor neighborhood. These efforts are of differing intent, scope and quality. They are all subject to evaluation. They are all relatively well financed and supported (or were). Probably not many of today's new clergymen are working in these places. But they illustrate alternative types of ministries possible even on a large scale.

The new clergyman must do what his own locality requires. He may be a community organizer who takes as his task development of a community legal service office. He may be the manager of a building or a business in which neighborhood residents find opportunity. He may be studying management or investment so he can address his efforts to those in the business establishment. Clergymen are doing all of those things at this time. Such efforts may not find support among traditional religionists, or even among the persons whom they serve. Appropriate skills and funding have to be found. Competence is required with no assurance that viable communities will result.

Perhaps it is useful to cite the writer's own experience. Although imitation is contrary to the spirit required of new clergymen, examination of comparable material can be of assistance for pondering a potential course of action.

When I came to work for a summer at St. Mary's Church in 1964—at that time still intending to complete my Ph.D. in History of Religions at Columbia University—members of the congregation were talking about what would be done with their "new" Ackley Center. Even then the five-story school building was more than sixty years old, but to the church which had just acquired it in 1963 it was new. The big event during the early part of that summer was the time a group of parishioners came together to paint one of the building's larger rooms. Falling into the jargon denominational bureaucrats were using, people joked about the new "educational plant" and speculated as to whether the Sunday school would fill all those rooms. Not long afterward, on a Sunday morning, the radio newscasts carried reports of fires and looting in Harlem. Some of us drove across 125th Street to see the damage done by the "riot." The Sunday school never did fill all those rooms —but the riot did!

The church might have been expected to respond to disaster by providing temporary shelter for the homeless and comfort for the weary. The Ackley Center was never needed for that kind of literal response to riot, but its function was to be more profoundly affected. The riot in Harlem, and others in Watts, Newark, Detroit and urban ghettos the country over, produced the political response of the "War on Poverty." Although the government appears to have settled with the enemy on terms the Viet Cong could envy, the effort did endorse the rhetoric of "maximum feasible participation" by the poor whose safety and security were at stake. Residents of the poor communities had their own notions of participation that surpassed the government's commitment to the concept. The riots only indicated how great the gap had become. As an instrument of national policy, community participation has hardly held its ground. For St. Mary's work in its neighborhood, however, such participation became the purpose and focal point.

The transformation of concept and function of St. Mary's Church that has occurred since 1964 is remarkable. Its congregational life continues with worship services, Church school, parish dinners, etc. Baptisms, marriages, burials and sacramental matters are carried on as for generations. But now a major portion of the Church's money and energies is engaged in an effort that few other churches even dream about. Under the heading of St. Mary's Community Outreach, the church sponsors a cluster of projects for the benefit of its neighborhood. That building that once might have become a Sunday school facility has become the daily recipient of hundreds of persons engaged in community service efforts.

My position is that of Pastor of Community Outreach. I do participate in congregational activities, but my principal responsibility is administration of our community programs. The purposes and work of my organization are set forth in a small brochure recently prepared called: *Community Outreach; A Church's Response to its Neighborhood.* I share several extensive quotations:

It is impossible briefly to describe the wealth of programs supported by *Community Outreach* . . . they range from Headstart and Day Care, to youth recreation, college counseling, and Alcoholics Anonymous. A typical day might witness:

The Afro-American Caravan writing, editing and publishing books on black history (they have already done books on Benjamin Banneker, Nat Turner, and Harriet Tubman);

The Citywide Coordinating Committee of Welfare Groups organizing welfare mothers for a demonstration at City Hall;

St. Mary's Community Services representing a parent and student at
a suspension hearing;
The Youth Employment Service helping a high school graduate find
a job;
The St. Mary's Cadet Corps practicing for a parade;
The Youth Evening Center preparing a newsletter to publish stories
and poems by the young people themselves.

This list could be expanded to represent all the programs included in
St. Mary's *Community Outreach,* and together they constitute a vigorous
and sustained attempt to make Manhattanville a better place.

What can St. Mary's really do for programs operated by other groups
of neighborhood people? First, of course, it provides space. Cheap office
space is rare in New York City, and the programs in Ackley Center can
hardly afford much rent. Without the existence of a *Community Outreach* effort, many of these groups would be out on the street. More to
the point, several of them would be bitterly remembered ideas that
failed for want of even minimal space and supportive services. Typical
of an organization given a lease on life through St. Mary's support is
the Harlem Parents Committee. In its early days, even had it been able
to pay, HPC was considered too radical and unruly by landlords to occupy space in their buildings. The current respectability of HPC—most
of its old demands are now state and federal laws, and its former chairman is now a member of the New York City Board of Education—
hardly suggests the sense of uncertainty that its members had when
they approached St. Mary's for assistance.

The building itself is more than space for these programs. They cannot spare scarce resources for furnishing offices, setting up maintenance
and security, and arranging for meeting rooms, reception duties, etc. A
function of *Community Outreach* is to meet nearly all the physical and
organizational needs of its component groups.

Equally important are many more intangible forms of support. First,
it serves as a beacon of hope to neighborhood groups. As an acknowledged friend of the community, St. Mary's interest and support can be
sought without threat during the critical early stages of program development, before ideas have been thought through and proposals solidified.
Second, the pastors and staff of St. Mary's are able to offer advice and
counsel—both programmatic and personal—in a variety of areas, they
develop outside contacts useful to the individual programs, and they

have an overview of programs that encourages coordination of the programs for common goals. Third, St. Mary's also serves as the friend within "the establishment" to clear up difficulties with city, state or federal agencies. Thus, St. Mary's has been able to undergird local leadership without taking control of this leadership.

In addition to providing services for its own programs, *Community Outreach* responds to new community efforts. Short term support for incipient neighborhood projects can nearly always be arranged. New groups need a place to meet, or a telephone connection, or the use of a mimeograph machine for leaflets. *Community Outreach* has provided all these things—sometimes on very short notice—for people who were fighting for their neighborhood's welfare. For example, a "freedom school" was once housed in St. Mary's—classes held, lunches prepared, and children escorted home—by community groups engaged in educational reform. *Community Outreach* has participated in the beginning of many of the established groups throughout the Harlem area.

The programs housed in Ackley Center are only part of St. Mary's *Community Outreach*. The pastors and the staff in their own right set aside major portions of their time for community affairs. For example, some of the roles played by the staff as individuals are: board membership of HARCAP, a program to assist high school students with college preparation and admission; leadership in the Manhattanville Renewal Association, which has recently secured support from the New York State Urban Development Corporation for new housing and health facilities in the Knickerbocker Hospital area; initiation and organization of the United Federation of Black Community Organizations, a coordinating body to maximize the efforts of many local groups. These examples are only illustrative of the staff's wide-ranging activities—activities that take them to the evening center some nights, to community meetings on others, to the Board of Education during the day, to rallies on weekends—that, in short, make all of them integral parts of community life.

My real role in the development and operation of St. Mary's Community Outreach is unlikely to be chronicled by any present or future historian. In moments of unbridled imagination, I may flatter myself with notions of theoretician or master planner. Probably more to the point would be images of midwife or handyman. I have stood by while it happened, trying to be attentive to the directions and consequences of various occurrences, while hoping that my tinkering would help, not hinder, the process. Acceptance of the less glamorous designations implies no great modesty; rather, it is an acknowledgment that conditions of the nation and neighborhood have a far greater bearing on anything that happens than do thoroughly crafted proposals or strokes of genius. I have had to keep looking to discern where currents seem to be flowing, to keep thinking to produce plans that take account of those currents, and to keep working to make realities of ideas. My particular input has varied from time to time. What has remained constant has been my perspective of one who looks at the workings of St. Mary's organization from the top, with a sense of responsibility for nudging its elements into purposeful and effective relationship.

My work is informed by three intellectual perspectives. In a very real sense I am a practicing social scientist. Although the careful methodology imputed by my undergraduate professors is a long-lost luxury, a sociological view of community movements has seemed to me almost indispensable. My responsibilities require constant sizing up of groups, attitudes, and other phenomena of social interaction. The objectivity of a sociological perspective is necessary insulation against the emotional and partisan moods that characterize much of community action.

I am also what in my younger days I vowed never to be—a business administrator. It has become evident that righteous causes and willing volunteers often lack effectiveness and endurance. I have had to learn personnel selection and supervision, administration of properties and budgets, program planning and fund-raising.

Finally, I am a pastor and humanist. I care about human beings as more than the sociological ciphers that I otherwise observe them to be. I care about their spiritual depths and their whole humanity. I care enough about these qualities in life to do what I can to create an atmosphere in which they can flourish. I have tried to develop a pattern that utilizes my talents and these perspectives in a meaningful process towards a religious goal.

The writer's experience ought not to be misread. A colleague who has largely congregational responsibilities can be every bit as much a new clergyman. The significance lies not in the choice of a social action pattern, but in the willingness to modify conceptual and organizational structures for the accomplishment of religious ends.

Another type of experience that may be widely emulated is that of the radical Catholics. The Berrigan brothers, the Melvilles and others have forthrightly manifested a religious criticism of the society. In certain respects these persons have splendidly demonstrated qualities needed by new clergymen. Even their opponents and detractors can hardly deny the profound and heroic quality of their witness. However, even more than a general caution against imitation seems warranted when considering the radical Catholics in respect to new clergy purposes. Although their criticisms are made from a religious foundation, the force of the group's efforts seems intended for the political arena. These efforts are valid expressions of religious convictions, but in themselves they hardly seem sufficient bases for sustenance of any religious community. Some radical Catholics are concerned with institutional reform and theological advancement. In those respects their work is simply comparable to that of other new clergy or their supporters and seems to warrant no separate treatment here. In the realm for which they are best known, they should be applauded, supported, and even followed. But judgments of them should surely be related to the effectiveness of their politics, not for their leadership of religion.

What, then, are the requirements of the new clergyman?

Given the onerous conditions of the task, the new clergyman must first of all be sure of his self. If he is to retain his critical perspective on the society, he cannot afford to be subsumed under one of the stereotypes provided by the tradition or the community. To search within one's self for what is authentic requires a fumbling and painful procedure. One can hardly be clear where his feelings and perceptions are distorted. A constant testing precedes the sense of a coherent reality. But knowledge of an internal reality is the only true bulwark against the slings and arrows of an impersonal world. To know that there is a part of one's self that does not belong to the world outside may really be the beginning of the religious attitude.

The new clergyman must develop his own religious feeling. He must certainly acknowledge the temptation to use his own experience as the standard for others. He must go to the tradition and the community for the wisdom that they hold. But in the sense that "deep calls out to deep," the authenticity of his own experience must relate to that of others. His own religious experience is not the cause of his profession, but it is the rationalization of it. The rituals, Scriptures, songs, prayers, and expressions of the community are amplifications of his own sense of being. Without his own sense of the realities involved, he is reduced to intellectual one-upmanship or the manipulations of party struggle. Battles fought for issues without substance can produce only hollow victories or meaningless losses. When there are so many struggles to be waged, one ought to have some assurance that he is joining a real issue. More important, however, experience and sharing of the religious attitude is the true motive for formation of a religious community.

People in their religious and other communities must be understood for what they are. Obviously doing that is no simple task. Clergymen can expect to be no more astute in their judgments than the bulk of mankind. But the difficulty of the effort should provide ample caution against hasty or demagogic actions. Yet it is precisely this failure that has wrecked the hopes of many who would be new clergymen.

Clergy have developed a new understanding of the meaning and implications of the Christian faith. They have not succeeded in communicating this understanding to laity. The frustration and failure of most clergymen to succeed in this task has led many of them to withdraw from the task. The fact that the amount of church involvement has little impact on attitudes toward racial justice and a large number of other social issues would seem to me to be rather serious evidence of the clergy's failure to communicate the meaning of the faith as they understand it. . . . I have come to feel that involvement has become the easy way out for many of them. Facing the jeers and insults of an angry crowd of racial bigots or war hawks may be easier than facing a congregation that feels the Christian gospel is a source of comfort and protection from a troubled world rather than a radical charge to go into the world and make it more human.*

So concluded Jeffrey K. Hadden after a sociological survey of nearly 10,000 clergymen. It is apparent that many clergymen are caught in a moral squeeze. As they view the evils of the society around them, they are easily impressed by the society's departure from the principles avowed by their religious communities. Not to speak out is to bear within one's self a burden of guilt for contributing to the continuance of evil. To speak out where one's words will not be heard is a pathetic waste of effort. But to spend the time required for a thorough communication process seems a criminal fiddling while the world burns. Whatever his decision the clergyman will be subject to hurt. That is why he needs certainty of self, that is why he must move with only the best judgments he can make.

The new clergyman cannot forget his people and their weaknesses, but neither can he be bound by them. One who seriously holds to a religious attitude can hardly doubt the

* Jeffrey K. Hadden, *The Gathering Storm in the Churches.* Garden City: Anchor Books, 1970, pp. 260–61.

priority of reconciling that perception with the life and organization of his community. However, community has many roots. Whatever authenticity of attitude may remain within any religious community, it is evident that for increasing numbers of people there is not enough. Both because of the inherent limitations of a traditional community living in a changing world, and because of the unfounded sets of values that have become so well established, the historic religious communities are found wanting. There is need for discovery and development of impulses in other sources. Time must be spent plumbing the minds and souls of persons and groups outside the community. The same standard of deep calling to deep must obtain in all situations.

A sense of pluralism and a spirit of adventure are the keys to the new clergyman's ministry. Without forgetting his community ties and the requirements for preserving them, he will seek out needs and opportunities elsewhere. He must develop a pragmatic attitude with respect to new possibilities, and learn to work where there are no patterns. He will need to develop skills and connections foreign to the traditional modes. He may need to become poet, accountant or mechanic. No technique that can be lifted from the secular world should be despised if it can help to impart a desired quality in life. The new clergyman cannot lose himself in the outside world, but he must immerse himself in it. He must learn to do well what he does, so that he meets the world on its own terms even while he does not accept them.

Eventually the new clergyman must probably give up his profession. That does not mean that he will cease to function in it. It means only that the profession will cease to provide his primary identification. The world may know him as a banker or lawyer or musician. If he is successful, he will be related to a religious community that may have a good many of the traditional characteristics—or it may not. Except for his personal preference, it will probably not matter very much whether it does or not. He may never preach a sermon, or he may do so every week. He will support himself according to his skills and opportunities. At one time he may be paid by a congregation for specified tasks, traditional or otherwise. At another time he may draw a salary for some other skill or operate his own business.

When conditions in the world at large have eroded the societal and cultural bases on which particular professions were founded, professions can become self-serving and irrelevant. That has happened to the clerical profession among others. To argue the need for religious exemplars, teachers or leaders is not to argue the need for a profession of religion. Irrelevant definition, stagnant stability and self-serving internal standards are not needed for the exercise of religion. Clergymen can exist without their profession.

The clerical profession might be reformed. There are constant pressures for that to happen. But the profession has become too cumbersome. From each age of its history it has accumulated "essences" until its requirements have become formless lumps of tradition. Many of its functions may be necessary ones, yet they are held together only by the cement of historical sequence. Once the profession's bonds have been loosened, its elements will not hold together. Indeed, they need not do so, and many advantages could result from greater cultivation of certain of the elements. Therefore, to focus on reform of the clerical profession seems a misguided effort, motivated primarily by yearning for tradition. If human needs and their social structures produce situations which can be benefited through well-defined professions, better to allow for a multiplicity of related professions than to strain for a single, ineffective one.

The disappearance of the clerical profession could mean the rise of a cluster of new professions. It seems better, however, not to presuppose even that. The types of knowledge and standards implied by professions obviously can be useful, but they must be meaningfully related to the purposes they serve. That seems to require a more searching exploration of those needs and a greater openness to their requirements than is possible in the traditional context. Giving up the profession does not mean giving up its concerns, only its trappings. The new clergyman must be conceptually and organizationally "stripped for action."

Anyone who seriously wishes to become a new clergyman should have no difficulty becoming exposed to the point of view. Most major seminaries, and even many college religion departments, provide learning experiences in the elements of religion and criticism needed for a basic framework. While one who espouses a new clergy point of view might do well to by-pass small or rural denominational seminaries, the problem is not so much where to go as how to avoid distracting tangents. Seminarians are notoriously subject to movements and fads. To follow the tide is to risk being swept away. On the other hand, seminary faculties may be too much limited by tradition and too compartmentalized to offer good guidance. The secret is in selection of course offerings and experiences. Offerings should be selected that sharpen one's wits, that provide varying perspectives, that deepen one's understanding of self, society and religion. If a seeker can discipline himself, he should have relatively little difficulty finding enlightenment.

If acquiring a new clergy viewpoint can be done expeditiously, practicing the same will be more difficult. Certification bodies for ordination and pastoral relations committees (who do the hiring) are not notably sympathetic toward new clergy aims. Also, most congregations have tended to winnow out those who might have been edified by the leadership of a new clergyman. In addition, inflation and taxes will almost certainly reduce opportunities for full-time, paid clergy positions. Thus, pressures from within the religious communities may exclude new clergymen from the clerical profession before they remove themselves. Some congregations are already sympathetic to new clergy aims, some can be taught to be appreciative, others may be formed from those "separated brethren" who were welcomed out of their previous congregational associations. The situation is not hopeless, but it could hardly be said to be promising.

Where can a potential new clergyman go for information and support? The answer is not at all obvious. New clergymen have been coming from a variety of seminaries. The interdenominational seminaries, or those in urban areas that permit cross-registration, are the best possibilities for study that inculcates new clergy ideas. The magazines *Christianity and Crisis* and *Renewal* will be of interest if financial circumstances allow their publication. Books and articles by Professor Harvey Cox and Stephen Rose open up a number of stimulating possibilities with respect to contemporary ministries. Clergy associations favorable to this point of view are sometime things that may flourish or falter at any moment. For those interested, guidance must be sought. With perseverance it can be found.

The role of new clergyman raises problems of training, organization and understanding. A look at ossified denominational structures at first glance seems to offer little hope. Religious communities are not promising to break through at any time with throbbings of new life. Old orthodoxies and conservatisms are not ready to fall away.

But new clergymen are out there. Some are in parishes in Indiana, some are working in banks on Wall Street, some are in publishing houses, some are on the streets of the nation's ghettos. They are working in the world at large. They do not necessarily know each other, though they may recognize each other if they meet. They are no secret society. But they are out there looking for forms with charisma and power that will offer a judgment on the society in which they live. One must hope for them.

Changing
the
Professions
of
Change

The New Political Activism

by DAVID HAWK

David Hawk has emerged as one of the prominent leaders in the anti-war movement. His first organizing experience was in Hattiesburg, Mississippi, in 1964 where he worked on voter registration and political organizing for the Mississippi Freedom Democratic Party under the auspices of the Student Nonviolent Coordinating Committee. A related experience was community organizing in the black community of Cordele, Georgia in 1966 to develop a tenants' council in a low-income city housing project.

He worked as a minor "advance" man in the McCarthy for President campaign in New Hampshire and Wisconsin. After the campaign he was a student anti-war organizer for the National Student Association and then one of the three coordinators of the Vietnam Moratorium Committee. During this period he also refused induction into the army and organized local support around his resistance.

He is currently a student at Union Theological Seminary in New York City and is continuing to organize against the war.

MUCH OF the history of the decade of 1960 was made by political activists. This is a new and provocative phenomenon, for history is usually made by generals, statesmen, politicians or scientists. Yet, as Americans look back on the 1960's, and as they consider the changes that occurred in the social system, much of what they will see is the product of ordinary people and the efforts of anonymous organizers of those ordinary people. The civil rights, anti-poverty, university reform, anti-war and ecology movements were organized by political activists; and the social forces set loose by that political activism, and the reaction of the social structure to those forces, describes to a large extent what the past decade was all about.

The efforts for social change begun in the sixties had a substantial initial impact: They exposed raw injustice, raised issues, and changed the consciousness of nearly an entire generation of Americans. Those activists, striving to restore quality, direction and control over their life situation, established a pattern for a wide spectrum of Americans. Many people, struck by similar dismay over the course of the country, now want to be something that resembles a political activist. It is only necessary to look back to the early sixties, when leaving school or business to go South and work was a very drastic, almost unheard-of step, to recognize how new and different the present situation is.

As a new, influential and radical force on American politics and institutions, it may be helpful to look at this political activism, to examine the boundaries and presumptions, and the skills and functions of political activism.

CAREER SITUATION

It seems to me that young people about to enter the "career" market, as well as many older Americans, have, broadly speaking, a basic choice about what they will do with their lives. One choice is to work for the technostructure; the other is to do work that has positive and constructive political consequences. Working for the technostructure, that is, the corporate or state bureaucracies or their extensions, has, in most cases, little positive political, cultural and moral consequence. One can spend one's time convincing the American public that they need yet another revolutionary new mouthwash or deodorant for yet another part of their bodies, and be well paid for it. Or if the state bureaucracy is preferable to the corporate one, one can administer some program that is as much a part of the problem as it is the solution. This kind of work may be steady and remunerative, but it does little except reinforce the existing institutions and enhance their stability.

If the corporate or state technostructure lacks appeal, one can work in ways and in efforts that are socially, culturally, and politically positive and enduring. Doing this can entail nearly everything from carrying a new attitude to one's present job to totally dropping out. There are several ways to approach work and vocation that are politically active—dropping out, turning to the new professionalism, and political organizing.

Dropping or opting out of the upwardly mobile escalator is now a viable alternative for the simple reason that thousands of young people are doing it. The drop-out or alternative communities that are currently taking root on the borders of large universities, rural towns and cities, are becoming sufficiently large to require and to support new systems of delivery of goods and services. These new institutions need to be organized. To the extent that they do not develop into an ersatz form of "hip capitalism," the building of these alternative institutions and sub-systems is political.

A second form of political activism is the kind of "new professionalism" discussed in other chapters of this book. In this case, one pursues a more traditional profession but uses those skills in new ways—public interest or poverty law, street ministries, free medical clinics—while organizing a new infrastructure or caucus within that professional association, i.e., Computer Scientists for Peace.

The third category is political activism, and the form which will be considered below is that of the political organizer—a person who spends his time organizing people or communities around a set of grievances or issues or goals. Apart from the need to build new institutions and to reform existing structures, as long as the country continues in its present disastrous and runaway course, it will be necessary to do various kinds of organizing. The issues around which people and political pressure groups need to be organized are fairly easy to list: the continuation of the war in Indochina; a foreign policy based on intervention and the preservation of American economic and political hegemony; the pursuit of an absurd arms race; the persistence of institutionalized racism; the economic exploitation of unorganized sections of the labor force; poverty and the maldistribution of wealth; consumer fraud; the despoiling of the environment; the rights of women; the concentration of power but diffusion of responsibility of corporations and conglomerates.

All of these issues have several things in common, one of which is that in nearly all cases the vested interests are better organized than insurgent movements against them. This is not the only reason the status quo remains as it is, but it is a very important one. For example, anti-war sentiment has always been considerably more widespread than our success in organizing that sentiment into an effective pressure for peace. People have to be organized around residential and occupational concerns as well as lines of interest.

WHAT POLITICAL ACTIVISTS ARE AND ARE NOT

Since many people lump all protesters into one large group of misfits, it may be helpful to distinguish between different types of political activism. A useful typology of activists is found in Harry Edwards' recent book, *Black Students,* where he discusses several distinguishable types of participants in the black student revolt. In addition to the "conforming Negro," there is the "radical activist," the "militant," the "revolutionary" and the "anomic activist." The "radical activist" is middle class in background, essentially a reformer, being willing to compromise on minor points, and politically more experienced and sophisticated. He is the starter and developer of organizations. The "militant" is younger, conversant in the rhetoric, and stylistically identified with the Movement. He is involved in politics primarily at the time of crisis, and then is strongly inclined to heavy and self-conscious reliance on the rhetoric and cultural trappings of black nationalism. The "revolutionary" is the zealous, well read, but dogmatic ideologue, who feels that premeditated violence is a necessary tactic for change in America. Like the militant, the revolutionary—except for ideological study groups—does not become visibly politically active until a crisis situation has developed. The "anomic activist" is the personally alienated, younger, and often lower-class "rebel without a cause," whose personal existence is marked by diffuse anger and rage. It is the "anomic activist" who will most often perform the acts of both premeditated and unpremeditated violence when a political crisis provides a focus and a target for otherwise diffuse rage.

The different categories of this typology are also, with little alteration, operative among young whites who participate in political action in the broadest sense. The radical activist organizes the committees and develops the programs. The militant attends demonstrations or provides the political muscle in a confrontation. The revolutionary discusses and develops his ideology and comes to demonstrations largely to demand his turn at the podium. The "anomic activist," the barely political but very alienated youth, violently retaliates against the society he despises when a political action gives focus to his constant anger.

While not denying the periodic utility of the other types of political participation in the process of social change, it should be made clear that the present discussion concerns the first type of participant—what Edwards calls the "radical activists" and what we discuss as the "political activist" or "political organizer."

POLITICAL BELIEFS AND ACTIONS—THE
PROPHETIC AND THE POLITIC IN ACTIVISM

The German sociologist, Max Weber, in his essay "Politics as a Vocation," made a fundamental distinction between the "political" and the "prophetic." The necessity of politics, especially in a democracy, is compromise. Politics is the art of the possible. The politician deals with power realities and power relationships. The politician is the bargainer hedging bets, keeping options open, trading a loss here for a gain there.

The prophet, on the other hand, is the person who deals with ethical norms and values. The prophet speaks precisely the language of right and wrong. He does not ask whether it will sell in Peoria, or how that unyoung, unpoor, unblack, middle-aged housewife of the Midwest machinist who is the statistically derived focal point of the real majority will respond. The prophet cannot compromise what his conscience or moral standards hold to be the truth. Evil is not to be compromised with or participated in.

The political activist is, in a very real sense, a blending of the prophetic and, to a lesser extent, the political. The prophetic assumptions which underlie much of the political activism of recent years has been well stated by David Harris, the draft resister. His idiom is that of the draft and the war, but it could as easily be the idiom of the other Movement objectives. Because he articulates what many activists feel that they are about, it is worth quoting at length:

> As we in the Resistance look out on a world that is really a merry-go-round of blood and misery, and as we look out on that world of widows and orphans and young men shipped home in boxes and little children with their chins melted to their chests, as we look out on that world, there is one statement that has cogency and meaning. That statement is a very simple statement, but like most simple statements, is a very

complex problem to try to live. That simple statement is: *All men are brothers.* And the problem that we have taken on ourselves is the problem of building brotherhood into a social and political reality. . . .

. . . One of the things that you and I constantly look for in this world is really an adequate tool, something with which one can bring about change in the world . . . the tool that you and I have is not a new set of words; it's not a new slogan, a new candidate, a new set of officers. The tool that you and I have is the tool of a life. . . .

. . . instead of dealing with the abstract notion of social problems and sitting down in all your academic regalia and presenting analyses about the various social problems in America, to understand that the social problem of America is people. It is time to understand that you are a people, and that there is a very direct connection between those social problems and the way you choose to live. For those social problems are nothing more than the way Americans choose to live and if you want to speak to those people's lives, then you have to speak to them with a life.

The second thing you should remember is that you can do that. This is not an abstract program for someone else. It's something that each of you can do. I think what faces each of us is a question about allegiance. What we in the Resistance have said is very simple. We owe allegiance to no piece of colored cloth. We owe allegiance to no musty set of political principles, or any musty set of people that may run those political principles. What we owe allegiance to is the fact of people's lives around the world. The fact of those lives is that those lives are wrapped in a chain of death and oppression. If you want a symbol for that, then take that widow, take that orphan, take that young man shipped home in a box, take the young child with his chin melted to his chest, and say *that's what we owe allegiance to.* . . .

. . . It's time to say, I'm given one thing on the face of this earth. That is my life. I intend to use my life as a way of building the lives of my brothers. It's time to say, I'm given a choice in the modern world today. That choice in a way is a simple choice. It's a choice between all those forces in the society and in the world that have become synonymous with man's death and oppression, and those forces which really offer hope for people. You must choose between them. You can't serve a god of militarism and war and serve a god of brotherhood and love. You choose and you serve one or the other, but the existence of one is the absolute contradiction of the other. That's the choice you and I get to make.

The political activist is not, however, purely prophetic. While the best of activism strives not to lose the prophetic idealism expressed by Harris, activists do strive to organize political power or muscle to change policies. They have to deal with the moral dilemma and paradoxes of wielding or attempting to wield political power. Activists must choose between strategies, tactics and persons. Because the resources of protest are scarce, there is political competition. This process nearly always involves a degree of manipulation. Though the internal politics of movement activists can be rough, a humane process of politics—often at the expense of efficiency, clarity and time—is usually a goal among activists. The political instinct, what is effective, lies not too far behind the prophetic instinct, what is right.

In practical terms, if the process of political power in America continues to be one of cajoling, pressuring, pushing or capturing the "middle" of the political spectrum, the role of the political activist is easily differentiated from that of the politician. The politician, if not directly fronting for "special interests" as many of the powerful ones do, usually takes a "middle-of-the-road" position, one that is the least offensive to the largest number of constituents. This process explains the reason that so little political leadership comes from our elected officials.

The political activist starts from a different position in the political process. The activist will organize in direct and stated opposition to the special and vested interests that maintain the status quo. The activist will, at least in most cases, at the initial stages expose social sores that a majority may well wish to remain hidden. The activist, at least initially, espouses solutions that are not popular. The extent to which the politician tries to "co-opt" the forces or the issues that activists have put in motion is a reliable gauge of the effectiveness of the political activists.

THE POLITICAL SITUATION OF ACTIVISM

Despite the fact that almost any public discussion by political activists will be followed with the inevitable question: "What can I do?", there is no lack of things that can be done. The necessary precondition for political activism is a general sense of direction and an analysis which reinforces the belief that social change is possible.

The belief that political change can work is particularly important at times like the present. Many people have briefly flirted with politics (and it is no more than that, really) by attending an anti-war demonstration or two, only to "turn off" to politics because they haven't stopped the war. For a number of reasons, there is much currency to a theory that we are in a kind of "post-political" situation; that all one can really do is try to find one's own inner peace, preferably close to the land.

The "post-political" part of this notion stems primarily, I think, from a misunderstanding of political change. Put simply, a march to Selma will not end segregation. A march to Washington will not end the war in Vietnam. An ecology fair will not stop pollution. It just never happens that way.

What must be recognized at the outset is that social change never comes easily and never comes cheap. This is especially true in a country like the United States where the vested interests are so deeply rooted in all the major social institutions and processes. Although it is not uncommon, the notion that change should be easy because it is desirable or even necessary is unrealistic.

The Abolitionist Movement agitated and organized for twenty years before they raised the moral issue of slavery to proportions of a national political crisis. The labor movement organized for years before unions gained legal status, and then worker organizing had to continue for many more years before unions gained economic leverage. The Vietnamese have been fighting for nearly thirty years to win national independence from a succession of imperial powers.

Social change just does not come easy—nor will it come cheap. In our own time, men have had to die to achieve the "right" to vote. In our parents' time, many working men were killed and wounded by police management goon squads before the major steel, rail and automobile industries could be unionized. It is difficult to think of a serious movement for fundamental social change—regardless of that movement's dedication to nonviolent philosophies or tactics—that did not have its leaders and workers ostracized, brutalized and murdered. The established order believes in itself. Those who maintain it profit from the status quo. The political and economic bosses have never demonstrated leniency or nonviolence to those seeking change. Presidents will applaud and congratulate construction workers who beat protesters of the President's policies. Mayors will covertly organize and publically condone police riots. A serious movement and serious political activists must expect this.

Social change doesn't come cheaply in another sense. It is the accretion of layers of work, painstaking and painful, by many who labor sixteen hours a day for months and years at a time. Yet when people think of political organizing efforts, they are prone to think first of the excitement of a political campaign or of a demonstration or march. However, much as it sounds like a truism, it is necessary to say that the publicly visible part of organizing is only the part of the iceberg which is above water. Thousands and thousands of man-hours of hard patient work have gone into the preparation of the exciting or dramatic event.

Although an activist must expect change to be difficult, he or she must expect it to be possible as well as desirable. Since many young people dabbled in political action only to give up because they felt idealism is wasted on America, the possibility of political change deserves further examination. In desperation over the current state of affairs, many overlook the real and important changes that have taken place as a result of the political activism during the decade of the 1960's.

In the early sixties, the civil rights movement broke down a legal and social system of racial apartheid second in severity only to South Africa's legal subjugation and suppression of blacks. In virtually every aspect of their lives, Southern blacks were held down by law. In the course of a decade of lawsuits, sit-ins, freedom rides, marches, voter registration drives, and community organization, the oppression of legal apartheid was destroyed. The civil rights movement was never able to move North or West, or to successfully take on economic deprivation, but few will deny that a deep and fundamental change has taken place in American race relations.

In considering the possibilities of change, the anti-war movement should also be examined. The peace movement has not as yet ended the war in Vietnam. But its strength, when politically organized, forced an incumbent president out of office. That is no small accomplishment for a political movement organized largely by political novices. The peace movement has spread opposition to war policies to virtually every level of American society. The anti-war movement has helped to break down the foreign policy consensus of cold war anti-Communist interventionism that dominated policy makers for over twenty years. Although the balance of power has not shifted to the anti-war and anti-militarist forces, the peace movement has become a major force in American politics during the last five years.

Similarly, in even less time, the ecology and conservationist movements have grown into a very powerful force in American politics.

The examples of the partial success of the civil rights movement and the past growth of the anti-war and ecology movements are not meant to imply that because of their past efforts the issues they raised have been resolved. But the predominant recognition must be that there will be no change in America without political activists who try year after year after year to reverse policies and change institutions.

THE TASK AND GENERAL DIRECTION OF POLITICAL ACTIVISM

Political activism is not something that takes place once every two or four years, as an election comes around. Nor has electoral political action extended the most productive lever for achieving social change. Indeed, both parties still basically apply a cold war conservatism or cold war liberalism to problems and situations that are not amenable to either the outlook or analysis of the Cold War or the New Deal. Further, Congress is still inhibited by the seniority system and other procedural malfunctions. Thus, while many of the important decisions that affect people's lives will continue to be made in Washington, electoral political activity forms only a small part of long-term strategy for change.

The necessary changes in the social structure are not the kind of superficial alterations that take place by laws or resolutions coming from the top of the society or from the seat of political and economic power in America, only gradually to filter down to people.

The starting point for many of the changes activists seek is in the institutions close at hand that affect our lives. Many changes in national policies will come only as we build up a series of new constituencies for change and a parallel structure of new and drastically reformed institutions and subsystems.

Only a portion of the ills that beset our national life can be traced to policies of the national government. A large portion of our national sickness can be traced to local, private and nongovernmental institutions. Does anyone doubt that the bar and medical associations act contrary to the public interest? Does anyone doubt that the banks, insurance and power companies are ripping off people at every turn? The corporations have produced war materials every time they could make a buck. The churches are wealthy institutions that have rarely applied ethical criteria to their financial stewardship. Colleges can recruit athletes or they can recruit minority students. Universities can train the officer corps for Vietnam or they can educate people for peaceful ends. Scholars can continue to study the life styles of the poor and the black or they can study the malfunction of the establishment and provide alternatives. Grade schools can track and program working-class children into vocational programs. But they don't have to.

The fact is that virtually every American institution and subsystem is badly in need of fundamental reform: the judicial, criminal and legal processes, the educational institutions, the churches, the financial and monetary institutions, the labor unions, the professional associations, the media. Most institutions have simply developed so that their normal functioning naturally reinforces the status quo.

What is necessary is what some have called "the long march through American institutions." Social and political policies do not perpetuate themselves in a vacuum. They are rooted in and protected by institutions, private as well as public. As new institutions are built or existing ones are reformed, and as caucuses or movements for change are organized within and against vested interests, the constituencies for change will be organized for pressuring or replacing the policy makers.

VARIETY AND STYLE OF ACTIVISM

Activism can and must take place at a variety of levels—all the way from community organizing, or even smaller subdivisions like precinct organizing, to regional or area groupings to national levels. Activists operating at any of these levels do pretty much the same thing. Outside of understandable differences in scale and the resources involved, the largest difference is that the more "national" the organization, the more abstractly one deals with things and the less one deals with "real" people. For example, activists who work for a national anti-draft group will deal with the Congress, the major court cases, the conscript vs. volunteer army debate, and, in addition, try to stimulate local organizing. An activist working with a local anti-draft group will work with the young man who has the very personal problem of dealing with his draft board.

An interesting consequence of this distinction between organizing at "local" vs. "national" level is a difference of perspective. The local organizer who lives and works with real people who are being exploited and badly hurt by the society is often considerably more militant than the organizer at the more abstract national level where one deals with less personal social forces. Anyone wanting to be a political activist should seek both kinds of experience.

Political activism can be virtually open-ended—improving the condition of minority groups, ending the war, cutting down the power of the military. Or, activism can be very specific and limited and immediate—stopping a particular plant from polluting the local river or defeating a particular bill.

There has been among political activists a running debate between "single issue" vs. "multi-issue" organizing. In many cases, an organization will begin organizing around a single issue. Then, over a period of time, after an organization has developed an "identity," political organizations will enlarge the scope and range of those efforts. The basic force behind this is the genuine interrelation of issues: the costs of the war necessitated the end of the poverty program; the draft oppresses the poor and the black; the buying power of the Pentagon is used to break citizen boycotts of nonunion lettuce and grapes; the same politicians who are reactionary on one issue are, with exceptions, reactionary on others. Thus, what is needed are activists and organizations that can adopt different strategies, coalitions and programs with changing situations. The most important factor in these ongoing discussions is the development of concrete programs that activists from different fields can participate in and organize around. If there isn't such a programmatic element, the "positions" of a given organization will make little difference.

HOW ACTIVISTS GET STARTED

Apart from a proportionally small number of political activists who grew up in politically active families, most activists are regular people who became so concerned and outraged over the state of affairs that they dropped out of more regular academic or commercial pursuits to work in the Movement. The civil rights, anti-war, anti-poverty, ecology movements are filled with people who went "South" during a vacation for a few weeks and "stayed" or who went to New Hampshire to work for McCarthy for a weekend and "stayed." Many have gone to an anti-war march or rally and decided that trying to stop the war was more meaningful than what they were doing before, and so went to an anti-war office to volunteer for part- or full-time work. Others became activists after first working with student governments or newspapers or campus-based committees.

As a person works as a volunteer or staff member for a variety of groups and committees, he or she learns the techniques and skills of organizing—how to run and repair the mimeo machine, how to talk to people, how to deal with the telephone company, how to write leaflets and contact the press. Simultaneously, the beginning activist gradually learns how the Movement works, how decisions are made, and gradually meets a wider spectrum of people who will know of another "going" project or another committee that needs help.

HOW DO ACTIVISTS SUSTAIN THEMSELVES?

This is undoubtedly the most difficult question facing would-be political activists, because the answer is, in honesty—poorly. To begin with, political programs and efforts on the whole pay basically subsistence wages, and missed staff paychecks are not at all uncommon. Except at the level of presidential and senatorial politics, activists or organizers rarely end up with money in the bank.

Secondly, political activism, except for a small number of staff positions in a few permanent national organizations, is a rather seasonal occupation. That is, there are periods during which a major effort or campaign may be mounted. At these times, staffs expand dramatically. Then, after the target date is passed, the election won or lost, the bill passed or failed, the confrontation mounted, the pace and momentum slackens. In fact, political organizations are formed, grow, if successful make their impact, and then fade from the arena with considerable regularity. Even in the relatively few stable organizations there is a fairly constant turnover of organizers. And surprisingly or not, political organizations are not immune from general economic conditions. If money is tight, Movement groups have to tighten their belts as well.

When this happens, activists have to seek alternative ways of sustenance. Lawyers or ministers or teachers can rely on professional training. Other activists need to seek part-time jobs, return to school, or drive a cab. Other activists of longer experience write, speak, or seek consulting jobs to sustain themselves. Finally, within the last several years, some activists have banded together to establish political communes or collectives. Sometimes, under these arrangements, an activist with professional training will seek full-time employment and will turn over his earnings to support the other organizers associated with the group.

Given the instability of the situation, the rapid turnover of organizers is not surprising. One of the main traits activists need to develop is a certain disregard for financial security and stability. It's rarely possible for activists to know where their paycheck will come from six months hence.

FUNCTIONS AND SKILLS OF POLITICAL ACTIVISTS

What is it exactly that political activists do every day? Regardless of whether it is a political campaign, issue organizing at a national or regional level, or local community organizing, there is a common core or function which the political activist performs. What follows is a brief description of those tasks, although not in order of importance, for that will depend on time, circumstances, and on the specialization of function with the group of activists:

Developing contacts: Developing the working network of contacts is the most basic and most important function of organizing. Except for a very few independent spokesmen such as Dr. Spock or Ralph Nader or media manipulators such as the Yippies, it is only the strength of a working network of concerned and organized people that allows activists to raise the issues and press for social change. This is done in a variety of ways: calling a meeting and starting with whomever shows up; seeking out the ministers of a town to see if they will cooperate; approaching other and related organizations for local contact lists; negotiating with other groups to develop working coalitions; canvassing a block to seek out the like-minded and sympathetic; holding neighborhood block meetings or "coffee klatches"; setting up a telephone tree for fast communications; house-to-house surveys; setting up a literature table and signing up interested passersby. It is the network of contacts on a block-to-block basis for community organizers, dormitory to dormitory for campus organizers, city by city for movements that are national in scope, that provide the base for extending pressure for change. It is this base which must be extended and developed.

Research: The more an activist knows about "how things work" the better able he or she will be to discover the most vulnerable pressure spots, and the easier it is to organize. In terms of community organizing, there are several guides to "researching the local power structure." One needs to know such questions as who owns the local industries and banks and newspapers. Are they controlled locally or by a distant parent corporation? What powers does the local mayor or city council have? Who controls the local political parties? Who are the influential ministers and lawyers and what are their interests? What are the politics of the national unions that have locals?

An activist also needs to know the particulars and the history of the issues he is attempting to organize around. What are the relevant laws? How has a policy or institution developed over time? What were the options that were not chosen and why?

A large and efficiently coordinated constituency will provide little pressure unless it is organized effectively around strategies and tactics which exploit the opposition's weakness. The more one knows about how the political sytem and a given institution or policy works, the better able one is to find that weak point and organize effectively against it.

Communication: Nearly every activist is involved in getting out leaflets, calls to action, and newsletters. Activists need also to find out costs and procedures for billboards, radio and TV spots, and how to get invitations to civic clubs, churches, high schools, and the local talk shows.

Press: Most of what activists do will be interpreted to the general public through the eyes and biases of the media. Activities that have political impact will, at some point, generate news. Thus, activists need to get to know the deadlines, appropriate TV, radio and newspaper reporters, and, if possible, editorial writers and columnists. Reporters often follow events quite closely and are quite knowledgeable. If one is organizing at the level of national issues, it is necessary to follow news quite closely. Not only to follow the events and statements of appropriate people, but to follow how the media "cover" the events. It is not only necessary to know what *Foreign Affairs,* the *New York Review of Books* and *The New York Times* says about the war, it is equally important to know what *Time, U.S. News and World Report,* Cronkite, Brinkley, and the local newspapers are saying. Those are the sources of opinion that activists at various times have to counter. The press is not by any means the focal point of organizing efforts, but in many ways the way the press covers issues determines the context and parameters in which activists have to organize.

Legal: Regardless of what the issue is or what is the strategy or tactic to deal with that issue, an activist will spend considerable time with legal counsel. Lawyers are necessary whether one is incorporating a group, seeking a demonstration permit, or, indeed, in almost any contact with the establishment.

Arrangements: A large amount of the time of a political activist is spent in simply making arrangements. Any event or conference entails a myriad of details which have to be checked and double-checked. These details are more thoroughly pursued in political campaigns which have more resources and run at a more hectic pace than most organizing projects. But simply consider, for example, the activities that surround the visit of an outside national spokesman or organizational leader to a local area. An activist will have to attend to air-line scheduling; transportation; lodging; finding the best meeting place; public-address systems for the speech; a press conference; individual interviews with the local TV, radio and writing press; private meetings with constituents; fund-raising parties; advance publicity.

Fund-raising: Although this is one of the least attractive jobs, most activists have to devote some time and energy to this function. Varieties of fund-raising activities include gaining access and introduction to potential financial backers, churches, labor unions or foundations; art and poster sales; concerts; and neighborhood fund-raising parties.

Hassling: Since most activists and organizations operate on the borderline of financial stability, a considerable amount of time is spent borrowing from Peter to pay Paul to stay one step ahead of the landlord, the phone company, the printer, the post office and a myriad of other creditors.

A brief description of how the national office of the October 15 Vietnam Moratorium was organized perhaps can give an idea of how the functions and skills of political activism are integrated in a working situation. The purpose of the national office was twofold: the most important job was to stimulate and minimally coordinate local organizing; and the second job was to try to provide a political focus and climate that would foster maximum participation and political impact. Thus, the office functioned at two levels.

The first level was the operation to stimulate grass-roots organizing against the Vietnam war. There were approximately a half dozen "student" organizers, each of whom maintained constant phone and mail contact with students in a several-state area. There were approximately a half dozen students who worked as "community" organizers, maintaining phone and mail contact with church, peace and civic groups within a given geographic area. The student and community organizers who covered the same area would exchange local contacts and information to fill in gaps in activity. Both would seek out a local contact and discuss the local situation and the problems as they developed. Later, the student and community organizers made field trips to their regions and established regional offices. A mailroom operation and speakers bureau backed up the student and community organizers, sending out bumper stickers, posters, pins, and helping to find speakers for local rallies.

The second level was an attempt to establish a focus and tone for the Moratorium Day demonstration. Much of this work was done by the national coordinators, who attempted to establish relationships with and support from elected political officials and national peace, church, political, civic and labor groups. This part of the office developed newspaper ads and held periodic press conferences and interviews to make public statements of endorsement, support and participation in order to establish development and momentum.

REWARDS AND EFFECTIVENESS

If political activism is usually performed at subsistence wages with no fringe benefits or security, what are, in the face of the many unnerving frustrations activists live with, the rewards that compel activists to carry it on? There are several.

At the most immediate level there is the satisfaction of watching something that we believe in and that we are building grow and develop. Building the network of working contacts involves much dull and tedious work. For every answered phone call there are six "not at homes." But at the end of the long day, if you can say "we now have a contact who will work on sixteen more campuses" or "we now have four housewives in the twelfth precinct who will hold block meetings in their homes next week," that is a really good feeling. That's the stuff of which social change is made.

Secondly, there are minor victories along the way. Carswell was defeated. LBJ was forced out of office. Federal registrars were finally sent into the South. Anti-pollution codes are being strengthened. Polls show increasing numbers of people in favor of ending the war immediately. These things happen only because people have worked very hard. Such victories reinforce the sense that we can prevail and make up for an equal number of setbacks and losses. The logic that either the just, humane and peaceful society or fascist political repression is imminent is unimpressive. The struggle between Nixon's and Mitchell's vision of America and ours will go on for some time yet.

Basically, however, the "reward" for political activism is the ability to answer when our children ask us what we were doing when they were murdering the Vietnamese, brutalizing the poor and despoiling the earth. If that war can be shortened by one life, then all the marches, petitions, committees, campaigns, prison sentences, boring meetings and repetitive rallies will have been worth it. If a poor or black child is able to grow up with dignity, then all the blood, sweat and lawsuits will have been worth it. If our children can find a natural stream or lake to swim in, then all the drudgery it takes to stop the corporate polluters will have been worth that. If, in 1971, this sounds hackneyed or trite or futile, then that is too bad.

It is difficult to grow up in America and acquire a sense of meaning and purpose in our lives. We no longer believe the myths of technology, Horatio Alger, Grosse Point, or the white man's burden. A place to begin to restore the dignity denied us by the crisis in our national values is by saying "no" to the order of things that allows children to be hungry or cold—or napalmed.

Political activism in the long run or final analysis may not accomplish anything. We may choose the wrong strategy and blow it. Or the opposition may just be too strong and too entrenched. Only the American government indubitably sees the light at the end of the tunnel. Activists know better. But one thing is certain. A decent and livable America and one that lets the rest of the world live in peace will not be built by the likes of Nixon, Mitchell, Bill Bundy, Nate Pusey, Hewlitt-Packard or the Chase Manhattan Bank. We may not be able to do it. But if we don't try, nothing will happen at all.

The New Journalist

by NAT HENTOFF

Nat Hentoff is the closest thing we have to a conscience for American journalism. He has earned that role through a careerlong commitment to honest reporting, social justice and professional autonomy.

Hentoff's column in the *Village Voice* was one of the first, and is still one of the best critical reviews of the performance of the press. In it he has constantly pinpointed the errors, lapses and biases of the nation's newspapers, especially the one from which we all rightly expect so much: *The New York Times.*

As a journalist in his own right, Hentoff wrote a series on methadone which changed public policy; a profile of a New York City school principal, *Our Children Are Dying,* which was one of the first books to awaken us to the tragedy of urban education in the sixties; and many other effective and compelling stories. He has also written fiction, jazz and film criticism, and books for young readers.

Currently Hentoff conducts independent study courses on the impact of the media as Associate Professor at New York University's Graduate School of Education, as well as continuing his own writing as a free lance, a *Voice* columnist, and a staff member of *The New Yorker.*

WHEN I was in college, it was customary for the professors—even the few who knew something worth learning—to use "journalism" in a distinctly pejorative sense. There were serious writers, and there were journalists. A piece of work was dismissed as too "journalistic." And when I told an English professor that I intended to continue being a journalist (I was editing the college paper at the time), he looked at me somewhat as if I had told him that I had chosen heroin addiction as a career.

None of this official deprecation of journalism impressed me a bit. I knew better. As columnist, then feature editor, and finally editor-in-chief of the *Northeastern News,* I had learned more about the actual morphology of higher education than from any course I'd had on the subject. Since we were muck-rakers, I also learned more about racism and anti-Semitism through doing stories on them than from the bland courses in sociology I took. And none of my courses in ethics taught me as much as our struggle with the administration to retain our autonomy as journalists—and as ourselves. I and several colleagues eventually resigned from the school paper rather than accept administration mandates on what we could and couldn't print—and that was a useful lesson, too.

After college, there has never been a period of my life when —whatever else I might also have been doing—I have not been engaged in journalism of one kind or another. Although I take time to write novels and nonfiction books and to teach, I cannot conceive of ever abandoning journalism. I agree entirely with Jean Schwoebel, diplomatic editor of *Le Monde,* that "We must have citizens able to choose representative people in any field of activity. And they can do so only if the citizens know the real facts—the factors of every situation. If you don't have that, it is a caricature of democracy. That is why we say that only a society which has highly qualified journalists can progress."

From time to time, I have wondered whether I'd trade a political life for a writer's. Nobody ever did ask me, so the question was academic, but I come down again in consonance with Mr. Schwoebel: "Political men may be very authentic men, but they are dependent in large degree on the man who elects them, and it is on journalists' courage and quality that we depend to raise the quality of citizens."

This is not to say, of course, that we ever have nearly

enough journalists of courage and quality. In the past, many who have begun with the potential to demonstrate both attributes have been flattened by the nature of the newspapers and magazines for which they chose to work. For a very long time, the conventional wisdom—and it is, alas, still widely operative among far too many publishers and editors—has been that expressed succinctly, and utterly wrongly, by Geoffrey Wolff of *Newsweek*. In reviewing a book on *The New York Times*, Mr. Wolff proclaimed that a newspaper—in this case, the *Times*—"is chained to great events and can do little more than reflect them. It serves as a mirror; its function is its limitation."

There is no such limitation, except in the limited perspectives of certain publishers and editors. The most cursory history of journalism reveals the stubborn strain of muckraking, investigatory reporting and fiercely committed editorializing that distinguishes those newspapers which are part of the news from those which indeed are only mirrors and therefore of little use to their readers.

The New York Times has massive faults, but there, too, journalists have functioned who have done much more than "reflect" events. Consider the impact on American opinion of David Halberstam's reporting from South Vietnam early in the war (journalism so revealing that President John F. Kennedy tried unsuccessfully to have Halberstam removed from that post). Some years later, Administration lies about the nature of the North Vietnamese and about what we had done to that country were devastatingly skewered by Harrison Salisbury's reporting from North Vietnam for the *Times*. Domestically, Tom Wicker has for a long time been one of the country's most valuable awakeners of the citizenry to the systematic assault on the Bill of Rights being conducted by Congress and the Executive.

It also ought to be remembered that one of Ralph Nader's roles has been that of a journalist, and he can hardly be described as a passive mirror of events. In my own experience, I have seen the more widespread use of methadone in the treatment of heroin addiction come about in part because of a widely circulated series of articles in *The New Yorker* I wrote on the subject. In a later series for the same magazine, I focused on a principal of an elementary school in Harlem, and it was directly because of those articles that his promotion to District Superintendent of the Lower East Side—where he has more scope and power to try to humanize education—was successfully demanded by the community there.

I do write in order to try to bring about change, and I reject entirely the view of journalists which holds that they must be such finely calibrated balancers of facts that their own positions ought never to be discernible in their stories. However, I do not mean by this that facts ought to be distorted, glossed over, or invented. False reporting is indefensible, let alone counterproductive, whether it comes from the Right, the Left, or any sector of ideological conviction. A widely published writer I know, usually identified as a "New Left journalist," has very little influence because he has scant patience with the basic hard work of getting his facts straight. He has been proved inaccurate so often that he is the veritable personification of the Boy Who Cried Wolf. If Tom Wicker were to write that he had seen the CIA's plans for a Doomsday machine, the country would be in turmoil. If this other writer were to come up with the same story, it would be given about as much credence as a Tiny Tim declaration that the Martians are coming.

But once you do have all the facts you can dig up—especially those that subvert your preconception (*any* reporter goes into a story with some kind of preconception)—then there are conclusions you have to make unless you've turned into a machine.

In so far as there is a "new journalism," it is most durably characterized by this insistence on having a point of view. The stylistic adventures of some of the new journalism—from the rococo stunt-flying of Tom Wolfe to the laser-beam penetration of Norman Mailer's *Armies of the Night*—are far less important than the increasing determination of a wide spectrum of journalists to make judgments on the facts they have collected.

One of the most useful journalists in America is Richard Harris of *The New Yorker*. He is not in the least a "personal" writer in the sense that Tom Wolfe or Norman Mailer or most of the "underground" journalists are. But his calm, judicious writing on the dangerous ignorance of Congress concerning the most fundamental civil liberties of us all (*The Fear of Crime*) and his carefully detailed analysis of the transmogrification of the Justice Department by John Mitchell into a possible tool of a police state (*Justice*) have been of critical importance in making hundreds of thousands of people conscious of ominous developments that the daily press has covered fragmentarily when they have covered them at all.

It is this kind of new journalism—not really new, but largely in disuse during the 1950's and much of the 1960's—that I am sure will be more and more in evidence in the years ahead. I mean basic investigatory reporting which can be written in any number of different styles but which validates itself by the unassailable accuracy of the research, the depth of the analysis, and the persuasive conviction of the reporter that it is essential for the citizenry to understand exactly what's going on.

As I noted before, this is not "new," but until recently, for several decades, there were only a relatively few reporters committed to this kind of journalism. A prime exemplar is I. F. Stone. Any issue of his biweekly newsletter contains a number of illustrations of how productively informative hard digging can be. In the summer of 1970, for instance, Stone, so far as I know, was the only journalist in the country to report this specific example of how "the Establishment" can interlock to shut out the citizenry from information they should have: "Senator

Young of Ohio told the Senate June 29 that during the week of May 15 the White House asked a group of reporters, including (James) Reston of *The New York Times,* 'not to embarrass the Government by printing the details' of U.S. air raids over Cambodia, Laos and North Vietnam the previous weekend after they became known through news dispatches from Hanoi. But no paper reported his remarks or the pressure from the White House."

The key question, of course, for the journalist coming newly into the profession is where he can publish such investigative reporting without its being emasculated by an editor or a publisher. Stone is his own boss. So are Andrew Kopkind and James Ridgeway of *Hard Times.* But while it's much easier economically to set up your own journalistic shop than it ever has been before—3,000 copies of a black-and-white, eight-page tabloid can now be produced for $100—it remains exceedingly difficult for a new publication to get sufficient distribution to ensure the most minimal income for its editor and staff. Robert J. Glessing points out in *The Underground Press in America* (Indiana University Press) that "most underground newspapers have a lifespan of approximately twelve to eighteen months if they attempt weekly publication." And if you don't come out fairly frequently, it's hard to sustain the kind of continuum—of coverage and readership—that effective investigatory journalism requires.

I do agree, however, with Marvin Garson, an occasional publisher-editor from the underground, that more and more new papers will be started in the 1970's and beyond. And, even given the forbidding law of averages in this field, more will survive.

But there are alternatives for new journalists who would rather avoid the highly uncertain economics of do-it-yourself journalism. My own route of preference is free-lancing. Obviously that too is risky in terms of size and frequency of income; but if you do have the skills to function as a free lance, it's a superior way of continuous self-education without having to worry about printers' bills, and revenue, and the hectoring of contributors to your own publication to make their deadlines.

Working as an independent journalist enables you to pick the places in which you want to publish particular kinds of stories with regard to their maximum effect. I write, for instance, press criticism and political commentary for the *Village Voice*, but I have preferred to do long interviews with Joan Baez, Eldridge Cleaver, William Sloane Coffin and William Kunstler for *Playboy* because the latter has a huge audience, much more heterogeneous than the *Voice*'s and much more likely to contain sizable numbers of readers who are not familiar with what Baez, Cleaver, etc. are really all about. On the other hand, when I want to do carefully detailed, analytic reporting on education (a subject in which I'm greatly interested), *The New Yorker* is for me the optimum publication because of the time it affords for research and the space it will give a writer if his story warrants it.

As for how to break into free-lancing, the best entry point—provided you can write—is through one or more areas of specialization. I consider majoring in journalism a waste of time. Depending on his main spheres of concern, an aspiring journalist is far wiser to major in economics or political science or some branch of the natural sciences. Even on daily newspapers, the time of the general assignment reporter is, I'm convinced, fading fast. The geometrically accelerating quantity and complexity of even the most routine news is such that a generalist hasn't the time to learn enough to do an illuminating interpretative story. To critically cover housing, prisons, the courts, pollution—to cite just these beats—requires a considerable amount of specialized knowledge to be able to fit whatever facts you gather into a gestalt that will provide the reader with more than another barrage of confusing "information."

If you're able to start as a journalist with some background in one or two fields, you're immediately more valuable to an editor than the average bright, eager journalism major who may have a lot of energy but no focus. Furthermore, since serious journalism is always interdisciplinary, you'll find that if you begin, let us say, with a moderately advanced knowledge of housing, you'll quickly be drawn into gathering expertise on the symbiotic relationship between housing and municipal and state politics, the internal and external politics of construction unions, the rhythm cycles of banks and other lending institutions, the civil rights ramifications of zoning ordinances, the hiring practices of employers and unions, the changing demography of the country, and much more.

A basic corollary point—equally applicable to free-lancing, setting up your own shop, or a staff position with a paper or magazine—is that effective journalism-for-change is not in the least synonymous with free-expression polemics. While it may well be transiently self-gratifying to compose "revolutionary" philippics against The System, The Police, The War, All Wars, Sexism, Racism, etc., the way to move out of your own head and have your writing actually make a difference is factual exposure and prescriptions for real alternatives on the basis of what you've learned.

A third route for this kind of journalism is joining the reporting staff of an established newspaper or magazine. There are writers who have carved out sufficient autonomy in the straight press to enable them to keep their self-respect as journalists who are much more than mirrors—among them are Harrison Salisbury and Tom Wicker of *The New York Times* and Nicholas von Hoffman of the *Washington Post*. But there are as yet very few places for that degree of independent journalism in the large, hierarchical newspapers and news magazines. The usual ambience has been described by Gay Talese in his book on *The New York Times, The Kingdom and the Power:* "Each step up, it seemed, cost the individual a part of himself. With greater power went greater responsibility, more caution, more modesty, less freedom. . . . The *Times* had seemed to become a much less personal place in recent years, more coolly corporate as it had grown larger and more important."

Essentially, the same description applies to most other prestigious newspapers, and certainly to *Time* and *Newsweek*. I would say categorically that either of those last publications is a cul-de-sac for an exploratory journalist. The news magazines are hostels for team players, and it is precisely this institutional spirit (people truncated into personnel) that any journalist of quality instinctively combats wherever he finds it. To have such a temple of white bread as a working base is professional suicide for the new journalist. If, however, you have unusual resiliency, self-confidence and quite unique expressive powers, you may become a Wicker or a Von Hoffman on one of the better daily papers. But the odds—as of now—are against you.

However, if both of the first two alternatives—instant proprietary journalism or free-lancing—appear too hazardous at first, a regular job with a straight newspaper is worth the effort, if only for the experience to be gained that can be put to later, fully independent use. For all my strictures about the straight press, it is changing. Not nearly pervasively nor fast enough, but with an inevitability linked to what it's going to take for most papers to survive the rest of the century. Television has largely preempted the "entertainment" and shallow spot-news functions of the daily paper. Increasingly, readers want to know what the news *means,* and they can't learn that from television.

Accordingly, there has been a rise in the amount of newspaper space given to interpretative reporting, and the proportion of such space is certain to increase as there are ever more clumps of complicated data to try to make some sense of. And in this respect, it is possible for new journalists to acquire useful training on such papers as *The New York Times*, the *Washington Post*, the *Los Angeles Times*, the *St. Louis Post-Dispatch* and the *Wall Street Journal*.

The problem is that, for the most part, reporters are considerably more advanced that the editors of these papers in understanding the gulf that still remains between the rhetoric and the actuality of interpretative journalism. Consider, for example, a full-page promotional essay in the March 20, 1970, *New York Times* by that paper's Managing Editor, A. M. Rosenthal. It pretends to be an explication of how the *Times* is adapting to the new journalism.

"Law reporting," Rosenthal writes, "used to be simply what went on in the courtroom. We still report that, but we know that we must also report on the relationship of law to politics, law to civil rights, law to labor, law to poverty, the difference between law in the courtroom and law in the squad room."

An admirable homily. Unfortunately, however, the *Times*'s reporting on every single one of those relationships remains either inadequate or invisible.

Rosenthal continues: "In education reporting it is not enough to write about the business of education—teachers, unions, taxes—but of the process of education. What is being taught in their classrooms and by whom? How has the teaching of history, sociology, economics changed? Why? The relationship between student and teacher is a whole new field of news."

Again, Rosenthal is exactly correct in prescribing how education ought to be covered in the new journalism, but the *Times* has yet to seriously undertake a single one of the explorations he lists.

However, if enough restive reporters on the *Times* were to exert pressure for just such coverage in education and other fields—and were also to turn in vital stories, unassigned, to prove what *can* be reported—Rosenthal's rhetoric could be transformed into real copy. The same is true on other papers.

And there is the beginning of a movement among young reporters—and some not-so-young—on the *Times* and at other dailies to organize from within to press for substantative changes in the quality and depth of coverage of not only law and education, but also such largely virgin fields as the way judges are elected and the manner of their functioning; the innermost workings of the military-industrial-labor-academic-technical-bureaucratic-intellectual complex; the economic returns to those who contribute lavishly to political campaigns; the fantasy world in which the State Department and the reigning Henry Kissinger of the moment make foreign policy; and the fundamental contradictions between the continuation of even mixed capitalism and the survival of the planet.

One possibility—and I can only be speculative at this point —is that an increasingly inquisitive and sophisticated newspaper readership in combination with a new breed of journalists moving into the straight press can eventually leave management no choice but to thoroughly change its policy so that the normative approach to journalism will be what A. M. Rosenthal preaches but does not yet implement: "We have learned that news is not simply what people say and do, but what they think, what motivates them, their styles of living, the movements, trends and forces acting upon society and on a man's life."

Yet, for this to happen on enough papers will really require, I'm convinced, the sharing of newspaper management and policy-making by the people who write for it. This fundamental revolution in journalism has already begun in Europe, beginning with *Le Monde* and extending to *L'Express* in France and *Der Stern* and *Der Spiegel* in Germany. Similar movements are under way in Italy and Britain. At *Der Stern,* for one illustration of how shared management can and ought to work, a two-thirds majority of a journalists' committee is needed to approve the hiring or firing of a chief editor or the letting go of editorial employees. And it is mandated that "no staff writer or contributor may be required to act or write against his convictions."

When asked by the *Columbia Journalism Review* whether he thought shared management would ever take root in America, Jean Schwoebel of *Le Monde* answered: "Very possibly it could happen some day at *The New York Times,* the *Christian Science Monitor,* and maybe the *Washington Post.* But . . . it is much more difficult for American journalists than for us because in such a society as yours it is not regarded as a scandal that economic processes control the press. In European societies it *is* looked on as a scandal. . . . In my view, control of the press by economic processes is completely anti-American. In ten years I am sure this philosophy will have taken root in America. . . ."

I wish I were nearly so sure, but I have no doubt that shared management and policy-making is a goal that self-respecting journalists, especially new journalists, should begin organizing to achieve. And as more of them move on to the staffs of the *Times,* the *Monitor,* and the *Washington Post,* among other papers, Mr. Schwoebel's prophecy may begin to appear to be less fanciful.

I mean by new journalists, I should point out, those writers in agreement with FCC Commissioner Nicholas Johnson, who told a group of reporters in the spring of 1970: "You have to decide . . . what you are going to do with your lives because the resource that you represent, the talent that you represent, is a scarce commodity in our country. It does make a difference what you do with your life. It does make a difference what standards you hold."

The new journalist is more accurately defined as a free journalist. He exists in the underground press, among free lancers and, increasingly, he is moving into the straight press. But he cannot survive in freedom there unless he transforms the established press. If he succeeds, the mass of the citizenry will finally have the information on which to act to transform other institutions. If he fails—there'll be all the more work for journalists on the outside to continue to do.

I doubt if there has ever been a more challenging or fulfilling time in history for the practice of journalism. Free journalism. Who but the journalist can make clear to everyone else the interconnections between what is and what should be during a period in which nothing less is going to be determined than whether man has any future at all? And in America, whether—if man does survive—democracy also can.

And if democracy doesn't survive, valuable stories have always been smuggled out of prisons.

The New Teacher

by NEIL POSTMAN

Neil Postman's career as a teacher of teachers and as an educational reformer has carried him from what might be called old-style educational "innovation" to his present role as a catalyst of student action to improve schools.

In the early sixties Postman was a leader of the curriculum reform movement pioneered by the new math and the new physics. In a series of highly regarded textbooks he created a language arts curriculum for secondary schools which was based on "discovery learning" by the students, and the use of relevant, contemporary materials. He also wrote an introduction to linguistics for teachers, showing how this discipline pointed toward a revolution in language instruction.

In the course of the sixties, however, the deepening crisis in the schools forced Postman to a more radical position. In *Teaching as a Subversive Activity* he proposed a new role for the schools which went far beyond merely revising the curriculum. And in *The Soft Revolution* he appealed directly to students, rather than teachers, to change their schools drastically through potent but nonviolent action.

Currently, Postman is professor of English Education at New York University, and director of its graduate program in Language and Communication.

AT THE beginning of the last decade—1960, in fact—I was commissioned by the National Council of Teachers of English to write a book on television. Its purpose was to encourage English teachers to give some serious thought to the stuff their students were seeing daily, and to show them how they might help their students develop what are called "critical standards." The National Council of Teachers of English was then, and is still, the largest organization of "subject matter" teachers in America. Thus, my book was a matter of some professional significance, especially because it was to be distributed free to the entire membership, and was intended to be a sort of policy statement. As a consequence, my manuscript had to be approved by a committee of important educators. As I recall it now, the committee asked for only one change in the manuscript—a change involving a quote from Bennett Cerf to the effect that "television is the greatest invention since mother's milk." I was asked to remove that line from the book because it would offend Suzie Zilch. And Suzie Zilch, I was informed, was the very backbone of our profession.

Who was Suzie Zilch? Since I had written something which would offend her, I needed to know. Here's what I found out about her: She teaches in Omaha, or Des Moines, or Anaheim, or some other place that is alleged to be culturally deficient. She is somewhere between forty and sixty—always has been and always will be. She is unmarried and virginal. She wears her hair in a bun, takes her nourishment from chalk dust, and is never so much at home as when she is foraging in the supply closet. If she had any political opinions, which she does not, they would be somewhere to the right of Attila the Hun. Above all, Miss Zilch is the guardian of good manners, good grammar *and* good taste.

Back in 1960, I argued with my committee of editors that Miss Suzie Zilch did not exist, and never had. I argued that we were being victimized by our own stereotype; that, in a sense, Miss Zilch was a self-fulfilling prophecy: We alleged her existence and then confirmed it by offering only those ideas that would appeal to a Zilch-like creature. (You see to what lengths an author will go to defend a single sentence in a manuscript of his.)

I lost the argument, back in 1960. I was told that the phrase "mother's milk" suggested female breasts, and that, in Miss Zilch's mind, nothing could be more blatantly uncivil than a reference, however veiled, to an actual part of the human anatomy. I suspect that, under similar conditions, I would lose the argument in 1975, as well. Stereotypes have a way of clinging, of becoming part of the popular wisdom, and therefore they have no trouble in spanning decades.

I do not propose in this essay to help create another stereotype. It would be easy to assert that Suzie Zilch was the old teacher, and that Charlie Swinger is the new—Charlie being, in effect, Miss Zilch's revealed libido, what with his long hair, peace buttons and heady talk about freedom. It just ain't that way. Suzie Zilch never existed, and Charlie Swinger doesn't. What a teacher *is*, at any given point in time, is largely a product of the assumptions underlying the educational system in which he/she functions. To the extent that any set of "old" teachers is different from any set of "new" ones, the difference can be traced not to some inherent characteristics of each, but to the arrangements that society makes for what they are supposed to do.

I am sure you recognize that I am taking a rather Lysenkoish line here. I am asserting that environments make people what they "are," and that it is rather senseless to talk about the character of teachers unless we talk about the roles and rules of the system we call schools. I am not unaware of certain recent claims and even "proofs" to the effect that the world is being visited by a new type of person. For instance, Professor Charles Reich tells us that we can expect our educational system, along with other social institutions, to be soon overrun by people who have attained a state of Consciousness III. They are radically different in temperament, understanding and motivation from the groups of people who preceded them, and they will change everything by the sheer force of their life style. Professors Margaret Mead and Marshall McLuhan have also explained how and why this breed of mutant has suddenly appeared. While I find the hypothesis pleasurable to contemplate (God knows we can use a new breed of anything!), I regard it as mostly nonsense. The boys sitting at the tables down at Morey's may indeed be something the world has not yet seen, but my own experience suggests that among any group of college students today you will find roughly the same number of conventional fatheads and sloths as you will find at any meeting of the Pasadena Chapter of the American Legion.

So the question, Do we have a new kind of teacher? is misleading. What we need to know is, Do we have a new kind of education? And if we do, where does it come from, and what kinds of teachers will it require?

Well, of course, we *do* have a new kind of education, which means a set of assumptions different from those that have formed the schooling we have had in the past. Probably the best way to depict these differences is to list, side by side, selected examples of each set of assumptions. Here's what they look like:

Old Assumptions	*New Assumptions*
1. The best way to prepare a child for the future is to have him study the past.	1. The best way to prepare a child for the future is to have him practice developing questions, hypotheses and predictions about the future.
2. The most important intellectual skill for children to learn is how to get the right answers to predetermined questions.	2. The most important intellectual skill for children to learn is how to formulate creative and answerable questions.
3. The most important information children need to know is in the areas of literature, language structure, mathematics, history, geography and science.	3. The most important problems children need to investigate are war, poverty, ignorance, prejudice and disease.

4. All children should learn the same things, in roughly the same way.

4. Each child should investigate the problems most interesting to him, through the medium he feels most comfortable with.

5. For someone to learn something, he must be taught it in a systematic and organized way.

5. For someone to learn something, he must be aware of and interested in solving some problem or answering some need. He will then organize his own learning experiences in his own way to solve that problem or answer that need.

6. The learning process is logical, lineal and sequential.

6. Learning is psychological, random, simultaneous and integrated.

7. Learning is facilitated when the information to be learned is organized into discrete "subjects," each with a specific and stable "content."

7. Learning is facilitated when the student starts with a problem he is interested in and finds out or invents what he needs to know to solve it.

8. Adults know more than children; teachers are smarter than students.

8. About some things, yes; in others, students are smarter than teachers, and in others still, students and teachers are equally ignorant—or smart.

9. Teachers are better qualified than students to determine what students need to know and how they can best learn it.

9. People don't learn things well that *they* don't think they need to learn—no matter how powerful the arguments from outside sources.

10. The best teacher of a subject is someone who is thoroughly versed in the facts and skills of that subject.

10. The best teacher is someone who shares a student's interest in a particular problem and who can help the student formulate a program of inquiry which might lead to some solutions.

11. Children learn best from adults, and especially from adults who have no connection with the child's social life.

11. Children learn best from their peers and from those adults with whom they have a strong positive emotional relationship. They also learn from anyone whom they perceive to be experienced with some problem they are trying to solve.

12. Children learn best when they are grouped with other children of the same age, I.Q., and skills.

12. Children learn best when they have available the greatest range of interpersonal experiences.

13. Children learn best in competitive situations.

13. Children learn best to cooperate in the solution of problems by practicing cooperation in the solution of problems.

14. The experience and expression of emotions interfere with the learning process.

14. The experience and expression of emotions cannot be divorced from the learning process. Feelings are the proper subject of learning.

15. Learning takes place most effectively when the learner is isolated from his community in a centrally located building.

15. Learning takes place most effectively when the learner is immersed in the environment where the problem is that he is investigating.

16. Learning takes place primarily when the learner is sitting still, either reading or listening to the teacher.

16. Learning takes place in all kinds of places and activities, so long as the learner is engaged in problem-solving.

Now, the first thing to say about most of those assumptions listed as "new" is that they aren't. They began to be formulated early in this century by men and women who became the leaders of what we know as the Progressive Education Movement. By and large, they were not especially young, and

such consciousness as they achieved was simply a consciousness of the fact that the nineteenth century schoolroom had
reached the end of the road.

The "new" education, in other words, has been here before.
And it has been resurrected in our time for essentially the
same reason it was born in the first place: the inability of the
schools to adapt to a changing society. At the turn of the century, America was well on its way toward becoming an industrial society, after two hundred years as an agrarian one.
Today, we have moved—with unprecedented rapidity—from
an industrial society to an electric/electronic one. Thus, the
function of the "new" education today is the same as it was
then: to harmonize the educational process with the needs of
people. In particular, the primary need of most people—in
both an industrial society and an electronic one—is to be dealt
with as a whole human being, not as an abstraction which can
be processed to suit some sort of economic or political or social function. If you will look again at the list of "new" assumptions, I think you will see that most of them invite a perception of children which highlights their uniqueness, their need
for freedom, their creative potential.

This brings me to the second thing that must be said about
the assumptions listed as "new": It is unlikely that they can
become operative in most of the public schools around the
country. At present, the best exemplification of the "new" education can be found in what is known as the alternative or free
school movement. This is an uncoordinated network of independent, small, and privately (also erratically) financed
schools whose teachers, for the most part, reject the old assumptions—particularly those that have to do with coercion,
punishment, restraint and competitiveness.

As I see it, the alternative school movement has two uses—
as "reality" and as metaphor. As reality (i.e., a continuing,
practical education alternative), the movement does not have
much of a future. Let me put it this way: If you took all the

kids in the United States and Canada presently attending "free" or "independent" schools, then doubled the number, they would just about equal the number of kids who live between Coney Island Avenue and Ocean Parkway in Brooklyn. Or, to take an example of an "alternative school" within a large public system—the "classroom without walls" experiment known as the Parkway School in Philadelphia: If the Parkway School had the capacity (which it does not) to accept all the kids who applied to it last year (about 11,000), you would still have 240,000 kids attending conventional Philadelphia schools. In other words, unless there occurs a structural transformation of American society of an unprecedented magnitude, we cannot expect the alternative school movement to grow to a size where it actually offers what its name promises: a really different mode of schooling for a substantial portion of our population.

I say this regretfully, but the fact does not make me despondent. In the first place, there are an awful lot of kids who live between Coney Island Avenue and Ocean Parkway in Brooklyn, and if free schools can offer even that number an alternative route to education, the effort is worthwhile. (It has been estimated that there may be as many as 340,000 kids attending free schools by 1973.) In the second place, I may be wrong. "Community control," vouchers, constitutional changes permitting public funding for private schools, the rising cost of building and maintaining large centralized schools—these developments and others may lead to a restructuring of the schooling process, even if not accompanied by similar changes in other social institutions. But I doubt it, basing my doubt on an analogy with the Progressive Education Movement of the first thirty years of this century.

The Progressive Movement began as a reaction against a system of education just as stultifying and oppressive as the present education machine. In fact, more so (due to the fact that the schools at the turn of the century were pre-Freudian). The leaders of that movement were as charismatic, and clever, and committed as those of today. If you made two lists, consisting of the top ten people in each movement, and then compared them—man for man—the comparison would be embarrassing to the moderns. John Dewey, William H. Kilpatrick, Boyd Bode, George Counts, Harold Rugg, Goodwin Watson and early Sidney Hook, all by themselves, would be a match for the entire subscription list of the *New Schools Exchange Newsletter*. Moreover, although the figures are hard to come by, there were probably as many alternative or experimental schools generated by the progressives as there have been by the moderns. In fact, the progressives had *whole cities* go "experimental." For instance, Gary, Indiana, and Menomonie, Wisconsin. (It's hard to conceive of it today, but fifty years ago, "Middle America" was a most congenial region for radical ideas.) With all this going for it, the Progressive Education Movement, as reality, was pretty much washed up by 1940. Just about all the experimental schools were gone, and those that have hung on through the years—like the Walden School and Bennington College—long ago lost their radical spirit and have become elitist institutions.

What happened? Why didn't the Progressive Movement leave behind a structure for alternative education? There are many reasons, some having to do with the internal working of the movement; for example, its leadership became fragmented. But mostly, the movement failed because of external factors. There were just too many kids to educate. There were all those buildings that had to be used. There weren't enough teachers who understood. And there weren't enough teachers, period. And then, the philosophy of the progressives, in its purest application, just wasn't acceptable to most of the population. (Dewey, Counts, Watson, Hook and Jane Addams, among others, eventually found themselves listed in Elizabeth Dilling's *The Red Network*. In fact, so was the Progressive Education Association itself.) The philosophy of the Progressives did not take into account the fact that most people do not want *too much* spontaneity or creativity or even individuality for their children. Neither do most people despise the Great American Dream Machine, and they very much want their children to "fit in." In other words, the conditions which made it impossible for the Progressive Movement to sustain popular support and to become a continuing presence are very similar to the conditions of today.

So, as I said, I could be wrong about the prospects of the present movement, but I doubt it. Nonetheless, as I also said, I am not discouraged—and mainly for the following reason: The Progressive Education Movement did not leave behind an alternative school structure, but it did leave us several important things. First, it left us evidence, in the Eight-year Study and others, that "open" education works, and works better than conventional schooling. Second, it left us models of education (e.g., Dewey's Laboratory School, Marietta Johnson's Organic School, Kilpatrick's project method, etc.) which, whether present-day reformers know it or not, are the blueprints for just about all the varieties of alternative schools currently in existence. Third, it left us a vocabulary and an ideology which make it possible for education criticism to be conducted on a continuous basis and in the most vigorous terms. Holt, Dennison, Kozol, Kohl, Leonard, et al. (including me), would hardly be able to talk if not for the Progressives. Finally, and most germane to the point I want to make, the Progressive Movement influenced the conduct of conventional schooling to an extent not fully recognized. For somewhere between thirty and forty years after the movement reached its crest, American schools *were* better than they had been. Not as much as everyone had hoped, but better, nonetheless. Schools were more child-centered. Discipline was less harshly imposed. Teachers were less authoritarian. There was a greater variety of "subjects," including "vocational" education —which, in its time, was considered a plank in the Progressive platform.

And that brings me straight to my point: Like its predecessor, the present movement has its most promising opportunity as *metaphor*, rather than reality. All the reforms that will take place in education in the next decade will have their origins in the present alternative school movement. The movement is creating and re-creating vivid images of what education should be like or could be like, when it puts the individual at the center of the process. The conventional system will accept those images, reduce their intensity, distort their shape to some extent, and then remake itself along the lines those images suggest. The alternative school movement is to the American school system what the Socialist Party was to the Democrats and Republicans. I have been told, although I haven't verified it, that the platform on which Republican Dwight Eisenhower ran for President in 1952 was very similar to the platform on which Socialist Norman Thomas ran in 1928. In any case, it is well known that America became a kind of socialist country during the first fifty years of this century, and that, while it was moving in this direction, *socialism* remained an undesirable word. And this is how I can see education reform happening in the decade ahead. The movement will provide the ideas. The education machine will resist and denounce them, but ultimately accept them in some bowdlerized form.

The process is well under way. During the time I was writing this article, there appeared on the education page of the Sunday *Times* several advertisement articles by Albert Shanker, President of the UFT. In them, Shanker denounced the "destructive" education critics (Kozol, Kohl, Friedenberg, et al.), then went on to praise the concept of an "open classroom"—while reminding his readers that not all teachers can work effectively in such an environment. He did not mention, of course, that the most useful book around for teachers who want to work in such an environment is Kohl's *The Open Classroom*. Neither did he discuss the rationale for *having* an open classroom. His main purpose was to reassure his constituents that they are doing a good job, that everything is under control, and that it wouldn't hurt them to experiment a little. Probably not a bad idea. In any case, one must not demand too much from bureaucrats such as Shanker. They are the agents through whom education will be reformed, and presumably they know how to do it. It is probably unreasonable to expect them also to know *why* they are doing it, and what are the sources of the ideas they must work with. We are all specialists. Shanker's specialty is in changing a system. The specialty of the leaders in the alternative school movement is in knowing why the system needs changing and in what directions it must go.

What are the ideas most likely to be used by the public school system in the years ahead?

The first is the deprofessionalization of education. The movement is demonstrating that reasonably intelligent, highly motivated adults need no special "training" to be effective "teachers." Even as I write, this trend is under way. In New York City, for example, the Board of Examiners is under attack, and will not survive the next three years. Certification laws are being loosened in most states. We may even see the end to the bachelor's degree requirement, and by the second half of the seventies it may be commonplace for high school seniors to be teaching.

The second is the de-emphasis on grading and record-keeping. The movement has not yet shown how it would be possible to manage a large school operation without labeling kids, but it has pointed up the dangers of the labeling process —particularly grading. We may end up, before the decade is out, with some sort of pass/fail coding system—an entirely inadequate compromise, of course, but better than what we presently have.

Third, there will be a redefinition of what constitutes the "basic skills." At present, the schools, for all practical purposes, equate intellectual competence and interest with skill in reading. The experimental schools, though, have tended to let kids display their intelligence through a wide variety of communication skills—e.g., photography, motion pictures, video-tape, audio-tape, and so on. This fact is sure to have an influence on the assessment of student ability in the future, as well as on the definition of what the "fundamentals" are.

Fourth, there will be a redefinition of what it means to "teach." Experimental school "teachers" are providing a variety of models as alternatives to the subject-matter, test-centered, talk-centered, information-giving teacher. By the end of the seventies, we may find that the "teaching" styles developed in experimental schools will be as common in the public schools as are the more traditional modes.

Fifth, although the experimental schools have not emphasized the teaching of "subjects," the interests of teachers and students in the movement are much inclined to ecology, film, race relations, urban affairs and other "subjects" not commonly treated in conventional schools. As a result, we can expect to see such "subjects" infiltrating the public schools very soon. (They already are.)

Sixth, the free school movement has changed the role of parents from pests and interlopers to participants and decision-makers in the whole education process. This fact will lead to greater militancy on the part of parents of children in the public schools. Their militancy will be a form of education in itself—for them, for their children, and for the school community. By the mid-seventies, we may see the end of afternoon teas and cake sales sponsored by the PTA.

Seventh, the legitimization of emotions is one of the major contributions of the alternative school movement. That is to say, in the experimental schools the feelings of students are not viewed solely as a matter of social concern, but are taken to be a legitimate area of inquiry on the part of student and teacher alike. At present, about the only concession the public schools make to the emotional lives of children is to hire people known as "guidance counselors." But by the end of the seventies, it is entirely possible that most teachers in the public schools will be at least as much concerned with their students' acquiring self-knowledge as any other kind of knowledge.

Finally, if a structure for alternative education does exist by, say, the end of the seventies, I expect it will take the form of the school-within-a-school arrangement. The Parkway School is an example of this. So is the Village School in Great Neck, and the 3 I's program in New Rochelle. In these instances, you have an educational program based on entirely different assumptions from those of the conventional schooling process, but which is connected legally and financially to the conventional system.

I trust that nothing I have said will be taken as a criticism of the alternative school movement. The movement is, of course, necessary, because bureaucracies cannot reform themselves. Moreover, alternative schools must experiment with the most far-out styles of education they can invent. If they don't, their metaphorical function—their image-making role in the change process—will be diluted, and their chance of ultimately influencing the education of millions of children will be considerably reduced. And *that* is the point to keep in front of us: Unless the "new education" can make a difference for most kids, it won't make much difference at all.

There still remains the question, What will our teachers be like? Those who gravitate toward the alternative schools will have to learn, among other things,

1. to live on less money than most teachers get;
2. to use their imaginations more than most teachers do;
3. to relate to children more as "concerned adults" than as "teachers";
4. to relate to parents as equals;
5. to avoid the temptation to "instruct";
6. to listen with uncommon attentiveness to children; and
7. to distinguish between their own emotional needs and those of their "students."

I say "will have to learn" because, as things stand now, some of the "teachers" in the alternative school movement should not even be allowed to have house pets, let alone be placed in close proximity to children. I am referring here, of course, to an earlier point I made: It is a great mistake to assume that because a person is young, wears dungarees, sandals, beads and long hair, he or she can do any of the things listed above (not even live on less money than other teachers). But if the *structure* is there, the chances are good that many teachers— young and old, freak and straight, poor and middle-class—will learn how to behave within its requirements.

Most teachers, of course, will go directly into the existing system. Because "the system" is under such serious attack, they will find that there are increasing opportunities for them to alter their procedures and orientation along the lines I suggested earlier. These teachers will get very few books written about them; they will function in *mostly* conservative ways; the changes they make, and which are made *in them*, will barely be visible. But then, they've got twenty million kids to worry about, and forty million parents to answer to, and that means they've *got* to mind the store as best they can. Nothing new about that. But something kind of nice, anyway.

So if you are a teacher, or if you want to become one, you will need to know what kinds of alternatives are available, which ones you are suited to work in, and what kinds of changes are needed to improve your situation—wherever you are. Here's a school of suggestions that may be useful:

1. Write to the Teacher Drop-Out Center (Box 521, Amherst, Massachusetts 01002) and ask for their list of alternative schools. As of this writing, for a fee of $17, you will get a state-by-state listing of about 1400 experimental or "free" schools. You can get a similar list from *The New Schools Exchange Newsletter* (301 East Canon Perdido, Santa Barbara, California 93101).

2. To keep yourself informed about the kinds of new struc-

tures that both students and teachers are inventing, you ought to read *regularly* the following publications: *This Magazine Is About Schools* (56 Esplanade Street East, Toronto, Ontario); *Outside The Net* (P. O. Box 184, Lansing, Michigan 48901); *After Schools S.A.C.* (1643 Dwight Way, Berkeley, California 94703); *The Teacher Paper* (280 North Pacific, Monmouth, Oregon 97361); and *The New Schools Exchange Newsletter* (at the address above).

3. If you are not sufficiently informed about the major criticisms of the conventional schooling process, you ought to read: *How To Survive In Your Native Land,* by James Herndon; *How Children Fail,* by John Holt; *Compulsory Mis-Education,* by Paul Goodman; *Death At An Early Age,* by Jonathan Kozol; and *36 Children,* by Herbert Kohl.

4. If you want some ideas about alternative rationales and philosophies of education, as well as suggestions for effecting change, read Herbert Kohl's *The Open Classroom,* George Dennison's *The Lives of Children,* Charles Silberman's *Crisis in the Classroom,* Harold Taylor's *How to Change Colleges,* Saul Alinsky's *Rules for Radicals,* and *The Soft Revolution,* by Charles Weingartner and your humble servant.

5. If you want to keep clearheaded on the subject of education, make every effort to avoid using any of the following sentences:

a. "The school is dead as a social institution." (It may or may not be, but the *kids* in school aren't. Don't write them off.)

b. "You can't do anything to change the system." (You can, and people are doing it every day.)

c. "Our educational system is merely a reflection of other institutions in the society . . ." (It is, but so is everything else, and so what?)

d. ". . . so what we really have to do is change the whole nature and quality of life in our culture before we can

change the schools." (You'll be dead if you wait for that
—in which case, you'll have missed all the fun.)

e. "They don't want anything new or different." ("They"
sometimes do, and *"they"* are sometimes us.)

6. If you will look again at what I have listed as the ideas
most likely to be used by the public school system in the years
ahead, you will see that each one of them has sharp implications for the working lives of teachers. For example, on the
matter of deprofessionalization: If you want to become a
teacher, you should become less concerned with accumulating
credits than with gaining wide experience working with kids
in an authentic way.

On the de-emphasis on grading: You should begin to discipline yourself to be less evaluative in your responses to
people. You will need to become a good *describer* of behavior,
less of a judge.

On the redefinition of basic skills: You ought to try to become more literate in non-print media. If this means taking
film and television courses in college, do it.

On the legitimization of emotions: You ought to familiarize
yourself with what's happening at Esalen and other centers of
emotional inquiry. It would not be at all a bad idea for you to
try to get in touch with your own feelings—through an encounter group or some other situation which has that as its
purpose. Any efforts you would make in this direction should
include your trying to find honest answers to the question,
Why do I want to become a teacher?

Finally, you will be of great help to yourself, to your students, to the new education, and to the concept of a new
teacher if you rigorously avoid becoming a fanatical advocate
of any *single* learning structure. Remember, it's *alternatives*
that are needed, not The Alternative.

Humanizing
the
World
of
Business

The New Businessman

by HOLLY HENDERSON

Holly (MacNamee) Henderson had a unique opportunity to observe the current changes in American business as editorial associate on The Record, the monthly magazine published by The Conference Board, a nonprofit business research organization. Few people in the business world ever get the chance to learn about such a wide range of issues, or to become familiar with the workings of so many different companies in diverse fields.

Among the problems which have particularly engaged her attention, and to which she has drawn widespread attention via articles in the business press, are: the implications of consumerism, the hiring and training of the hardcore unemployed, and the inadequacy of the official poverty standard as a measure of people's needs. Her abiding concern has been for the role of the individual, not only in business, but in modern society in general.

From The Conference Board Holly Henderson went to her present position, as special assistant to the president of Brooklyn College. But she refuses to be type-cast as a careerist in either business or education, remarking that she continues to be, among other things, "a Sagittarian, a philosopher queen, and in love most of the time."

BACK IN the dim reaches of time, somebody was bartering to fulfill a need and ended up with something more valuable than what he had traded. Thus was discovered another need: to do somebody out of something, since called "making a profit." In our society it far overshadows "making a product"; the foremost goal of American business is to amass

213

large sums of money. Ideally, of course, business should have several considerations besides the rate of return. Is the company flexible enough to change its outlook, product, market? Can it easily adapt to inventions, discoveries, environmental requirements? Is it making and/or selling something useful? Well made? Creative? Aesthetic? Is it using profits to improve life for anybody at all? Contributing to education, charity? Doing research on social problems? Do employees, consumers, stockholders, community people have a voice in company policies? Does management much care whether a life-time association with the company is fulfilling, shattering, or deadening?

Some cultures have understood more clearly than others the results of preoccupation with profit; in some, making a large profit has been illegal. Once people lose sight of trade as the exchange of needed goods and services, and view it as an abstract method of gaining money (an abstraction in itself), quality deteriorates. Competition, touted as the automatic regulator of quality, instead becomes the vehicle for agreed-upon downgrading. The buyer becomes quarry, the seller an opportunist who hits with a shoddy product and runs. He may not have to produce something good enough to be purchased more than once by any one customer, and he will still be "successful." The customers often don't know where the buck stops—and if they did, would find themselves effectively barricaded on the other side of a welter of secretaries, private offices, etc. The seller who concentrates on profits chooses things over people; he feels free to perpetrate planned obsolescence and useless crummy junk because he assumes the supply of buyers to be endless—just like the supply of clean air and water, lumber, minerals, and other resources. "There's a sucker born every minute . . ."

Now, however, it is obvious that there isn't room on this planet for an infinite supply of suckers; those already here threaten the remaining resources. Business talks gravely about

planning, systems analysis, forecasting—and daily adds pollution to the air we must breathe, the water we must drink. Executives say we must find the level of pollution below which it
is not "profitable" to go. Inescapably, slavery was "profitable,"
as racism continues to be. War is "profitable"; so is poverty.
The businessman accustomed to hit-and-run profits doesn't
understand the cost of poor education, slum life, barbaric jails,
understaffed hospitals and other wretchedness. How come
money means so much to him? It doesn't. Neither does "what
it can buy"—the reason he advances for wanting it. If it did,
as soon as he had amassed all the money he could spend, he'd
quit and do so. What he wants is not money, but power—and
he has it. Few doubt that business runs the U.S.A., crucially
affecting laws, politics, war and the quality of life—if not determining them. Businessmen uphold the image of democratic
America, where everybody is free to Make It, as they did. But
they also seem to believe that some people's interests are more
valuable than others; a little nudge in government's ribs is still
in the spirit of '76. Business lobbies, threatens, bribes, hires,
persuades. Peace is not good for munitions and other growing
industries. Countries with rich resources are "protected" at
the urging of companies which, oddly enough, use large quan-
tities of those very resources. Everybody knows by now what
alcohol and tobacco and guns and exhaust fumes do to us—
and what alcohol, tobacco, gun and automobile lobbies do to
Congress.

Why can't businessmen stop meddling behind the scenes, if
they "believe in democracy"? Why can't they offer what
people need, instead of trying to make products *seem* desirable or indispensable? Because they see themselves and their
products the same way; they feel that nobody could really
value them as they are; they feel they would never be accepted if they didn't "fix" things. They sell products the way
they sell themselves—not on genuine merits or lasting usefulness, but on illusion. They have learned to present (advertise)

themselves as boundlessly optimistic, "normal" creatures (all parts guaranteed), living irreproachable (packaged) lives of single-minded service to The Corporation—which exists for and through them, and simultaneously preys on and rewards their anxiousness and double-dealing. Businessmen further aggravate their insecurities by buying yes-men, whose adulation is mixed with fear.

Businessmen believe they can gain respect through what they have, instead of what they are. And they do—from others who believe that what one has makes up for what one isn't. But the need for respect can't be satisfied by this flimsy imitation. No amount of it solves the problem of feeling unworthy; such a person never has enough power, or possessions, or money. Instead he has heart attacks, ulcers, too many drinks, too many tranquilizers, an unhappy marriage, and children who don't want to be like him: you.

So you already affect business—and businessmen. They are not able to ignore you, partly because you have lived in their houses, and partly because you haven't been buying what they thought they could sell you—themselves, their products, their jobs. This has begun to worry them. They see that the brightest of you aren't unduly moved by high salaries and job security. Instead, they have had to expand or create social service programs to attract you. You are not buying the products they expected you to want. You buy top quality stereos and musical instruments—and jeans from a surplus store. Your idea of status has nothing to do with mink coats, costly jewelry, luxurious cars, expensive homes. Generally, you're interested in things for what they are, do, or look like—not for what people will think of you if you have them.

In other words, you are in many ways the antithesis of the traditional businessman who still runs this country, and if you don't want mayhem you're going to have to find a way to deal with that conflict. The men I have been talking about are insecure people with no real self-respect; they see you as relaxed, easy-going people who enjoy what they were taught to despise. You have everything they wanted, from enough money to sex before marriage. And you don't care at all about most of the things they hold up as important. In a mild word, they resent you. They don't realize that the end result of their resentment is death; even confronted with Vietnam, Jackson, Kent and Augusta they can blind themselves with packaging, advertising, guarantees. And when you denounce that blindness you are denouncing them; they become furious with your "disrespect" and the cycle begins again. Somebody will have to do some defusing; somebody will have to build some bridges and do some educating. Somebody will have to take the whole thing out of the realm of anger, unless there is to be more killing. It isn't going to be them.

You have to reach business to change the shape of society. (Minority group people have told the legions of young middle-class whites who want to help that they can be most useful by educating their own parents and those who surround them.) You aren't going to do it by denouncing businessmen and driving them into corners; they will only come out of them fighting. And whether or not they have any answers, they *do* have weapons. You may see businessmen (and/or parents) as omnipotent beings purposely ignoring human concerns, who could make things right if they were willing to; people who have the means to change things but criminally lack the motivation. You're right, in some cases, but many simply don't *see* the reality of other people's suffering—usually because they can't. They are alienated from it by their own sickness. College students are in the double bind of being viewed as children, but held responsible as adults. Businessmen are in the double bind of being disturbed, and being held responsible for what they are hindered by their disturbance from seeing.

Asked for advice to young activists entering business, many older activists said they would offer the following: "Don't." This despite their own successes—establishment of education and sensitivity programs for foremen and other blue-collar workers, a course to prepare minority group employees for college, a day-care center for employees' children, credit unions, sensitivity training for middle management, appropriations for charity, and so on. Most feel that their biggest achievements aren't measurable, at least for some time, because they involve one-to-one relationships with co-workers or management people.

They work at many levels (president, vice president, management consultant, market research manager, distribution manager, education director, economist, publishing assistant, secretary) in many fields (light industry, publishing, management, chemical industry, hotel, utility). In every case they feel business badly needs people with conscience—and in every case but one, they feel they can't be identified without risking the progress they've made, along with their jobs. (The exception is president of his company.) Most of business' effective reformers, apparently, are hired for reasons other than their deep social concern. Much of their achievement is *sub rosa;* some think of themselves—usually ruefully—as infiltrators. In spite of their accomplishments, most are deeply pessimistic about business' ultimate response, and though the prospect of young activists joining with them generates great enthusiasm, they feel it necessary to warn that progress is torturously slow and incredibly frustrating to achieve.

The most important advice they feel they can offer: Get your head together. If you want to work in business, and you don't want to find yourself selling out, you have to see what's around you clearly, and what's inside you even more so. Your first requirement has got to be your own growth. It's easy, in the business world, to see yourself as pure and everybody else as corrupt. Learn to recognize a disturbed person when you see one, but don't be fooled by your own "virtue." It's easier to see the failures and moral weaknesses of business if you did not grow up in the anxious, insecure days of the Depression; if

you are not an immigrant who couldn't get work at home, or
went hungry here; if you were not a child in the days when
business was presented as a glamorous, manly, socially responsible career. Profiteering is no less repugnant, power hunger
no less sick; a person who feels he can't afford morality is no
less bankrupt. But in the rage business directs at youth's well-
fed, well-educated condemnation, there is some justification.
What may be clear now was not necessarily clear at the time;
doubtless we do not correctly interpret all the influences of
the present upon our own courses of action. It took us a while
to understand the causes we stand for.

Not being a psychiatrist, you probably can't rid businessmen
of their hang-ups. But if you are aware of the hang-ups, and
aware of businessmen as people—however lacking you may
personally find them—you may be able to change business.
You may be able to find a way to replace the ersatz reward
with the real one; to offer businessmen respect based on what
they are and do that's worth respecting—and this might
enable them to give up their insane need for profits and the
power to bully. You might in time replace the whole structure,
with usefulness to the human family as the coveted goal.

Do you want to be a doctor, teacher, ambassador, secret
agent? Activists in business see themselves in various ways—
and all are needed. The kind of business you should go into,
the size, the job to look for, and your attitude will all differ
according to what you want to accomplish and how you think
it can best be done. You might want to build a business from
scratch, employing only those who have a sense of business as
an organism which must serve the interests of buyers as well
as sellers—and those who can't afford to buy. Obviously, if
you have a special interest or skill, find (or found) a firm that
will give you full scope. But decide whether you'd be most
useful in a company that's trying to solve the problem, being
forced to, is aware but resistant to change, or is unaware of
the whole issue. Depending on who you are, any of these

could be your forte. Are you primarily interested in getting a company to improve its product or service, use profits to more socially responsible ends, open itself up to greater participation in policy decisions by employees, stockholders, consumers? Maybe some combination? Be as clear as you can about what you want to do.

If you decide to work through business, there are at least four alternatives:

1. You can find a firm which has already begun to take some responsibility for social reform.
2. You can choose one which needs to do so, but has not yet begun.
3. You can found your own company along socially responsible lines.
4. You can involve yourself with consumerism, as a vocation or as a concerned citizen.

If you want a firm which has already begun, ask recruiters about company involvement with issues you are interested in. Don't put much stock in vague do-goodery; what was a good sign a few years ago is merely fashionable now. Ask for figures; when you get them, ask for others to put them into context. (If a company has 500 black employees, is that out of 2,000 or 20,000? What's the percentage of blacks in the surrounding location(s)? How many executives? How many work in the stockroom? How many are seasonal employees, or fall into other fancy part-time classifications which may serve as an excuse to deny them health protection, life insurance, vacations, holidays, sick days and other regular employee benefits?) If a company can cite examples of social concern, has its involvement been recent, fairly recent, present since founding? If recent, does evidence suggest its stance is more for public relations than for action? If fairly recent, was management a leader or a follower? If since founding, has management generally been sufficiently flexible to focus on the most relevant and urgent issues of each era?

Don't hesitate to make clear that you are also doing the interviewing and that your emphasis is on the company's social achievements. Most firms that have begun will appreciate such an attitude. Remember, though, that you are offering your work in exchange for the good you can do and the salary you will receive. Make it understood that if the company does offer you an opportunity to help deal with the issues that concern you, you will not be merely a critic in residence, but will do the hard messy work that change requires, and do it well. They will not hire you if your crusade is only a verbal one, and you will have contributed another pebble to the façade of clichés that enables them to see you as worthless. They will extend that judgment to the causes you espouse.

It's often worth interviewing the interviewer even if you lose the job; this is a public service which has an effect in itself. Companies confronted with constant questioning of their commitment dust off old programs or start new ones. Businessmen aim products at specific markets; their ears are tuned to respond to repetition. Any attitude they frequently encounter gains in significance—and respectability. At a recent moratorium, the biggest banner said "Businessmen for Peace," and supporters from several cities accompanied it. Explaining your commitments to recruiters will have a double effect—it will inform them that those commitments are widespread, and it will wake up their marketing instincts. You are their potential labor pool *and* their potential market. They cannot afford to ignore you. Businessmen were raving (in their crewcuts) about the degeneracy of long hair a few years back. How many crewcuts have you seen lately? Any assemblage of businessmen, even the most conservative, now has a distinctly hairier look. Do they know where they got it? I don't know. But they did get it. And if it's co-option, they nonetheless thought it worth their while to co-opt.

If you don't work through recruiters, you can get some idea of which companies are socially responsible by checking their ads. Many publicize conservation, employee education, housing subsidies, minority hiring, and other efforts. A few have come out as anti-war. Check also to see which companies sponsor what programs on radio and TV. Caution: A public service stance does not necessarily mean anything more than a desire to look heroic; keep asking for concrete facts at the interview. If the subject gets changed unreasonably often, or your persistence creates first uneasiness and then irritation, chances are the big heart was only a come-on. But make sure you've done *your* part in sincerely answering what the company wants to know about *you*. Be as honest as you can about your commitments. (One exception you may—or may not— want to make: Big Business is still not ready for psychiatry! If you see a shrink, that means you're sick. It may be wise to wait at least until you're hired to reveal this interest in your health and well-being.)

Decide whether working for a socially useful company is enough, or whether you must have a job directly related to social change. These are few and far between, but try employee training or hiring, community or industrial relations, honest public relations (a particularly perishable job). Some industries which have begun, according to consultants, make pollution control equipment, or hard- and software for education, or are cooperatives of various kinds, or are in communications. Look for a company with a stake in its community. Public corporations are just beginning to form government-business combinations which may offer opportunities, particularly in their early days, for shaping policy. Companies that deal *with* government are required to meet certain standards (minority hiring, etc.); one consultant suggests it would be useful to work for such a company to make sure that these contract terms are not violated. You might consider banks which finance minority businesses, make mortgages available at low cost, and lend money for worthy causes at little interest or for collateral others find insufficient; also, the insurance industry has been plowing impressive sums into ghettoes.

But be wary. No total industry is virtuous (or infamous, unless you write off weaponsmakers and sellers). A Little Goody Two-Shoes in one area may be Simon Legree in another. This is why I name no names, though a few firms seem to be doing outstanding work. By next week they may not be—or I may have discovered that a company campaigning for peace decided to do so because cessation of hostilities would make it easier to plunder resources. There are companies investing in job training for black people here while supporting apartheid in South Africa. Etc., ad nauseam.

Top management will be involved, if a company's commitments mean anything. Interestingly, top management is more often socially concerned than one might guess; it is in the middle layers of many firms that apathy and resentment stifle action.

This is also common in companies which have not begun. If you state your objectives in interviews at these, your chances of being hired may decline, particularly if your appearance differs markedly from that of their typical employee. Whether you should explain your concerns anyway depends on your philosophy. If you feel the important thing is to join that particular firm, however covertly, and work from within, then don't. If you feel that hiding your goals is a form of denying them, or that business will see the handwriting on the wall eventually if it's made plain enough often enough by people like you—then do.

Firms with little or no sense of responsibility tend to be small or middle-sized. Big corporations (whether because of genuine concern, or because they can't hope to escape notice) generally have some kind of program. Again, while top management tends to be intelligent and aware, there is that thick layer of middle management which is sluggish. Those at the top, particularly if they built the firm on the strength of a product or process, usually began with a skill or an idea—something for which they could respect themselves. Those in the middle, if they can point to such achievements at all, still feel dwarfed by those ahead and challenged by those behind. On the other hand, top management in the middle-sized corporation is often similar to middle management in the top corporation. So while it may be better to get a spot near top people in the larger firm, in the smaller you may be more effective if you can discover who might be responsive and work there, without regard to the company's hierarchy.

Small companies have little time for training programs—they prefer to put you into a slot directly—and little capital for "frills" (i.e., experimental programs). Big firms have rigid, unresponsive frameworks and do not implement any one person's ideas without a lot of red tape and watering-down. The repercussions of what you do will be felt much faster, and on a larger scale, in smaller companies—but you are highly visible, and if you frighten or antagonize, you will be disposed of much faster, too. If you're more interested in sensitizing people, you may prefer a larger company where you can meet many people, talk to them over an extended period, and perhaps have lasting—if indirect—impact on them and their thinking.

Proselytizing, as many religious sects have discovered—often through decimation—has little or negative effect if it is simply propaganda shoved down the throats of people in whom one plainly has no real interest. Ranting about imperialism and fascistic warmongering is not going to turn anybody on to real situations and concrete problems. If you feel you are not good at communicating directly—and try to be objective about it—do some work on yourself or place your focus elsewhere. When you work with people, listen to them, talk straight to them; never treat them as audiences. When you don't like the way someone talks to you, figure out why; check to see if you make the same mistake.

Making people around you aware of social problems is a major contribution, along with whatever else you happen to be doing. Most activists include it in their job conceptions.

Interestingly, even the *idea* of this kind of communication panics business. An SDS document written for students involved in sensitizing industrial workers was picked up and widely circulated by the business press, which treated the idea of such "infiltration" *as though it would result in the business world's downfall.*

Another way to contribute is through any influence you can have on company policies to benefit employees, consumers and the community. Whatever you can do to improve product safety, quality and usefulness is obviously a service too.

Any job may have important (and often unexpected) leverage; the truly useful spots may not be apparent from the outside. Somebody doing market research can initiate a project on paint, say, that will ultimately disclose the extent of lead poisoning in ghetto children. Somebody doing mail pickups may be in a better position to see a cross-section of the company than the president—and may see more of the president than the rest of the company does. Someone in personnel work can drastically affect minority hiring, employee benefits, on-the-job training. And as anyone who has ever been in business knows, secretaries and switchboard operators often run their bosses—and know more of what goes on.

Wherever there are opportunities to make friends with a broad spectrum of people, there is a broad spectrum of possibilities. Avoid the job in which you'll have no contact with anybody who has a real voice in company affairs, or the job in which you may meet such people, but clearly they won't listen to your ideas. Ask the interviewer exactly what you will do, with whom you will come into contact, and what other jobs may open up if you prove yourself in the first one.

Stay flexible; go in with the idea of seeing what's around, not with the idea that you're beginning a career. Don't get established too early. Showdowns based on differences in integrity—an unavoidable part of an activist's life in industry—are much less excruciating if what you have to lose is a job, not an "indispensable" step in a life plan you've carefully mapped out. Take your time.

You will probably have to do a lot that isn't directly relevant to your goals, and will have to check yourself and your integrity daily for symptoms of sell-out. (Do you often say things at work that you don't mean? When you describe your job to someone you admire, do you feel you're not being strictly truthful? Do you let a lot of ugliness and decisions that harm people go by for the sake of some vague larger value that never materializes?) You will also have to put up with friends who don't understand, and possibly parents who will be triumphant about your "capitulation." You will have to cope with far more disappointment than accomplishment. Not many have the fortitude (and strong stomach) of the late Whitney Young, Jr., who worked with white people for black people, and whose towering achievements were obscured for many of both races by their mistaken idea that he was a "house nigger." He knew very well what they thought; his position was often lonely, and yours may be too.

If you think the frustration of all this outweighs—at least personally—the importance of opening up the most powerful, most stubborn sector, then avoid companies that have not begun. Maybe you should consider founding a company. Maybe you have an idea for a useful device (say, a pocket machine that clarifies unit pricing, or a formula to dissolve plastic bags without harmful fumes or residue). Maybe you have a concept of how a company should be, and you want to try it out. Maybe you see a way to influence society by exercising some kind of control over a product. (One young entrepreneur decided that educational toys are priced out of reach of the underprivileged kids who really need them. After first running his own restaurant, then his own toy store—and along the way a combination of the two—he now heads a large toy concern which can translate his idea into modestly priced educational toys.) Maybe you have a talent you could mass-market—selling posters of your photographs highlighting problems of American Indians, for instance. Or maybe your talent is for business techniques. If you have a lot of energy, ingenuity and mental freedom to take risks, you might go into business yourself.

A major consideration is money, since most new companies require financing. If you can't borrow from someone you know, you will have to deal with banks, loan associations, or the Small Business Administration, and you may have to modify your ideas to get financing. Make sure you don't sell out what you believe with the excuse that you're finding a way to *disseminate* what you believe. It may not be there anymore by the time you get set up. Keep in mind that you would rather give it all up at any stage than sell out your principles—because the number of businesses that survive without doing so is minute, and the pressure on those few is tremendous (and harder to resist, as the business gets closer and closer to becoming reality). Those that do cop out do a lot of harm; they reinforce the businessman's conviction that everybody has a price—which of course means that he is excusable, misunderstood, and even laudable when *he* sells out. Try, if you can, to set up your financing privately. At the moment, though, if you're black, you may have better luck and greater freedom than is generally possible in getting funds from the SBA and from banks encouraging minority enterprises. You may not, too. Money may not be the root of all evil, but there is definitely a relationship.

Try to set up the company along lines that express your beliefs; devote some creative thought to giving everyone connected with it maximum amounts of freedom, satisfaction, and benefits. Don't fall into traditional business assumptions (nine-to-five, female secretaries only, five-day weeks). Try to see each element freshly, so that you're not bound by times, ages, sex, and skills in ways that are irrelevant and counterproductive. The company itself should function as a social gain.

A new management consulting firm with such ambitions will not hire anyone who cannot state at least one goal for his or her life outside of working hours. Spokesmen for the company say they make no attempt to influence these aspirations —though they do emphasize the importance of personal integrity, close family ties, and community relationships—but salary increases are partially tied to the employee's ability to demonstrate progress towards the goal(s) personally chosen. The important thing, says an executive, is that the employee have a feeling of accomplishment and growth. In their consulting work, these people seek to establish the idea of growth as an indispensable part of executive outlook; they hope (and work to realize their hope) that more and more companies will take the shape of their own. Their stated ideal is to make their clients successful not only in business, but also in family and community life. When the profit motive overshadows a person's basic objectives, the executive says, it becomes destructive of the person. Whether this firm succeeds or fails, whether it becomes too rigidly paternalistic or so loosely defined that it falls apart, it certainly is an attempt to inculcate in business a greater consciousness of the totality of human beings.

Take a good look at where the money in your company will go; try to see through any rationalizing you may be tempted to do about why you should have more than anybody else (after all, it's your business, isn't it?)—once you get hooked on the profit motive, it's a business like any other.

Some new businessmen and women see their enterprises as extensions of themselves—ways of learning, spreading an idea, or sharing something they enjoy. They are, in a sense, professionless, in that they refuse to tie themselves permanently to any venture, no matter how profitable. The business exists as an expression of a period in their lives, or provides a growth experience. When that period ends, when the firm no longer offers the personal enrichment something else might, when the extension is outgrown, the company is sold or dissolved. Two enormously successful young entrepreneurs, a rock mogul and a magazine publisher, independently offered such explanations when they recently divested themselves of assets still very valuable—commercially.

Make sure your product is useful, creative, well made, or has a socially conscious aspect, even if you have to take some losses. If we can't make such things commercially viable—if not outrageously profitable—in the last analysis we may have to examine business' contention that "we're only giving the people what they want." In the meantime, give the people an alternative. Maybe they want that too.

Exercise your own right to alternatives, through consumerism. This field expands faster than it can be written about; concrete advice is likely to be dated by the time it appears. The best lead is still to contact Ralph Nader or Consumers Union. Many communities have—or soon will have—small consumer units, usually set up by local government. Now is a good time to get hired. Consumerism is still new enough to be malleable and to be influenced by creative thinking. Some legal training is useful but not obligatory.

Comparatively few firms have a department or even an employee hired to deal with (let alone represent) the consumer. The president of one which does, however, was the featured speaker at an important business conference and produced the figures to prove it profitable. So maybe things will improve—aided, of course, by class action suits and other consumer rebellions. In general, you won't find ads in the papers seeking you out to be the consumer's friend. You have to create this job for yourself. It requires a fine balance. You think you'll make the company more responsible; the company thinks it has a new PR person to placate irate customers. There will be great pressure in that direction; don't get sloppy.

You need self-confidence and a certain amount of salesmanship. Begin by picking out companies that drive people up the walls (utilities, manufacturers of appliances, huge companies of any sort). Instead of going through personnel, try to see someone at the top, and make a presentation on why they need you. It will help if you have some idea of the volume of complaints, or the amount of business lost through consumer dissatisfaction, but most companies are ostriches when it comes to this, and the information is difficult or impossible to get even inside the company.

Think out the functions you want to perform, and present them as a job description. Do you want the firm to advertise your name or a phone number as an oasis for distressed consumers? Do you want to follow up on sales, interviewing purchasers? Do you want to be available to local outlets on a regular basis? What departments in the company will you need to work with? (For instance, if most complaints are due to malfunctioning products, you will need to work with the people in the labs. In a utility, you will have to stay in touch with the service department; in any huge company, with the accounting or billing section.) You may want to suggest a program by which the company can recycle waste resulting from its own products, thereby earning the undying devotion of consumers and conservationists. Be sure you point out that the function of a consumer relations representative is not to temporarily delight the customer with fulsome phrases. Emphasize that *everybody* is a consumer; money not only can't buy immunity, it is likely to buy planned obsolescence, hazardous and defective merchandise, and bigger and better pollutants. He who thinks it's perfectly all right to sell a toy with sharp edges may not bring one home to baby, but he is still getting emphysema from factory-polluted air, his wife has been burned by a carelessly slapped-together appliance, and his child, who isn't allowed to play with the crummy things Daddy makes, gets cut on somebody else's.

You may want to give a flashy guarantee that you will increase the sales record, lower the volume of complaints, or whatever. Don't forget that there will be a time lag; don't promise results before they can reasonably be expected to show up.

Remember, if you get the job, that you are a liaison between the consumer and whatever aspects of the company are out to screw him/her. It's no good mollifying the individual customer if you're not modifying the company's methods to match. You also have to believe that whatever *has* to be done *can* be done. You will meet massive resistance in the company. Everybody there knows it can't be done, because it never has been. Resist.

One celebrated gentleman in government who went after industrial polluters reported that some of his culprits came back to offer thanks and even support, because his office, figuring out alternative ways to dispose of effluents, found a few more profitable ways than dumping them. (In all fairness, I am compelled to report that he was nonetheless fired when he went after too big a giant. This, however, is the occupational hazard of truly effective people.)

It is important, too, to recognize your individual responsibilities as a consumer, whether you go into business or not. Buy postage stamps in quantity, so you'll write more letters; send them to manufacturers whose products let you down, or whose policies let society down; to congressmen, consumer organizations, newspapers, the Better Business Bureau. It is a royal pain, true. But this is one area that has not yet developed so many coats of gluey bureaucracy as to be impossible. It may not seem as important as getting the hungry fed, but a small effort has a big chance of paying off. So mount one. Boycott bad products, and inform companies that you're doing so.

Consumer power can accomplish a variety of ends. One of the Securities and Exchange Commission's rules may be liberalized soon; this would give stockholders considerably more influence over company policies. Some universities and church groups are already using consumer and stockholder leverage. There are boycotts like the ones which have helped migrant workers achieve a better life—remember doing without grapes and lettuce? To dethrone profits as the be-all and end-all, demonstrate that human standards must be met if there are to be any profits at all. If you don't recognize your responsibility to deal with business from the outside as well as the inside, you aren't doing the whole job.

There are a number of businessmen's organizations whose names proclaim them to be socially concerned. It isn't safe, however, to give any blanket statements of approval. Motives vary, emphases shift. If you think working with one of these groups might be helpful, or if you think you might find someone you want to work for by checking out the membership, by all means do so. But look carefully at the people involved. Look, too, at how much the group has actually accomplished. Lip service is still far more common than hand and wallet service. But if you do find a useful group, and you join or work through it, don't get too far away and uninformed about it; six months later it may not stand for the same things, and you may, in blissful ignorance, still be supporting it.

Most really effective work seems to get done through networks of people of like mind, spread through business, education, government and the professions. Depending on mobility, opportunity and gregariousness, everybody is part of some size network. Yours will expand relatively automatically, both in size and influence, as you meet more people and as your acquaintances move up to positions of greater authority—a function of time as much as ability. Unfortunately, the network of visible business activists is less extensive than in other fields, because so many work "underground." Though you will develop your own contacts, to my knowledge there isn't a clearinghouse where you can check in and be put in touch with people like you in other firms. You can do a lot with cross-discipline networks, though. At some point, you or someone you know will need service or simply answers from

sympathetic lawyers, doctors, educators, housing experts, reporters and so on. When you meet somebody you like and feel
you can trust, take note of the profession and get an address
and phone number. Hopefully you will serve a useful function
in the network too.

Stay reasonably aware of what's going on in other fields and
the world in general. It will help you see more possibilities.
Hunches about where things are going can be translated into
effective action. There is always a better chance for real
change, real innovation, before red tape and bureaucracy
smother an idea. Some trends that might bear watching—and
thinking about—are the development of public corporations,
increase of multinational companies, possible moves toward
decentralizing decisionmaking in massive corporations and
conglomerates, and continual acceleration in the use of computers. Watch for a business attempt to control access to information technology; be prepared to fight it.

Keeping widely informed will help you remember that no
job is worth sacrificing your sense of self for; there is too much
work to be done everywhere to let yourself be blackmailed
into keeping any job. If you go into business, remember peri-
odically that you are basically a kamikaze pilot; you can't
afford to care that you won't have the security other employees are all bundled up in. Your job may prove useful, vital,
extraordinarily effective; you may be lauded for your efforts,
paid well, and may finally reach retirement never having compromised yourself, never having had to switch jobs. However,
this is only slightly less likely than the total abolition of all
forms of war as of tomorrow morning.

One reason business turns into such a fuzzy, mindless trap is
that it plays on people's need for security; it encourages employees to think that if they are quiet enough to escape notice,
and move through the years camouflaged by their desks and
the proper stacks of paper, they will emerge at sixty-five as
from a high-school initiation, smiling, approved-of, sponsored

by the company to live a full life at last. Often this life consists of a watch, a luncheon, an inadequate pension, bewilderment, and the relief of early death. But every year the company murmurs, "You have more of your life invested now . . . Don't rock the boat . . . Too much at stake . . ." Don't listen. Don't read the memos from the personnel department on how rich you'll be when you retire in the twenty-first century. Don't join the pension plan. When you find yourself reluctant to do things you know you should because you're uneasy about losing your job, move on. The company dangles raises and promotions (and the fantasy of Rising High); its game is to exact as much compulsive work, "loyalty," and conformism as possible, while actually doling out as few premiums as it can. Nevertheless, generally you will be paid very well for selling out; you will be offered much more than the people who don't concern themselves with questions like these. This is not a function of the devil out to get your soul (though if you sell out, he'll have it). It's those insecure people out there who can only be sure they're valid if everyone else thinks so too. They'll offer you pretty much anything they think you want if you'll give up and join them. You're safest if what you want is to be straight with yourself, to help other people, and to love and be loved. They believe that everybody has a price, and they're either awed by somebody who doesn't care about having a lot of money, or they see only a fool. You'll have an offer made to you that will include not only money, but something else you want, probably more—travel abroad, maybe. Try to look at the real price tag.

Remember that the business analogy of "family" works against you; you are the child. If you have problems with your parents (who doesn't?) business can psych you out from that angle, pushing buttons and muddling your mind with bogus authority.

Something should perhaps be said on the subject of getting fired. If you do, make it count for something useful, instead of something that begins and ends with you. A lot of firms see their employees as personal possessions: "It's *his* company, and *he* says you have to cut your hair (take down that poster, sign a time sheet)." You may be able to demonstrate that the quality of your work balances your "disabilities"—or even depends on them. Don't count on it. Whether to give in, or how much, depends on you. If there is absolutely nothing in the job, atmosphere, or working conditions that is congenial, and supports your sense of self, your stay should be limited (and doubtless will be). It is very difficult to find the point where individual satisfaction and achievement of larger goals balance. You can put up with less of one to achieve more of the other, but if the balance isn't close, there will be trouble. You should know clearly from the beginning that you're willing to quit or be fired over some issues. You don't even have to try to envisage what they might be—and you probably couldn't. But as long as you don't let your job become a security blanket, your alarm system should work automatically when your integrity is threatened. Be straight with everybody about why you're leaving, or why you're thinking about it.

There are times when announcing that you can't tolerate something and will have to quit over it will change the circumstances. Obviously, though, frequent declarations lose their effectiveness. The idea of quitting should never be a threat or a bluff; don't suggest it unless you're dead serious. In a publishing job, for example, an activist ran across purported reportage of an event she had witnessed; the author, highly respected, had distorted quotes and slandered a participant in a way that might have affected his entire life. The activist went to the editor and explained. He wasn't inclined to challenge the author, and, not surprisingly, was even less happy to have her do so. He told her she couldn't—as a member of *his* staff. She replied that she would have to leave the staff, then, and see the author as an interested individual; she added that if this didn't work she would advise the misquoted person to sue. The editor deleted the passage.

Before taking any job, tell the person making the offer that you will not do anything that seriously violates your own code of ethics. This usually gives rise to assurances that of course nothing immoral will be required of you—plus compliments on your character. (This is not hypocrisy; it's difficult for an employer to envision the kind of circumstance you are likely to react to.) Later, when the courtship is over, your statement provides a background when such issues rear their ugly heads.

To protect *your* head, stay close to people whose life style, sense of humanity, and general goals harmonize with yours. You may not be able to do it at work, but you can at home. Be sure you encourage friends you trust to confront you with signs of erosion in yourself. Self-examination is a constant necessity; a little outside help is a little outside help. How you earn a living should ideally be supportive of what you are and do otherwise; it shouldn't dominate your personality. Don't force yourself into any area just because the need is great; people are badly needed practically everywhere, and in the long run you will be of most use by finding the place where you will most fulfill yourself—as long as you have the idea of service (and *effectiveness*) in mind.

Don't neglect self-education and growth; examples of people who have are all around. Look at them when you feel lazy. Certain ideals never change, but contemporary manifestations of them do; you have to remain clear-sighted and flexible enough to recognize the shifting lines of social contributions. Everybody knows an old-line liberal who still believes that unions represent the most downtrodden people in society.

Beyond this, you'll pretty much have to create your own concept of what needs to be done and how to do it. To give detailed case studies of how business activists got where they are, as though there were a formula, would be unreal. Each found or made a route in a highly individual way. Like the entrepreneurs who see their ventures as extensions of themselves, activists seem to change jobs and functions as their commitments intensify. The idea of service becomes central to some before they ever have a job, while they are still able to direct their formal education toward specific goals. Others wake up in mid-career, and then either expand or change their jobs. Neither way lessens or guarantees effectiveness.

There are people in business waiting for you; they will help you any way they can. The most crucial thing, in their view, is to respect your self, try to see what's around you clearly, and understand what compromise means in terms of your self and your goals. Then you can be of use without damaging your self and what you stand for.

If you are to disprove the profit motive as the basis of society, you will have to disprove it as an individual. You'll have to prove that human well-being, and respect gained for what one is, are a much better bargain than Things, and the power to confine and to brutalize. You will have to make it obvious that people make people happier than money does. If we really do have a better way, we should be able to demonstrate that we do. Education is the process by which people come to see that others have something valuable to offer. Can we show business what we have, and give it free? Or will they continue to crucify us? Business has a lot of nails, a lot of power, a lot of need.

Social contributions have proved easier to make, and to get support for, in other fields. More has been done faster, and maybe more satisfyingly, elsewhere. All the consultants spoke —some wistfully—of teaching, law, social agencies, education. But they feel needed, and badly, in business, which has the greatest resources in the country locked up. They stay because it's obvious to them that the need for business reform is matched only by the need for government reform—and that business could initiate change faster and more efficiently, if it can be moved to do so. Its very resistance proves its need for change, and if that resistance discourages reformers, its power will be confirmed in the same old ways, strengthened by the lack of contradiction.

Business has the most concrete power in the country; it controls most of the money and resources; it utilizes management skills and efficiency. If businessmen can be reached, they can effectively end racial, religious, and sexual discrimination (at least economically), military involvement in Asia and elsewhere, poverty and hunger; they can construct housing on a massive scale, improve education, work for conservation and reclamation of the environment, and support drug rehabilitation programs and prison reforms. If they aren't reached, they'll continue to support (directly or indirectly) war, racism, the poverty of the many, destruction of the environment, and a value system based on money and material goods, dividing people against themselves and each other. If they aren't reached, but only antagonized, they will attempt to destroy whatever and whomever they see as a threat to their way of life. And because competition is their life-style, they will stand a good chance of succeeding.

They will have to be offered an alternative.

The New Engineer

by JOHN E. ULLMANN
and SEYMOUR MELMAN

In his critique of the engineering profession, John E. Ullmann speaks as very much an insider. Trained originally as a civil and mechanical engineer, he did his graduate work in industrial engineering. In fourteen years of active engineering practice, he gradually turned from the technical to the business problems of the mechnical, chemical and electrical/electronic engineering industries.

In his many books, monographs and articles over the past fifteen years, he has been able to predict most of those aspects of the impact of technology on society which have caused the most public concern. He was among the first to do extensive work on occupational conversion of weapons engineers; one of the earliest engineering economists to take an optimistic view of the favorable prospects of nuclear power; a strong dissenting voice against extreme views of the menace of automation (considering it self-limiting in many of its effects); one of the first to express concern over the technological backwardness and inefficient production methods in our capital goods industries; and one of the pioneers of industrial engineering applied to community planning. In that field, he is co-author of seminal works on industrial urban renewal, industrial development, urban logistics and environmental problems. He also writes on broader political and historical issues related to these.

Ullmann is professor of management and chairman of the Department of Management, Marketing and Business Statistics at Hofstra University, combining his academic duties with consulting for business and public agencies.

Seymour Melman is professor of industrial engineering at Columbia University. One of the best-known critics of war industries and Pentagon policies and management, he is the author of *Our Depleted Society*, *Pentagon Capitalism* and *The Peace Race*, and general editor of a six-volume series of studies on conversion problems of military to civilian industry, of the set of readings *The War Economy of the United States,* of the pioneering study *Inspection for Disarmament,* and other works on productivity and management methods.

> *How by an appliance many are able to remain for some time under water. How and why I do not describe my method of remaining under water for as long a time as I can remain without food; and this I do not publish or divulge on account of the evil nature of men who would practice assassinations at the bottom of the seas, by breaking the ships in their lowest parts and sinking them together with the crews who are in them.*
> —*The Notebooks of Leonardo da Vinci*

> *What has once been thought can't be unthought.*
> —FRIEDRICH DUERRENMATT, *The Physicists,* ACT II

MORE THAN three hundred and fifty years after Leonardo's famous, though little-imitated forbearance, the central problem of the engineering profession is still the same, only worse. It is the troubled relationship of the individual engineer to his profession as a whole to those who decide the training of its practitioners and the nature of its output. Leonardo himself knew all too well, for instance, the caprice of powerful patrons, and that weapons development can lead to more preferment than artistic achievement. And when weapons were available, they could not be scrapped; they were ordered used by the authorities because, like Mount Everest, they were there.

It would be pleasant to be able to report that, faced with such problems in modern dress and on a modern scale, engineers had taken energetic steps, both individually and collectively, to come to grips with the failures, insecurities and general malaise that besets them today. Such, alas, is not the case to any significant extent. Engineers at times sadly discuss some of their problems in their journals, but rarely is a crisis meeting well attended. Collective action is almost nonexistent; they seem to do their worrying in the privacy of their own homes. The pressure for new orientations in our intellectual effort and the recognition of its past misapplication also largely comes from outside their ranks. The prevailing passivity recalls Hilaire Belloc's admonition: "Learn from the pig to eat what fate and elder persons put upon your plate."

From roughly 1950 onwards, the servicing of military and space undertakings became the concentration point of the engineering profession. By 1970 more than 20 per cent of all engineers served military industry (aeronautical engineers, 59%; electrical engineers, 22%; mechanical and metallurgical engineers, 19%). In the vital research and development sphere, more than half of the nation's relevant manpower served the military-space operations. This concentration at once reflected and set the tone for the engineering schools of the nation. A preponderance of new engineers were directed to the new military-space agencies, firms and laboratories. The training for and experience in this work created a population of engineers with a special characteristic: a trained incapacity for the traditional civilian work of engineering.

By late 1970, modest military and space cutbacks had been enough to destroy the seller's market for their talents. Burgeoning unemployment reduced some engineers to such last-resort jobs as taxi-driving and franchise hamburgers. Communities in which their hard-hit industries are concentrated have discovered that the welfare clientele does not, as the fashionable political demonology has it, have to consist mainly of nonwhite ladies with illegitimate children; engineers have joined its ranks too.

Many of those affected by the Nixon-Laird budget constraints in 1970–71 would no doubt like best of all if the weapons jobs were to return in all their previous lucrative profusion, no matter what the cost. Though the SALT talks are proceeding at glacial pace and though Congress has not so far cut military spending significantly, in September, 1971, even the highly militaristic Senate Armed Services Committee became sharply critical of the unlimited cost escalations of weaponry. The hope of a new spiral in the arms race may thus be well founded, but it would be inadvisable to bet on it.

Anyway, most engineers as well as the general public can think of nonmilitary jobs which are obviously necessary. It is precisely the existence of this need for new tasks of unprecedented scope which gives grounds for hope for the future of the engineering profession. The problem lies in the degree to which the needs will be met, i.e., in the size of the investment which society will make. As these changes take place under pressure from much of society, engineers—new engineers able to solve new problems—will find a new and essential role for themselves.

Meanwhile, the problems of the old engineers and old engineering must have our attention. They are the datum from which change must proceed and, as a practical matter, in 1971 at least, both old engineers in specialties no longer needed in the job market, as well as recent graduates, have trouble finding employment. Inevitably, retrained or otherwise convertible old engineers will compete with younger ones for the available jobs. There is enough reluctance to hire those with wrong experience in the past, however, to make this competition more equal than might at first appear.

ENGINEERING AND ITS DISCONTENTS

The engineering profession is the leading creator of modern life. It was responsible for the industrial revolution, which in turn affected the totality of human existence far more than, say, the French, Russian and Chinese varieties. It can be argued, in fact, that the last two were the reactions within their respective societies to industrial development in particular and technological modernity in general.

But viewed in detail, the contribution of engineers is a highly mixed bag. They created the wherewithal for sweatshops and death camps as well as the domestic comforts beyond the dreams of ancient kings which are now widely enjoyed. They have created labor-saving machinery which reduced primordial drudgery and made possible a lot of jobs beyond human and animal strength and intellect. They have expanded the possibilities of travel, instruction and communication. But the self-same communication systems, their computers and their data banks, eroded those inefficiencies of tyranny which can sometimes make it bearable to its subjects. In this sense, technology which is designed to serve ruling elites is anything but a liberating influence. It has, in addition, bound increasing millions of people to a pattern of ever-intensifying consumption of irreplaceable raw materials, at the cost of polluting air, water and land. It thus negates a significant part of its own achievements in helping the world to a more reliable food supply by means of agricultural machinery and chemicals, and transportation systems.

Most crucial of all has been the decisive link between engineering and armaments. In Bernard Shaw's *Man and Superman,* the Devil says: "There is nothing in Man's industrial machinery but his greed and sloth; his heart is in his weapons." Shaw wrote this in 1903, that is, just about the time when the notion of inevitably benevolent progress was expiring; today we know that the literal and total destruction of life is technically possible. In all this, engineers are both problem and solution; the mess they have made is in large measure technical, and so are the remedies.

Unfortunately, engineers confront the future in serious disarray, compounded of defects in the structure, performance, control and ideology of their profession. There is first the matter of defining an engineer. He certainly does not have to have a degree from an engineering school, nor a state license. Many firms have "engineers" on their payroll who may not have a university education at all, but rather rose from the ranks of technical production workers and learned on the job to pick up a few simple technical routines which then earned them the job classification of "engineer." The presence of these non-academic entrants creates a significant dilution of the profession and makes it shade over into its own accepted paraprofessional occupations such as draftsmen, laboratory technicians, model makers and the like. To confuse the situation further, there have always been graduate engineers who never rose above that kind of work. The theoretical foundations on which the individual could build other technical careers are thus often very shaky and this raises serious questions of how much potential for useful conversion really exists.

The profession is thus fragmented in its educational levels; it is even more so in its ever-proliferating branches. These days, doctors are often alleged to have become too specialized; the old joke about the specialist on the left nostril is a case in point. Compared with engineering, however, the medical profession is a model of unity. In the course of this century, engineering has grown from its classical branches in civil, mining, mechanical and the beginnings of electrical engineering to the present situation in which, say, aerodynamicists are segregated by Mach number. Jobs are often advertised with so detailed a requirement for specialized training and experience as to give the impression of a joke to which only a very select few know the punch line. The effect of all this has been to make it difficult for engineers in many fields to communicate with one another. The concepts and vocabulary, or, more accurately, the jargon, have established barriers not only to effective cooperation but also to change where change is needed.

There is a third split which is perhaps the most serious of all: The engineering profession comprises within its ranks both employers or executives and employed engineers. Its work is frequently directed by nonengineers, and its own organizations are dominated by engineers who are also executives and supervisors.

Again, there is a sharp contrast here between engineers and, say, doctors, dentists and even lawyers, who generally determine their work content to a far greater degree than engineers and who are not encumbered in the collective actions of their professions by this particular dichotomy. Management is, in fact, the best way for engineers to burst through the salary "sound barrier" (about $20,000 a year) which they would otherwise face and which is not nearly as burdensome in other professions like law, medicine or accountancy in which individual practice is a viable alternative.

It is not, of course, necessarily desirable socially for a profession to be judge and jury in its own cause at all times. But for engineers, the limited control which most of those who work in the field exercise on their work content has serious implications for the conditions in which they have to function.

Furthermore, engineering has certainly had a bad press. There is first of all the technical performance of the weapons producers. The technical justification for much military hardware was itself spurious, but ultimately there were 65 major defense projects canceled from 1953 to 1968 on which $10.5 billion dollars had been wasted. Since then, there have been further billion-dollar fiascos of which the F-111 fighter aircraft and the C-5A transport plane are prime examples, both having been cut back after huge over-runs and bad performance. The weapons engineers also went along with all the other "systems" which were not canceled but which still cost far too much, work badly, and in any event contribute no increment to our safety in an age of overkill. Further exercises of the engineering imagination no doubt await the discovery by medicine of ways of killing people more than once.

In the course of developing and manufacturing these weapons, moreover, the engineers involved have learned work habits and attitudes which make their subsequent employment in commercial industry difficult. There is, for example, a degree of overspecialization which requires major retraining in order to make a change. There is a leisurely work pace and there is a lack of independence and addiction to "teamwork" which translates itself into a continual demand for "support services." This is another way of saying that nobody can do a job without asking umpteen others for advice. Individuals are, of course, often creative and scholarly, but what is called the "paper mill" grinds slowly—and lumpily to boot.

It is, therefore, remarkable that the existence of such overblown organizations is actually touted as a valuable resource, able to tackle large nonmilitary projects by means of the "systems approach," which views all aspects of the proposed task as a coherent whole and can manage the design and construction involved better than previous arrangements. However, attempts to realize this potential have been markedly unsuccessful so far. When the "systems approach" was applied to San Francisco's Bay Area Rapid Transit System (BART), for example, the "total" method of design resulted in the stipulation of a track gauge of five feet, which happens to make the system compatible with the railroads of Finland, the Soviet Union and Panama, but not with those of the Southern Pacific Railroad with whose commuter network the system ought to be integrated.

Further, even granting the necessity of such systems applications as the trip to the moon, something like NASA is a singularly poor model to follow. When it started, nobody knew how much a trip to the moon ought to cost, and therefore NASA was given almost unlimited financial leeway to accomplish the job. By contrast, we know very well the cost limitations of rapid transit systems, electric power, or even such more distant prospects as desalinated sea water. In the latter, we have been aiming at a cost of less than 40 cents per thousand gallons. So far, it is still above $1.00. The point here is that these new project management methods are demonstrably bad at coping with problems in which the criteria of effectiveness are to a great degree economic.

In assessing the state of engineering, moreover, what might have been must be examined along with what has been. The conditions and organization of engineering have served to deprive other technologically oriented industries of the effective use of engineering talents. The resulting depletion is clearly evident. The United States today has the oldest stock of metalworking machinery of any major industrial country. Having been a net exporter of machine tools during all of its modern history, with some individual machine tool producers becoming household words in the rest of the industrialized world, the United States became a net importer of machine tools in 1967 and has since then lost first place in this industry to West Germany. Nor is this the only instance: We have long learned to write off as terminal cases such once innovative and prosperous American industries as shipbuilding. By now, however, even such key contributors to the nation's trade surplus as the chemical industry are anticipating major difficulties in keeping up their growth rate and international strength.

The military concentration has also been a prime culprit in keeping the United States from strong participation in new technical fields, in some of which, to make things worse still, Americans had made the basic discoveries. The outstanding contribution of U.S. industry has always been the ability to take a device and, by successfully organizing its production, to transform it from a laboratory curiosity or highly specialized item into something that could be used in households, offices or factories with high efficiency and at relatively low cost. Since the days of the treadle-operated sewing machine there has not been an appliance, for example, that was not first developed into a commercially viable product in the United States—until the past decade, that is. Japan took the lead, and the small television set, the portable tape recorder, the transistor itself (an American discovery) as a mass production item, cameras with electronic instrumentation, etc., all had their origins in Japan and Japan dominates their markets today.

Some of these trends have been viewed with complacency by industrial spokesmen who argue that the United States should leave manufacturing to foreigners, at least at the low technology end, keeping the more advanced areas for ourselves. How to keep the lower orders in their place in such an arrangement is, of course, not revealed. The United States should become a "service economy," it is further argued. However, services based on engineering have themselves deteriorated to an alarming extent with the same symptoms of depletion as in manufacturing and product design. We have had, and continue to have, breakdowns in the electric power system, ranging from area-wide failures to the inability to repair equipment effectively. Telephone service is generally on a "trial and error" basis. True, many of these calamities were due to a lack of investment and sometimes to poor planning, but these are themselves engineering failures. In certain other instances, notably in the construction of power stations, environmentalists have become so concerned as to exercise a veto over virtually all forms of power generation, including the importation of power from distant areas by means of long-distance transmission lines. Here, past experience with environmental disasters has created a credibility gap between the public and the technicians; there has just been too much lying.

Engineering has for a long time inspired a whole spate of anti-utopias in which humanity is depicted as the victim of an all-encompassing technology, helplessly yoked to it the way a galley slave was chained to his oars. The standard methodology in confecting such analyses is to take a given development and extend it to extremes. By now, however, there is also a "system collapse scenario." All useful information on which society depends is stored in a computer which breaks down. The manager wants to get to the overworked repair service, but the phone doesn't function and, anyway, he can't see to dial because there has also been a power cut. And even if he could get through, the repair mechanic's car is in the garage and can't be fixed because there aren't enough garage mechanics either. And so technology ends, "not with a bang but a whimper."

THE BURDENS OF THE PAST

Past trauma is an imperfect excuse for present incompetence, but it still requires consideration. The cyclical nature of engineering industries, as well as their changing emphases, have created a professional, political and economic environment which bears on the scope of possible changes now.

Moreover, engineering has, in general, not been an outstandingly lucrative calling. The "working stiffs" of the breed have not fared conspicuously well compared with other professions requiring a similar training period. Neither in salary nor in employment security have they done as well on the average as, say, accountants, unless they became managers themselves.

Job instability has been a particularly frequent companion in the engineer's professional career. Throughout the last five decades or so, he has experienced a succession of harrowing business cycles which exposed him quite often to much the same game of occupational musical chairs as occurs in more obviously seasonal industries. One reason is that for a long time, the center of gravity of engineering employment has been in the design and production of capital goods, or in plant construction, and thus followed the ups and downs of that especially unstable industry group. Its members were in dire straits throughout the Great Depression. At the time, the industry also had a notoriously bad record of racial, religious and ethnic discrimination, which was to be alleviated only partially and slowly in subsequent periods.

Arms production in World War II gave us the first "engineer shortage." Peace found the American economy with a need to convert its war factories to the production of civilian goods of all kinds. The plants had been literally changed over to war purposes and all that was necessary now was to reverse the process. Engineers with some skills in the design of consumer goods and their production systems were in particularly high demand and the job was undertaken quite rapidly. By the end of 1948, it began to be apparent that this phase was essentially over. It had also coincided with the sharpest reduction ever in military spending, even though it never fell below $15 billion, a substantial sum in those days. For a few engineers, the kind of electromechanical instrumentation required for the more scientifically based weaponry of the time provided an employment opportunity. Much of the rest of the profession watched the backlogs of its employers shrink and could project fairly reliably the imminence of unemployment.

The outbreak of the Korean War changed all this. There was both a sharp rise in military spending and in industrial construction designed to assure improved supplies of strategic metals. A major objective was to reduce the risk of some of the material shortages which had plagued industry during World War II—an example of the old military tradition of always fighting the previous war over again. Though military in application and strategic in purpose, such projects nevertheless employed, in the main, a technical approach which did not differ materially from the commercial work of the day, i.e., from the design of other similar plants or of conventional industrial machinery.

The end of the Korean War was accompanied by a drastic

decline in new plant construction, and engineering employment suffered accordingly. At the time, for example, New
York City had a large cadre of highly experienced engineers
and draftsmen able to design the chemical, power generating
and other industrial plants which had been so badly needed in
the previous dozen years or so. It was a group as skilled and
unique in its own way as New York's renowned clothing de-
signers and workers. But it was dispersed as a result of the
slump. Many members of industrial design teams drifted into
other kinds of engineering, but mostly to the burgeoning technology of the aerospace industry.

The Russian launching of Sputnik in 1957 caused a well-
nigh hysterical reaction which had the result of pushing
greatly increased numbers of students into the engineering
schools and of changing the whole configuration of the field.
The movement received a further considerable impetus as a
result of the fake "missile gap" which was drummed up at the
time of the 1960 Presidential election, and which President
Kennedy shortly thereafter translated into a 20 per cent increase in the defense budget. In addition, he set the nation's
goal as getting to the moon by 1970, making the announcement only three weeks after he had asserted that solving the
problem of desalting sea water would make much more technical as well as human sense. Those were the days when recruitment ads leaned heavily on the *dolce vita* of the Southwest where the war industries were concentrated. Even a firm
in an unglamorous part of Indiana felt impelled to claim that
at least nothing was more than ten minutes from anything
else.

In early 1964, it looked for a brief period as if military
spending would be leveled off, and some preliminary reduc-
tions were made, only to disappear, and then some, in the
Vietnam escalation. However, much of the new spending was
for weapons to be used in a near future, and not for research
and development for which most engineers had been previ-

ously employed, or as the trade revealingly called it, "stock-piled." An index of demand for engineers compiled by the New York consulting firm of Deutsch, Shea and Evans, shows a steady decline since 1965. At the beginning, even troubles affecting a whole locality could be offset by jobs somewhere else, but by 1970 this mobility had vanished.

AS THE TWIG IS BENT

It is a common practice to blame education for the shortcomings of man, at least since Alexandre Dumas contrasted the number of intelligent children with the much larger number of stupid adults. In the case of engineering, there is some justification for the view that changes in education have indeed pushed the profession into some of its troubles, but, at the same time, one must also consider the qualities of the individuals who seem to be attracted to it.

Engineering schools have a considerable problem in setting their curricula, in that they must keep some reasonable continuity in subject matter within a discipline that is continuously changing and in which "practical experience" counts for a lot. The schools can therefore hardly be saddled with the whole blame for the fact that the utility of what an engineer has learned during his academic training diminishes throughout his working life and must be supplemented by later infusions of new knowledge. Many engineers neglect this aspect of their development. They are just too busy and confine their further work to the procedures, catalogues and specifications of their own companies. The diligence of their concentration on these is often awesome; it is also deadly when the time comes to change jobs. It represents an extraordinary degree of inertia in a society rooted as solidly in technology as the United States.

With rare exceptions, the engineering schools have followed rather than led the development of new engineering specialties, though they usually gave them academic homes. In fact, some of these waves of the future were overdone to the detriment of useful existing subjects. For example, during the rise of aerospace and military electronics from the 1950's onward, engineering schools generally added "applied science" to their names and curricula and thereby pushed out course work in production, product design, engineering economics and other applied subjects once firmly entrenched. However internally valid these new approaches were as scholarship, they had the effect of weaning engineers away from the original, essentially practical orientation of their profession by failing to teach them the methods by which its achievements and plans may be compared and evaluated.

The concentration on military electronics, aerospace and other weaponry has also determined very precisely the thrust of research and of graduate studies in engineering. The Department of Defense, the Atomic Energy Commission, and the National Aeronautics and Space Administration have supported and continue to support extensive contracts at various engineering schools. As a result of long Pentagon support, the universities became involved in wide-ranging activities on its behalf from basic scientific research to development of weapons and social control techniques. From 1963 through 1967, the Pentagon, AEC and NASA allocated $2.1 billion of federal research funds to universities.

As in the case of industrial depletion discussed earlier, a proper assessment of the impact of defense research and allied subject matter is obtained not merely by examining what work is done but by estimating what work is not done. A pertinent question is: What needs are not being met by universities? What lines of technology, for example, are neglected because of the current emphasis? The men who might have helped us out of a variety of technological predicaments are instead working on missiles, moon vehicles and the like, because that's where the "action" was. Under pressure from students and faculty in other fields, and in line with the federal cutbacks in funds for research, some of the university-based military and space activities have been phased out, and this process has in turn contributed to more engineering unemployment. The people affected often have a particularly bad time getting new jobs. The key word by 1970 was "overqualified." The misuses of engineering talent have thus called into question the very utility of the so-called "frontiers" of the field. No other profession can make this claim.

"I ONLY WORK HERE"

Engineers have long cherished a belief in the apolitical nature of their calling. They were, it was argued, a species of scientist and scientists had to be neutral. Engineers were led by these views into an ideology that justified obedience to the employer—any employer—which has at times not only been against their most narrowly defined self-interest, but inhibited the taking of responsibility for the results of one's work. Such responsibility is an essential feature of a "profession." Many thoughtful engineers have come to realize that their work is actually politicized to the hilt, from commercial product design to construction, but most weapons engineers appear as disingenuous in this respect as ever.

Their motivations have not so far been studied adequately. We can distinguish at least six modes of rationalization. The first of these is simply that what the boss feels like producing is his business, and that there is no moral issue involved; the second, which follows in part from the first, is "if I don't do it, somebody else will." A sort of nonpartisan "patriotism" animates a few, although it seldom stretches far enough to identify the waste of one's country's resources as unpatriotic. Most often, perhaps, we find simply the obedient employee; his attitude sometimes shades over into the fifth rationale which de-

couples the purpose of the weapon from its immediate technical complexities on which all attention is focused. The reality
of death is obscured in sophisticated mathematical formulae
and in the euphemistic jargon of modern militarism. Kill ratios
look a lot less bad when disguised as probability density functions. Finally, there is the view, or hope, to be more exact, that
military technology has potentially extensive commercial
uses. Even after all the disappointments which this "fallout
theory" has produced, hope still springs eternal.

There were material rewards for all this myopia, too. In
spite of often unimpressive salaries, for many engineers their
jobs produced substantial socio-economic upgrading relative
to their backgrounds. In a study done at Case Institute of
Technology and Northwestern University, it was found that
the new generation of engineering students mostly came from
working-class and lower middle-class families. Less than half
of the parents studied in the sample had completed high
school education, and a significant portion had gone no further than the eighth grade. Median family income was below
the national average, substantially below the average for the
parents of other college entrants. The chance to improve their
income level relative to that of their parents and to avoid a
low-level job was clearly a powerful motivating force. The
Case-Northwestern study included questions about the most
valued activities of their subject. Almost none of the group
chose community, national and international affairs.

This situation has recently led some observers to suggest a
technological decline and fall or significant social change for
the United States and for that other leading technocracy, the
Soviet Union. In the United States, it is argued, some of the
children of the upper middle class are exiting from conventional career building by way of Charles Reich's *Consciousness III*, and since blacks are likely to remain within a *de facto*
segregated and inferior educational structure, room will be
left "at the top" for the children of the lower middle and work-

ing classes, i.e., the small bourgeoisie and the hardhats, who will then run the technological establishment. Such groups, it is further argued, are less likely to be encumbered by moral baggage that would hinder their becoming willing servitors of a technological supermachine. But surely, nothing is new here; this is the same milieu which has furnished most of the existing engineers.

In a parallel assessment which can only be described as joyfully pessimistic, C. L. Sulzberger has argued that intellectual dissent within the Soviet Union would put a crimp in its own development and that "Russia will ultimately fall behind because there will be nobody to run the computer." There is, however, no evidence that engineers and senior technical workers have joined the brave initiatives of their colleagues in literature and science in any significant numbers. Not that the Soviet Union is unaware of the conversion problem. A Russian economist visiting at Columbia some years ago described defense work as a fine manifestation of patriotism, and then opined that Russian small-arms factories could always be switched over to making hunting rifles. In view of the awesome size of that industry, its output would surely be enough to furnish everything larger than a rabbit with its own personalized firing squad.

FUTURE CHOICES

The deep-rooted problems and inadequacies of the engineering profession as it exists today clearly call for a change—a renewal—and yet so far, it shows little sign of happening. The problems of the profession were, by 1971, overshadowed by the widespread unemployment in its aerospace sector, for which no significant aid has materialized.

This may easily foster the view that all the profession offers is an uncertain living, doing jobs for which moral blinkers are a major requirement. We would be very much less than honest if we did not point up the current troubles, not only because they exist but also because they tell us very clearly what we should *not* do—and that in itself can be very useful at times. There are, however, positive aspects as well, and to the extent that we implement them they have the potential of enormously outweighing the negative ones. There are, in fact, very few areas in which the possibilities of renewal are as extensive and as exciting as in engineering, and in which the results could solve so many real problems. Moreover, enough of a foundation exists to raise these prospects beyond the level of socio-political pipe dreams.

We view the problem of engineering renewal as one in which we have a great array of crucial tasks waiting to be done, on the one hand, and actual and potential skilled professionals on the other who would be able to carry them out. We do not believe, however, that current defense contractors should be given preference in organizing and doing the jobs. Their managerial inadequacies and wrong kinds of facilities surely argue against such a policy. The "market system" for *individuals*, i.e., finding an employer through one's own efforts, is obviously inadequate when the whole economy is performing poorly. If and when new tasks are put in hand, however, every *business* ought to have a chance, whether it is an existing commercial firm, a defense contractor, or a new enterprise. That much of a "market mechanism" is called for in the name of competitive efficiency.

Followed in the full tradition of Social Darwinism, such a policy would no doubt leave many communities stranded, because the aerospace-military-electronics complexes and the rest of the engineering industries are not concentrated in the same regions. Some movement out of the field will surely be necessary because there is no other industry which uses engineers at a comparable rate, like having from 20 to 50 per cent of engineers on the payroll. The volume of new business required to justify an extra engineer would thus be much higher because of this profligate use of technical staff. In the absence of growth in the same place of the "new" industries, those affected would either have to get out of their professions or out of town. Still, the people and the plants are there, and for those willing to undertake the new tasks, they are a possible resource to be used. The ones that do *not* deserve any favors are the managements of the defense contractors who can't adjust. But the government built many of their plants and gave them their machines. Let it now exercise reverter clauses, if any, or foreclose mortgages, or stop bailing firms out of deserved bankruptcy, or simply take the place by condemnation and give some more capable managements a chance to do something with the people and the machines!

To do otherwise would reduce the effectiveness of what is no doubt the principal asset in making the new engineer a reality. It is that the infrastructure of industries able to turn out those specific products likely to be most useful in a rehabilitation of our society is already in existence. There are firms making machine tools, transportation equipment, power plants, water treatment and pollution abatement facilities, even prefabricated housing. These industries are now largely in a depleted state, i.e., they have not been able to call on enough technical talent to keep up with new product design or create efficient production systems, but these are themselves technical problems which the new engineers will have to solve. During the public attention which ecology began to receive at the end of the 1960's, quite a few firms making the necessary equipment could point out, with every justification, that they had been in the business for decades, so what was new? To which one could reply, hopefully, "Extensive new markets"!

The second important aspect to finding new jobs for engineers is that the tasks which most readily come to mind are almost unlimited in scope. In many products—refrigerators, cars, etc.—we can define and estimate a condition of market saturation, but this does not hold, in practical terms, for housing, to take but one example. Theoretically, we could decide to tear down and rebuild every structure in the United States; nobody seriously suggests this, of course, but clearly an ideal answer would call for far more than the current starvation of housing construction relative to the country's needs.

A third aspect of helping engineers to concentrate on the improvement of our society is that investment in their work must be on a relatively much greater scale than for virtually any other profession. Unlike scientists in many other fields who can comfort themselves at a pinch with theoretical work under modest foundation grants, there is a limit to this kind of thing as far as engineering is concerned. We will later put forth one suggestion for a justifiably labor-intensive application of engineering talent, but in general it takes a lot of money before engineers can do their stuff.

The specification of the new action areas of engineering is not difficult at all. As the last two decades brought new planning tools to business, the feasibility of knowledgeably looking ahead was correspondingly broadened. J. F. Dewhurst's pioneering study in 1947, *America's Needs and Resources,* was followed in 1953 by W. S. and E. S. Woytinsky's *World Population and Production.* Individual companies were encouraged by such efforts to take a similarly broad-based look at their own environment, and we ourselves participated in such a study in 1957. In 1962, there appeared an extraordinarily succinct and prescient report of the Engineers Joint Council, *The Nation's Engineering Research Needs, 1965–85.* An important look at the nation's resource space was taken by Resources for the Future, Inc., in 1963, and in 1970 these projections were used in A. J. Van Tassel's important study, *Environmental Side Effects of Rising Industrial Output.* An additional important planning document of this kind was a program of new productive investment in the nation defined by the U.S. Council of Economic Advisers in the *Economic Report of the President, 1969.* The latter recommended for implementation by 1972 totals of $39.7 billion per annum and is designed to generate 5 million new jobs directly. A commitment of this magnitude on a long-term basis would speedily serve to orient business planners as well as engineering schools to the new prospects and benefits. All these works—and several others besides—range over the whole spectrum of national economic and technical neglect.

We can only offer a brief summary and identification here.

Energy Resources: Technical improvement and pollution abatement of "breeder" reactors, together with the development of secondary reactors able to consume the plutonium generated by the breeders; intensive work on fusion power. (As to the latter, the current conventional wisdom tells us to wait "decades." Do we really have to? Yes, indeed, if we cut the research budget in half as the Nixon Administration did in 1971.)

Transportation: High-speed railroads including linear motors, air cushion vehicles and magnetic levitation; fuel cells and other electro-chemical systems as substitution for automobile engines; new short-distance transport systems.

Water supply: Desalination of sea water and treatment of all waste water, including the elimination of phosphates and the even more dangerous nitrates. (Desalination, especially, received totally inadequate public sponsorship in 1971.)

Biomedical engineering: Hospital systems, prosthetic devices.

Air pollution: Abatement; air transport controls might be included here.

Information systems: Important problems remain to be solved here, notably information retrieval from libraries. (The field can be overestimated, however; a medical information system, for example, without medical personnel to implement its output can only improve the reliability of predicting demises.)

Housing: A virtually unlimited market as noted before; considerable difficulties due to conflicts between new technology, existing labor and managements and building codes; basic decisions on land use also await resolution, e.g., apartment clusters vs. one-family housing vs. rural reconstruction, which is virtually ignored now.

General Resource Utilization

The disproportionately large utilization of natural resources by the American economy calls for substantially increased work on substitute materials, as well as on increasing food production, which is not now at maximum level. The latter promises to be an important barter element in securing American needs in expected future times of global food scarcity. Allied to this is the whole problem of rural renewal, with important engineering factors in housing, logistics, etc.

All these fields could employ great numbers of engineers in both traditional and new fields of specialization. We should also undertake a concerted effort to improve the quality of manufactured products in the interests of both economy and conservation, and combine such an effort with a revitalization of our technically oriented export industries. To coordinate, and in part finance, the kind of rescue operation called for under this heading, it is proposed to establish a National Technology Foundation, which would act as a sponsoring agency for research on raw materials, design methodology, and applications, and would also assume that portion of "pure" research now sponsored by the Department of Defense that does not properly belong with the National Science Foundation. Its work agenda could tentatively cover the following:

1. Material and product-design studies with special reference to
   a. Economics and cost effectiveness of materials, including substitutability;
   b. Design methodology, e.g., stress analysis in products in which it is

not now widely used, such as enclosures of equipment; circuit analysis and development, including the use of computers;

   c. Systematic application studies of new materials and methods to replace the present rundown and inefficient technological fallout, e.g., integrated and molecular circuits;

   d. Reliability and robustness studies based on the kinds of test programs proposed but seldom fully carried out on materials of all kinds; applications to electronic circuitry.

2. Standardization and simplification

   a. Feasibility studies of modularization in producer and consumer durables;

   b. Cost studies, e.g., on economy of scale;

   c. Organizational studies for the systematic quantity manufacture of modules, including the legal environment.

3. Processes

   a. Automation systems for manufacturing and service industries;

   b. Maintenance and safety problems, including new automation systems justifiable mainly for safety reasons;

   c. Productivity and producibility studies, both intraindustry and international;

   d. Capacity studies on machine tools and metal-working machinery and on electronic component/circuit manufacture, including new material-machine configurations;

   e. Rationalization and reduction of job shop manufacturing; development of versatile small quantity production systems, "group technology" (the use of common physical characteristics in order to group the products into manufacturing subsystems, e.g., all shafts are made on one group of machines).

4. Information gathering and processing

   a. Information systems on design;

   b. Cost-effectiveness registry of materials, subsystems, components, etc.;

   c. Operating models for businesses, including inventory, market studies, etc.

This list is not meant to be exhaustive, but it does provide a useful beginning. Several of the items specified are likely to become of greater interest in the 1970's. Productivity improvement is particularly important, especially since some of our capital goods industries (e.g., those making machinery and other factory equipment) are little beyond the handicraft stage. International industrialization is an important market for these industries as well, but only if we become reasonably competitive again.

Another major growth area for engineering lies in many services, both public and private, virtually untouched by it so far. In some cases, it is only a matter of better paper and information processing. Such a task is well in hand in banking and, soon perhaps, it will be in the securities industry. In government, however, we are still at the very beginning. Jobs with complicated logistics such as garbage disposal, for instance, could benefit from the ministrations of industrial engineers; yet, little has been done so far. Their task would be especially vital if more extensive recycling were to be implemented.

Technical changes will also have to take place if the industrial safety legislation passed in 1970 is not to be honored more in the breach than the observance. Obviously, one way of solving safety problems is by reducing the number of people doing the dangerous jobs, i.e., by automating. The Foundation could act as a grants and contracting agency and its findings would be available to all American industry. In this way it would parallel the important public sponsorship of engineering research efforts in the commercial field carried out now in Japan, Western Europe and elsewhere.

This kind of a technical effort could absorb a great many engineers in work of real usefulness, although we recognize that the management of such an effort is not easy. One aspect of such technical investigations related to both these and other problems is the creation of public-interest engineering firms which could undertake the job of checking out technical arguments offered for public policy by governments and business firms making some claims on the public domain. By performing a task somewhat parallel to public-interest law firms, these organizations could provide a much-needed antidote to the *ex cathedra* snow jobs now regularly foisted on the public. The task is not too complex in many cases; an 8½ × 11 pad and a desk calculator in skilled hands can make mincemeat of the "analyses" involved. Consumers Union, for example, can often use simple tests in order to dispose of high-priced advertising histrionics; some of the public projects, weapons, etc., aren't "best buys" either, and there is a real need for somebody to say so, with full technical backing.

What advice can we offer to those now contemplating or completing engineering study? First, prospective "new engineers" should seek out the schools offering curricula or courses which would enable them to participate in the kind of work outlined above. Most major schools now offer such facilities, but it is important to relate their support and scope to other work done there as well. If the school is still beholden to or hankering after fat defense and AEC contracts, forget it! "Whose bread I eat, his songs I sing"—and if you want to be a new engineer you won't like the tune.

Secondly, the kinds of values and understanding of human problems which we have assumed as a prerequisite for effective participation in the new jobs for engineering must be carefully cultivated and based on fact and analysis. Hopefully, the era of the "value-free" social sciences is passing, and man will again take more seriously his obligations as a problem-solving animal. An analytic orientation directed at the finding of answers rather than the rehashing of problems is therefore an important guideline to the young engineer's study of the social sciences—which are, of course, quite indispensable to his profession.

Third, new engineers should be *entirely* warned off military work. Many a man who has regarded a good job in the defense field as a "temporary" arrangement has found the truth of the old French proverb that only the temporary lasts—until the cutbacks, of course.

You may ask, what if there are no jobs? The answer in 1972 must surely be that nobody is getting engineering jobs that easily, but that if anyone wants, and is able, to do the jobs we have specified, he will exercise his rights and powers as a citizen to make sure that they are done. This may sound cynical and recall what we said earlier on the political inclinations of unemployed defense workers. The fact remains, however, that when people know how to do a job well, they will fight for a chance to do it. And today it is far more important to fight for the rescue of our society than for more overkill.

Finally, engineers should see to the organization of their collective strength. This is of the greatest importance for the future of the profession. Engineers should become much more closely involved in both the public consequences of their profession and its economic environment. As the Talmud puts it, "If I am not for myself, who will be for me? If I am for myself alone, what am I? If not now, when?"

A profession which, as we have said, has given us the paraphernalia of modern life should neither be depressed nor concentrate on improving the mechanism of death. It will justify its continued existence only to the extent that it can build a new structure on the work and ideals of all those who have kept up the good work during what would otherwise be what Winston Churchill once called "a new dark age, made darker and more protracted by the lights of perverted science."

Selected Bibliography

Calder, N. *Technopolis*. New York: Simon and Schuster, 1969.

Dewhurst, J. F. *America's Needs and Resources*. New York: Twentieth Century Fund, 1947.

Engineers Joint Council. *The Nation's Engineering Research Needs, 1965–85*. New York: Engineers Joint Council, 1962.

Landsberg, H. H.; Fischman, L. L.; and Fisher, J. L. *Resources in America's Future*. Baltimore: Johns Hopkins Press, 1963.

A series of technical studies on conversion of industry from a military to civilian economy, edited by Seymour Melman and published by Praeger Special Studies, 1970:

Berkowitz, M., *The Conversion of Military-Oriented Research and Development to Civilian Uses.*

Christodoulou, A., *Conversion of Nuclear Facilities from Military to Civilian Uses.*

Lynch, J. E., *Local Economic Development After Military Base Closures.*

Mack-Forlist, D., and Newman, A., *The Conversion of Shipbuilding from Military to Civilian Markets.*

Melman, S., ed. *The Defense Economy.*
(See also this title for an extensive bibliography on the role of engineers and others in the conversion situation.)

Melman, S. *Our Depleted Society.* New York: Holt, Rinehart and Winston, and Dell Books, 1965.

————. *Pentagon Capitalism.* New York: McGraw-Hill, 1970.

————, ed. *The War Economy of the United States.* New York: St. Martin's Press, 1971.

Nieburg, H. *In the Name of Science.* Chicago: Quadrangle Press, 1966.

Schon, D. *Technology and Change.* New York: Dell Books, 1967.

Ullmann, J. E. "Conversion and the Import Problem: A Confluence of Opportunities." *IEEE Spectrum,* April 1970.

Ullmann, J. E., ed., *Potential Civilian Markets for the Military-Electronics Industry.*

U.S. Council of Economic Advisers. *Economic Report of the President, 1969.* Washington, D.C.: U.S. Government Printing Office, 1969.

Van Tassel, A. J., ed. *Environmental Side Effects of Rising Industrial Output.* Lexington, Mass.: Heath, 1970.

Woytinsky, W. S., and E. S. *World Population and Production.* New York: Twentieth Century Fund, 1953.

New
People
for
the
Professions

Changing the Professions:
The New Careers Strategy

by ALAN GARTNER
and FRANK RIESSMAN

Alan Gartner is associate director, New Careers Development Center, New York University, and the author of *Paraprofessionals and Their Performance*. He was formerly executive director, Economic Opportunity Council of Suffolk, and before that Community Relations Director, CORE. With Mary Conway Kohler and Frank Riessman, he coauthored *Children Teach Children*.

Frank Riessman was one of the first social scientists to draw widespread attention to the plight of poor children in American schools. For over a decade he has been in the forefront of efforts to awaken the professional and public conscience about the schools' failure to meet the needs of such children, and the necessity to find new ways to help them. His early book, *The Culturally Deprived Child*, was a path-breaking venture in this field. As the struggle to equalize educational opportunity became more heated, however, Riessman himself turned away from this term. He stressed, increasingly, the need to build programs to accent children's strengths. Moreover, he became concerned about the lifelong development of poor people, rather than just their children's school careers. For the past several years he has been director of the New Careers Development Center at New York University. The Center aims at providing training for poor people desiring to move up career ladders in the major professions.

FOR YOUNG people aiming to become New Professionals, or to established practitioners struggling to reform

their professions, powerful help is available from the paraprofessional or new careerist. They—both in terms of the work
they do and the challenge they bring to professional practice
—are playing an important role in challenging the limitations
of professional practice and in developing new forms of practice.

The new careers strategy seeks to change professional practices, roles, institutions, functions, values and attitudes. The
work of the paraprofessional improves both the efficiency and
the productivity of the system. They appear to have an effect
upon sensitizing professionals in the work place and, to a
lesser extent, in the training process. While not yet themselves
beyond the credentials barrier, paraprofessionals appear to
have direct and indirect effect upon professionals, upon human service practices, and upon the service consumer. It is to
each of these areas we will turn attention.

Everyone is down on the old-style concept of professionalism today: those who are served by professionals (especially
those who are poor and/or minority group members); the students who are preparing to enter the professions; the paraprofessionals who work in the service agencies; and finally, many
practicing professionals themselves.

All four groups agree that, in general:

1. professionalism has made a great deal of professional practice highly
   irrelevant to the needs of the community;
2. professionalism still values outmoded, inappropriate, rigid credentials;
3. professionalism is typically elitist and non-participatory;
4. professional practice has been, in too many cases, largely ineffective
   and nonaccountable to the consumer;
5. much of professional practice appears mystical, pretentious, jargon-
   based, over-elaborated and lacking in vitality.

The creation and development of new careers is aimed at
changing and improving the professions that serve human beings—health, education, welfare, corrections, mental health,
etc. New careers gives poor people a chance to move up a ca-

reer ladder by on-the-job education and training; they eventually become "new" professionals. The major goals are to reduce poverty and manpower shortages in the professions, while reorganizing the human services to make them more efficient, accountable, effective, relevant and vital, thus releasing these services from the confines of the old concept of professionalism.

DEPROFESSIONALIZATION

Professions have become largely deprofessionalized, primarily because of the distortions and limitations imposed on the idea of what professionalism means. The results of this deprofessionalism are very evident. Large numbers of professionals are functioning at a very low level. Teachers spend time helping children on with their boots, taking attendance, keeping order, filling out forms, erasing the blackboard, running a movie machine and so on. In essence, the professional is underutilized. He mechanically performs routine tasks; he has little initiative and he is bureaucratically controlled by the rules. His skills are wasted, and he becomes stultified and apathetic.

Another reflection of deprofessionalization is the failure of the professions themselves to grow, develop and change—essential requirements of a profession. The human service professions are lagging behind the new developments and new discoveries which could so dramatically increase effectiveness. They are not meeting the new demands of the population expansion. There has been little effective evaluation of the work that has been done in these fields. Old techniques, methods, and approaches continue to be utilized, even though they are inefficient or not reaching the wider community.

This lack of growth is evident in in-service training methods, or "staff development," as well as at professional conventions and in professional journals. In a way, the professional is *undertrained*, because he does not really learn how to do his job in a systematic, effective, professional manner. He is required to take a great many courses that are really not related to the job. He must pass tests which typically have not even been validated. His preparation is academically removed and prolonged, when it would be the simplest kind of training if it were an "on-the-job process," and it is usually unrealistic and inadequate. A teacher, for example, is forced to acquire the necessary techniques for survival in the classroom on the firing line.

Deprofessionalization leads to defensiveness and insecurity on the part of the professional. In order to protect his job he joins associations which supposedly maintain standards. Unfortunately, however, the standards are not performance-based, but rather credential-based. This satisfies the professional who is not really working in a professional manner; he hardly wants his performance to be judged. He prefers, of course, that the possession of a college degree and a passing score on the so-called "qualifying examinations" serve as criteria for his evaluation.

Deprofessionalization has its climax when the professional realizes that he is not serving the client. The *sine qua non* of the professional ethic is to serve; if children are not learning, and patients are not being rehabilitated, then the professional is deprofessionalized in the deepest sense. And too often the professional will shift the blame to the client in an effort to hide his own faults (see William Ryan's *Blaming the Victim*, New York: Pantheon, 1971). Or, he may seek refuge in one of the misguided, guild-like professional associations that are not concerned with the development of the profession but rather with the protection of short-range, narrow, vested interests. Many of the flaws in professionalism are intrinsically related to the way the professions are organized in our society, protected by these monopolistic professional associations. Colleges are similarly controlled and sheltered from the kind of change which is so vital.

Many critics have observed that the main defect of professionalism is the maintenance of autonomy—a kind of diplomatic immunity to any criticism other than criticism from peers. One such critic tartly states the doctor's view: "A doctor is accountable to his peers, a quack to his clients."

In a sense, professional practice can be viewed as a new industry which has quickly arrived at a semi-monopolistic phase, where the supply of services is *not* typically responsive to demand, and the character of the goods or services is shaped by the producer, not by the consumer's needs. Medicaid, for example, instead of providing a wider range of services less expensively for the poor, results in *more* doctor's fees. In education, much needed but misdirected increases in expenditures go for higher teacher salaries and more teachers, rather than for directly improving the learning of more children. This is deprofessionalization.

PARAPROFESSIONALS—FRESH HOPE FOR THE PROFESSIONS

There are various ways in which the paraprofessional can affect the professional. Contact with paraprofessional co-workers generally tends to increase the sensitivity of the professional to the demands of the community. In addition, the paraprofessional brings the values and needs of the consumer directly into professional practice. Of necessity, the professional becomes reoriented to the consumer in new and significant ways. The paraprofessional also affects the professional by raising new and constructive questions about how the various agencies operate. In this sense, the paraprofessional functions as an observer/monitor of the professional inside the work system. He also embodies new styles of work and new ways of relating to people, which to some extent may rub off on the professional.

Charles Grosser, looking at the effect which paraprofessionals had upon State Employment Services offices, noted that their employment "forces the agency to a degree of accountability to the client community [which] is contrary to the traditional pattern in all service agencies of professional self-regulation [and to] the Employment Service's view of its responsibility to the employer." Unlike the traditional focus which has been directed toward meeting the needs of the employer, the paraprofessionals "often alienate employers; they tend to demand rather than ask for job placements [for their clients]." *

Grosser remarked upon the contrast between what may have been the agency's intent in instituting a paraprofessional program, and the actual consequence.

The introduction of a program device as innovative as this one, even if the original intention is only to improve services, must soon produce strains leading to alterations in patterns of agency function. †

Not only does the introduction of the paraprofessional directly affect the service, it also affects the professional and the agency as a whole. Grosser suggested that "professionals in these projects are more effective with the poor than their counterparts in ongoing agencies."

Francine Sobey found that National Institute of Mental Health project directors saw paraprofessionals infuse the projects with a new vitality and force a self-evaluation by the staff which, although painful, led to beneficial changes for the field of mental health.

The work style and personal attributes of the paraprofessionals were important in this study, as they brought about:

* Charles Grosser, *The Role of the Nonprofessional in the Manpower Development Programs.* Washington, D.C.: U.S. Department of Labor, 1966, p. 48.
 † Ibid.

a change in atmosphere within the agency, and more lively and vital relationships among staff and between patients and staff. . . . Improved morale, better attitudes toward patients, definite improvements in over-all quality of service were other improvements reported. The addition of youthful, untrained personnel within several hospitals make the older trained personnel re-examine their own roles and the role, structure, and function of the entire hospital.*

There is another, perhaps even more powerful impact that the new worker may have on the whole professional structure. By performing "non-professional" functions hitherto performed by professionals, the new worker allows the formerly "deprofessionalized" professional to perform more advanced and different functions. In a sense the paraprofessional contributes towards a restructuring of the professional's work as the latter is freed of many of the less professional tasks. Indeed, as the paraprofessional takes on many of the tasks previously performed by the professional, the new situation may permit a fundamental analysis of the work to be done with a resulting new division of functions. Thus teachers may become master teachers, case workers become senior case workers, social workers become multi-purpose workers, nurses become unit managers. Moreover, in this new differentiated staffing, professionals may more often play roles as consultant, trainer, specialist and administrator. To some extent the introduction of the paraprofessional "bumps" the whole system, disequalibrates it, and frees the professional who has been performing all sorts of functions which do not require professional understanding or preparation.

PROFESSIONAL ORGANIZATIONS

Many professional organizations have strongly endorsed the concept of new careers as an important new manpower re-

* Francine Sobey, *The Nonprofessional Revolution in Mental Health*. New York: Columbia University Press, 1970.

source. The American Public Health Association in 1971 granted full "section" status to a group called the "New Professional Health Workers," a paraprofessional organization with bases in Philadelphia and Pittsburgh. In 1970, the APHA had first granted recognition to the group as a "conference" and had assigned a staff member to work with it to achieve the acceptance in 1971 as a full "section." The American Orthopsychiatric Association has voted by membership referendum to admit those, including paraprofessionals, who lacked a masters degree but presented equivalent work experience.

The largest professional education association, the National Education Association (NEA), has also encouraged paraprofessional programs, but has limited the paraprofessionals' participation in the Association. However, the NEA's competitor in organizing public school personnel, the American Federation of Teachers (AFT), has supported paraprofessional programs and has encouraged full membership of paraprofessionals in its locals. At the national level, AFT organizers have assisted locals in organizing paraprofessionals and have included paraprofessionals in its "20/20" plan. This plan limits teachers to 20 pupils at a time, 20 hours a day, four days a week, with paraprofessionals used on the fifth day. AFT locals in dozens of cities have organized paraprofessionals, often winning contracts which include both traditional "bread and butter" gains as well as the special career concerns of paraprofessionals. This combination is illustrated by the contract won by AFT's New York City local, the United Federation of Teachers (UFT). More than 12,000 classroom aides in grades K-12 are covered in a new contract with starting salaries for entry workers at $2.50 an hour and at $5.05 for those at the top of the paraprofessional ladder (a 140% increase over the life of the three-year contract), a guarantee of forty-two weeks of work plus a four-week vacation, a college career program, and full fringe benefits.

Unions have brought the concepts of the new careers program—particularly as they relate to career ladders and built-in education and training—to the "old" paraprofessionals, such as "nurse's aides" and "psychiatric aides," whose positions have existed for some time. The benefits which were provided to new paraprofessionals from the community through federal programs are now being sought and won for their old members by the unions. In 1968, a joint report of the National Association of Social Workers (NASW) and the Council of Social Work Education (CSWE) officially recognized "the inclusion of personnel indigenous to the client system as part of social work manpower." * The CSWE also moved away from its traditional sole concern with MSW programs and developed guidelines for two-year college programs.

The American Public Welfare Association (APWA) has also been a strong supporter of the use of paraprofessionals. In December 1969, the APWA endorsed paraprofessional programs, with the proviso that such programs must include released-time for education, must provide for education leading to college degrees, and must include career ladders.

The American Medical Association's House of Delegates, in December 1969, endorsed two avenues to advancement in new health occupations. In addition to the traditional route of academic preparation and training, they supported "advancement through practical experience and attainment of a high level of competence. . . ." †

NEW "PROFESSIONALS" VIA NEW ROUTES

Much of the positive impact that the paraprofessional has had on the professions is a result of the new route to professionalism which combines training, work experience and education.

* National Institute for New Careers, *New Careers in Social Welfare: A Status Report.* Washington, D.C.: University Research Corporation, 1970, p. 5.

† National Institute for New Careers, *New Careers in Health: A Status Report.* Washington, D.C.: University Research Corporation, 1970, p. 26.

These future professionals have been recruited differently, from new ethnic and class backgrounds, and are being trained by a different combination of work and study. Therefore, they become a new kind of professional by the time they reach the end of the ladder. In a time of racial confrontations and sharpened community consciousness, it is particularly dramatic for a group of nonwhite, nonmiddle-class people to move into the professions. Most importantly, they usually are not simply replicas of the old professionals:

> To avoid falling into the same bag that other community professionals have, we must be constantly aware of our ultimate goal: to get the Black community on its feet economically and medically. The only way that we can do this is not to allow ourselves to be sucked into the Establishment. We must not allow the Establishment to use us to pacify the community. We must always work for the common good of our people, not becoming flunkies doing the dirty work of our agency to "cool out" the poor, especially Blacks. We must continually intervene in systems that are not truly concerned about the welfare of our people.
>
> We are aware that the war isn't over just because we have won a battle. We must continue to fight each new encounter as if it was the first. However, we must not become paranoid in thinking that every confrontation is a fighting situation.*

Perhaps the outstanding program to develop professionals via the new route is the Career Opportunities Program of the Office of Education, which functions presently in 132 cities. This program allows paraprofessionals to move up a career ladder from teacher aide to assistant teacher to associate teacher to teacher in four years. They are awarded college degrees through a combination of college courses, in-service training and work experience, all of which is presented in an accelerated program. As yet, of course, only a small number have reached the end of the ladder, so it is too early to judge whether a truly different and better kind of professional teacher will emerge. The indirect effect of the influx of para-

---

* Robert Royette *et al.*, "The Plight of the New Careerist," *American Journal of Orthopsychiatry* XLI, 2 (March 1971): 237–38.

professionals into colleges, along with the large increase in enrollment of minority students, has yet to be fully assessed. There is little question that there are new demands for meaningful, integrated work-study programs and courses that are more relevant to the work situation. Also, contact between these new students adds a richness and depth to the education of both groups. Perhaps, also, there is an effect on the college atmosphere and the professors' sensitivity to community issues. But as yet we have little direct evidence on these matters, and they remain for the most part as hypotheses.

The new careers movement is very much concerned with changing the present credentialing practices. It is increasingly clear that paraprofessionals in their unions and professional associations are clamoring for new credentials and new routes to old credentials. Thus far this has been a slow process; most of the paraprofessionals are impacted fairly near the bottom of the ladders. There has been some significant movement, however, and the pressure is increasing.

HUMAN SERVICE PRACTICE

Human service practice has been made more efficient and productive via the utilization of paraprofessionals. Paraprofessionals simply provide more manpower to do the job. They serve people who couldn't be reached before—the poor, minority groups, the aged, etc.; sometimes in new jobs such as health advocate, parent educator, expediter, patient advocate, family planning assistant, neighborhood service center coordinator they do jobs that previously were more peripheral. Paraprofessionals may refashion work that was traditionally performed by professionals—changing the character of the service by providing a more humanized, down-to-earth, indigenous style; and of course they release professionals to perform more efficiently and improve their practice.

Any effort to evaluate performance in the human services is

complicated. The complications are increased immeasurably when we attempt to isolate the effect of a single factor, such as the role of paraprofessionals. Studies of performance are complicated by questions of what criterion is to be used. In education, for example, are reading scores a valid measure? What about the more subtle measures in the cognitive area, to say nothing of the affective domain? Thus, to assess the role of the paraprofessional upon the quality of the service, we must seek a variety of methods and sources, and express results with some caution. The conclusions which follow, collected from many sources, are the fruits of extensive research efforts in varied areas—both geographical and subject-oriented—and cover a wide spectrum of our society.* We believe that together they do what no single study does (or can do)—that is, make a persuasive, although assuredly not final, argument that paraprofessionals, through their direct impact upon students, patients and clients, positively affect their learning, health and well-being.

Education

In January 1968, and then again in May, in the Minneapolis Public Schools, nine kindergarten classes were selected and were given the Metropolitan Reading Readiness Test. Those classes with one paraprofessional aide made a 50% greater total gain than did those classes with no aide.†

Health

A Los Angeles program, funded by the Children's Bureau, sought to test whether indigenous health aides could success-

---

* Here we present one or two examples from each field of service. Several hundred studies are reported upon in Alan Gartner, *Paraprofessionals and Their Performance*. New York: Praeger Publishers, 1971.

† William Bennett, Jr., and R. Fred Falk, *New Careers and Urban Schools*. New York: Holt, Rinehart, and Winston, 1970.

fully counsel parents about iron-deficiency anemia. The aides' effectiveness was compared with that of middle-class professionals. Based upon evaluation of the extent and degree of the parents' compliance with counseling instructions, and their recall of nutrition information, *those parents counseled by indigenous workers performed as well or better than did those counseled by second-year medical students.*

Mental Health

Based upon a study of 180 NIMH-funded projects, Francine Sobey reports:

Nonprofessionals are utilized not simply because professional manpower is unavailable but rather to provide new services in innovative ways. Nonprofessionals are providing such therapeutic functions as individual counseling, activity group therapy, milieu therapy; they are doing case finding; they are playing screening roles of a nonclerical nature; they are helping people to adjust to community life; they are providing special skills such as tutoring; they are promoting client self-help through involving clients in helping others having similar problems.*

A highly significant and well-controlled experiment was conducted by Roland Ellsworth at the Fort Meade, South Dakota, VA Hospital.† This demonstration program indicated that increased interaction between paraprofessional aides and hospitalized male schizophrenics resulted in a higher percentage of post-release returns to the hospital than usual. An important aspect of this program seemed to be the increased participation by aides in decisions regarding the patients.

---

* Sobey, op. cit., p. 6.
† Roland B. Ellsworth, *Nonprofessionals in Psychiatric Rehabilitation.* New York: Appleton-Century-Crofts, 1968.

Court Programs

The Manhattan Court Project was designed

to intervene in the usual court process just after a defendant's arrest, to offer him counseling and job opportunities and, if he cooperates and appears to show promise of permanent change, to recommend that the prosecutor and the judge dismiss the charges against him without ever deciding whether he is guilty.*

The key project workers were ex-offenders used as counselors (called "Reps"), whose activities included interviewing prospective participants, carrying case responsibilities, making referrals, conducting group counseling sessions, keeping records, conducting liaison activities with the Project's Career Development unit, and appearing in court to make recommendations as to case disposition.

The "Reps" had prior prison records from two and one-half to nineteen years. Their power lay in the fact that "they speak the language of the streets, know the ghetto neighborhoods, and are themselves extraordinary examples of people once in the same circumstances as the participants but who are now visibly making it in, instead of outside, the system."

In twenty-three months the project has handled 850 participants, and, as a result of the intercession, 343 were employed, 29 were in training, and 51 were students; 427 were unemployed and no information was available.

Parent Education

The following two studies, one in Florida and one in New York City, involved indigenous paraprofessionals who trained poverty family mothers to work with their own children. Fif-

* *The Manhattan Court Employment Project of the Vera Institute of Justice, Summary Report on Phase One: November 1, 1967 to October 3, 1969.* New York: Vera Institute of Justice, 1970, p. 7.

teen disadvantaged women worked with nearly 300 mothers and their children in a program at the College of Education, University of Florida. The "parent educators" instructed the mothers in a series of exercises designed to provide physical, intellectual and social stimulation for the children, ages three months through two years old. As measured by the Griffiths Mental Development Scale, *the children whose mothers were trained by the paraprofessionals did better on all scales—locomotor, personal-social, hearing and speech, eye and hand, and general performance—than did those in a matched control group whose parents did not receive this training.* [*]

A New York City program, STAR (Supplementary Teaching in Advanced Reading), used paraprofessionals to train parents to read to their children. Studies of the youngsters, first-grade pupils from predominantly Puerto Rican families whose teachers identified them as likely reading failures, found that the *children whose parents were trained by paraprofessionals for one hour per week scored higher in nine different reading tests than did matched children who received two hours of remediation from professionals, or a control group.*[†]

It is clear that the paraprofessional can take over some of the functions previously performed by professionals; for populations hitherto unreached or only marginally reached, health aides provide more immunization services, teacher aides more opportunities for remedial reading help, mental health aides in community mental health programs provide additional group counseling for neighborhood residents, family planning assistants provide advice and other services to clients, and many day care centers for working mothers of the poor are being staffed largely by paraprofessionals. In addition to extending the services, entirely new services that appear to be

---

[*] Alan Gartner, *Do Paraprofessionals Improve Human Services: A First Critical Appraisal of the Data.* New York: New Careers Development Center, New York University, 1969, p. 20.

[†] Ibid.

useful and necessary for improving human service practice and professional practice are being made available; expediters who decrease fragmentation, client advocates who struggle against bureaucratic deficiencies in the system, and parent educators who encourage disadvantaged parents to talk more to their infants.

AFFECTING PROFESSIONAL PRACTICE VIA THE CONSUMER—AN INDIRECT EFFECT

We have already indicated a variety of ways whereby the consumer or client in the new careers system may affect professional practice: (1) As the consumer becomes a paraprofessional worker in the system, he may bring consumer values and orientations closer to the professional and thus resocialize him and provide him with a different kind of "sensitivity training"; (2) by functioning in his new roles, typically as an advocate for client needs, the paraprofessional again assists the consumer to be a force, to make new demands: (3) as the paraprofessional, functioning with his outreach approach, reaches new clients hitherto only minimally touched, he may bring new demands and new demanders into the system; (4) by functioning as a two-way communicator between the professional system and the community, he also brings a consumer orientation into the agency system; (5) by providing services in a more indigenous down-to-earth fashion, he expands the service network of the system in a way more directly related to the consumer; and finally (6) if the service is improved, the demand for the service may greatly increase.*

* See Catherine Kohler Riessman, "The Supply-Demand Dilemma and Community Mental Health Centers," *American Journal of Orthopsychiatry* XL, 5 (October 1970): 858–69; Alan Gartner, "Consumers as Deliverers of Service," *Social Work* XVI, 4 (October 1971): 28–32.

DANGERS

The new careers strategy for changing the professions and human service practice entails many potential dangers: (1) The new paraprofessional may be changed by the professional without influencing the latter very much; in other words, instead of having cross-socialization in which both parties are affected, the impact may be largely one way, and the paraprofessional, moving up a career ladder may, by the time he arrives at professional status, be a replica of the old professional; (2) movement up the ladder may not occur and large numbers of paraprofessionals may only be impacted at the bottom; (3) the efficiency of the human service system may be increased somewhat by the addition of the new manpower but the system may not be really reorganized, so that professionals really perform essentially the same function as they did before, only with more hands assisting them; (4) in moving from an overly academic, abstract training model, there is the danger that the pendulum will swing too far in the other direction —the new workers will be trained in a simple type of on-the-job training and they will learn how to perform specific functions. They would thus be deprived of over-all systematic education of a professional kind. A corollary danger here is that higher education will be vocationalized and work-study will not really be integrated, but work will simply be added on as substitute for certain courses; (5) paraprofessionals may be used as a buffer between the community and the professions rather than being permitted to assist in changing the human service and professional systems; (6) paraprofessionals may be utilized to substitute for and even compete with professionals in order to save money for agencies; (7) a great variety of new functions may be added on to the paraprofessional's work as he moves up the ladder and may overload him; (8)

the paraprofessionals may be "compartmentalized," separated from the professionals, presumably to safeguard their indigenousness, but the effect, of course, will be to limit their effect on the professionals as well as to impact them at the bottom of the ladder.

The most important way to insure against the risk of misuse and the other dangers noted is to be sure that the paraprofessionals organize in employee associations, whether unions or professional associations. It is also important that they maintain alliances with the community organizations, and that they become politically involved on questions related to them.

The new careers approach *can* maintain its strong pro-professional ideology. To do so, it must continue to demand worker participation within all agencies so that the paraprofessional can have an input on all types of professional practice issues; paraprofessionals must maintain a concern for accountability, relevance and vitality stemming from their community background. They must make every effort to prevent the divisiveness with professionals that may be caused by cutbacks in the economy.

One of the great dangers is that paraprofessionals may be concerned only with their career aspirations; to counter this they must maintain a deep concern for the nature of the service and the associated professional practice.

New careers advocates must continue to fight in their professional associations, unions and caucuses for breakthroughs on credentialism—the need for recredentialing, new licensing, the removal of outmoded barriers, the development of new routes. Unless these positions are fought for organizationally and politically, the natural forces of inertia will be aligned with the specific resistance of defensive professionals to screen the new careerists out, maintain the old protective credentials, and allow professional practice to remain sterile.

In other words, it is essential that the new careers movement continues to emphasize the character of the service, the participatory involvement of the workers, and a pro-professional stance. One of the areas of great concern, of course, is the college arena, where paraprofessionals may be given a second-class vocationalized type of education en-abling them to function in the lower level technical jobs, but not to become full professionals. Paraprofessionals may be fooled by this because they are told that the high-level courses are irrelevant, academic, not related to work, etc. This anti-intellectual line can easily deceive the paraprofessionals un-less they are extremely alert and develop a powerful pro-professional, pro-intellectual outlook. *

CONCLUSION AND SUMMARY

We have outlined various new careers strategies for attempt-ing to change professional practices, roles, institutions, func-tions, values and attitudes. We have indicated that parapro-fessionals have had a definite effect on increasing the efficiency and productivity of the human services. This prob-ably occurs because they are performing new kinds of tasks, doing work that was previously undone, reaching populations that were previously uncovered, and freeing professionals to perform new functions.

Paraprofessionals probably have sensitized professionals to community needs, resocialized them to some extent, and raised new questions regarding agency practices. However, thus far, few paraprofessionals have become professionals, and there is as yet no evidence that when they arrive at the new role, they will perform it differently and become genu-inely new professionals because of their origins, community base, and the new routes by which they have become profes-

* See the editorial "The 'Vocationalization' of Higher Education: Duping the Poor" and the special section "High Education and the Poor," *Social Pol-icy*, II, 1 (May–June 1971).

sionals. Moreover, the credentials barrier has been difficult to pass and, for the most part, paraprofessionals have been impacted at the lower levels of the career ladder. They may be able to affect practice from these bottom rungs, but they themselves are kept from reaching the higher levels. There are some exceptions to this, notably the Career Opportunities Program of the Office of Education, where paraprofessionals are moving up a ladder to become teachers, but most of the other studies indicate that paraprofessionals, while earning more money, affecting practice, etc., do remain in nonprofessional positions.

While some 20,000 paraprofessionals are now attending college, we do not yet know the effect of this on the college or professional practice. We again hypothesize for the future a series of indirect effects, nonspecific in character, whereby the students, the courses, and the professors will be affected by this influx of new students.

We have outlined a series of dangers that may impede the new careers strategies for affecting professional practice, and we have indicated some of the counterforces that may insure against these dangers or limit their occurrence. Four main strategies were identified:

Strategy I: Paraprofessionals may affect professionals by working alongside them, changing the atmosphere of their agencies, sensitizing them to demands of the community, and participating in professional organizations and unions.

Strategy II: As paraprofessionals move up a career ladder to become professionals via new combinations of training, work and education, they may become different kinds of professionals at the end of the route. In addition, as paraprofessionals take over the functions previously performed by professionals, the latter have the opportunity of performing new kinds of functions—e.g., consultation, supervision, training, management, administration, diagnosis.

Strategy III: Paraprofessionals may change professional

practice by performing new work and new job functions such as health advocate, expediter, parent educator, program developer, thus providing a whole range of new human service practice.

Strategy IV: Paraprofessionals, in a variety of ways, may improve the performance, efficiency, productivity of human service agencies, and in so doing improve the professions.

We have indicated direct and indirect effects upon the professionals, upon human service practice, and upon the service consumer. The new careers effort strives to affect the professions in all three of these areas. It seeks to change the roles, values, norms, and attitudes of the professions; to affect the credentials, regulations, and professional organizations of the various fields; to redefine the work to be done, who is to do it, and why it is to be done; to change by the presence of paraprofessionals the composition of the work force at all levels of human service agencies. While significant steps have been taken in each of these areas, the new careers effort still has far to go to achieve the fullness of its goals in changing the professions.

Sources of Further Information

Useful sources:

New Human Services Newsletter. Published by the New Careers Development Center, New York University, 184 Fifth Avenue, N.Y. 10010.

New Careers Bulletin. Published by the University Research Corporation, 4301 Connecticut Avenue, N.W., Washington, D.C.

New Careers Bibliography: Paraprofessionals in the Human Services. National Institute for New Careers, 4301 Connecticut Avenue, N.W., Washington, D.C.

Judith Benjamin et al. *Pros and Cons: New Roles for Nonprofessionals in Corrections.* Washington, D.C.: Office of Juvenile Delinquency, Department of Health, Education and Welfare, 1966.

William S. Bennett, Jr., and R. Frank Falk. *New Careers and Urban Schools.* New York: Holt, Rinehart and Winston, 1970.

Garda Bowman and Gordon Klopf. *New Careers and Roles in the American School.* New York: Bank Street College, 1969.

Roberta Boyette et al. "The Plight of the New Careerist." *American Journal of Orthopsychiatry* XLI, 2 (March 1971).

George Brager. "The Indigenous Worker: A New Approach for the Social Work Technician." *Social Work* X, 2 (April 1965).

June Jackson Christmas. "Group Methods in Teaching and Practice: Nonprofessional Mental Health Personnel in a Deprived Community." *American Journal of Orthopsychiatry* XXXVI, 3 (April 1966).

Dorothea Cudaback. "Case Sharing in the AFDC Program." *Social Work* XIV, 3 (July 1969).

Alan Gartner. *Paraprofessionals and Their Performance.* New York: Praeger, 1971.

Charles Grosser et al. *Nonprofessionals in the Human Services.* San Francisco: Jossey-Bass, 1969.

Wilbur Hoff. "Role of the Community Health Aide in Public Health Programs." *Public Health Reports* LXXXIV, 11 (November 1969).

Laura Pires Houston. "Black People, New Careers and Humane Human Services." *Social Casework* LI, 5 (May 1970).

Mary Lynch et al. "The Role of Indigenous Personnel as Clinical Therapists." *Archives of General Psychiatry* XIX, 4 (October 1968).

Salvadore Minuchin. "The Paraprofessional and the Use of Confrontation in the Mental Health Field." *American Journal of Orthopsychiatry* XXXIX, 5 (October 1969).

R. A. Nixon. *Legislative Dimensions of the New Careers Program: 1970.* New York: Center for the Study of the Unemployed, New York University, 1970.

Arthur Pearl and Frank Riessman. *New Careers for the Poor.* New York: Free Press, 1965.

Frank Riessman and Hermine Popper. *Up From Poverty.* New York: Harper and Row, 1968.

Francine Sobey. *The Nonprofessional Revolution in Mental Health.* New York: Columbia University Press, 1970.

Demasculinizing the Professions

by CAROLINE BIRD

In 1970, David McKay brought out a second edition of Caroline Bird's 1968 account of the status of women, *Born Female: The High Cost of Keeping Women Down*. Both editions are in paperback as well as hard cover.

In an earlier book, *The Invisible Scar*, Miss Bird explored the lasting effects of the Great Depression.

In addition to her journalism career, she does a twice-weekly "Personal Report" over radio station WRFM in New York City in which she speaks her mind on a wide range of controversial topics. Miss Bird is Consulting Editor of *New Woman*, a national magazine published for "thinking" women.

Formerly on the staff of *Newsweek* and *Fortune*, she has contributed to virtually all the national magazines over the past twenty years, and was for many years associated with a large New York public relations firm.

In private life she is the wife of author Tom Mahoney, mother of a young son and a married daughter, and a grandmother.

Now THAT we recognize the high price we pay for the feminine mystique that keeps women down, it is easier for us to see the high price we pay for the masculine mystique that keeps women out of the professions. Gloria Steinem put her finger on the most obvious price men pay when she remarked that we would have gotten out of Vietnam quicker if we had had Margaret Mead for president, because she wouldn't have had her masculinity to prove.

The masculine mystique is a suit of armor that keeps the professions from doing what they know they ought to be doing. Physicians know they should treat the patient rather than the disease. Educators are all for teaching the whole child instead of the subject. Lawyers readily admit they should worry less about the rules and more about justice. But talk about these ideals makes established doctors, lawyers and educators as squirmy as a marine at a bridal shower. Nice ideas, of course, but what will they do to professional standards?

To be professional is to be objective, detached, impersonal, authoritative, competitive, stoic, tribal and tough. To be professional, in short, is "to be a man." I believe that suggestions for making professional practice more responsive, more concerned with social welfare, more people-oriented are resisted as soft, effeminate threats to professional "manhood."

It is, of course, this masculine mystique which limits women to 1 per cent of American engineers, 3 per cent of American lawyers, 7 per cent of American doctors, and pitiful minorities even in the helping professions, such as psychiatry, for which the virtues labeled feminine would seem a special qualification.

A mystique is a set of unexamined convictions which enforce conventional behavior and solidarity of the group which shares them. While the term is, strictly speaking, limited to codes like medieval chivalry or patriotism, the cult of masculinism is as arbitrary, as restrictive, and as exclusionary as those true mystiques, the medieval craft mysteries from which our codes of professional conduct are descended. The main purpose of the feminine and the masculine mystiques, of course, is to use sex as a stick and a carrot to get a lot of essential work done.

MEN'S WORK AND WOMEN'S WORK

Talcott Parsons, the Harvard sociologist, teaches that every culture, including the primitive tribes observed by Margaret Mead, assigns men what he calls "instrumental-adaptive" roles and women what he calls "expressive-integrative" roles. Men are "instrumental" or active in doing things to the physical environment, and "adaptive" in making policy for the family, the firm, the nation or the group. By contrast, women are "expressive"—or concerned with registering emotions and "integrating the group." To quote Parsons, women generally manage the "internal motivational tensions of the members of a group and their solidarity with each other." Parsons assumes that this division of labor is written in the very nature of males and females. Whether it is or not—and I tend to think not—it is a good shorthand summary of the sex labels on jobs.

Any work carrying power, prestige or money is earmarked for males, while welfare work is for women. Three other rules also apply: instrumental or mechanical, competitive, outside work is for men; expressive, helping, inside work is for women. Thus engineering, the most masculine profession (only 1 per cent female), is the only one that is literally instrumental and outside. It is thought of as dealing with machinery and the outdoors. (Since this is mystiqueland, the facts don't matter and are simply disbelieved when they don't support the rule: most engineers work indoors; women are better drivers than men; and, according to those who train airline pilots, their reflexes make them better pilot material.) Let's see how these criteria work out in practice.

1. *Profit vs. Welfare.* Because teaching and nursing, the lowest-paid professions, are defined as feminine, there are more women in these professions than in profit-oriented businesses, particularly manufacturing. But they are scarce, too, in

profit-oriented professions, such as investment banking, where the risks and rewards are high.

The United States is one of the few countries in which medicine is essentially a private enterprise, and in no country are physicians relatively so well off. Our doctors head the occupational list in earnings. Unlike physicians in other countries, our doctors have to pay for their expensive education (frequently in the "sweat capital" of working wives) and recoup their investment through fees. Since the feminine mystique discourages women from investing in expensive education, the United States has fewer women doctors than any other developed country.

Money is for men, welfare is for women. The rules apply within the professions. Surgery, the highest-paid (and most mechanical) medical specialty, has the fewest women. Women doctors are more apt than males to go into government service or teaching, less apt than men to be coining money in a plushy private practice. Women lawyers, too, are more apt to work in government or welfare organizations than in the lucrative law "business" of serving big corporations. In poverty law they even violate the outside-for-males rule and go to court. In 1970, seven of the nine women among Shearman & Sterling's 200 lawyers were in trusts and estates, according to a firm recruiter, because "women bring personal warmth to working with widows and orphans." Even in this big, profit-oriented law factory, women found expressive, welfare work to do!

In banking, women do escrow and trust work, the bank's welfare or unrewarding service work, but seldom become loan officers, where money is to be risked and made. Stockbrokers are paid in commissions. If a woman is a partner in a brokerage firm, she is likely to stay "inside" doing the thankless housekeeping of keeping the papers straight while the men go "out" in search of business that will increase their incomes. And so it goes, adding up to a significant pay gap, widening at the higher levels, between the earnings of professional men and professional women.

2. *Instrumental vs. Expressive.* Men gravitate to figuratively instrumental work as well as to machinery. They are interested in the methods, the rules, the theory, rather than the result. "The operation was a success but the patient died." In hospitals, doctors practice "medicine"—an abstract discipline—leaving the care of patients to nurses. Sociology deals with theories of society and methods—recently highly mathematical—for measuring it. Sociologists are mostly male. Social workers do the grubby work of dealing with the people society disadvantages, and most of them are female.

Philosophy, psychology, anthropology and economics are dominated by males who have been concentrating on statistical measures (they're *called* "instruments") and "value-free" theory rather than the rights or wrongs of the situation. Really "in" economists construct elaborate mechanical "models" of the economy, leaving to the laity—among whom professional economists count John Kenneth Galbraith—the political issues involved in who gets the lion's share of the pie. Really "respectable" scientists devote themselves to pursuing "pure" truth by "elegant" methods, and the more useless the more beautiful. It is no accident that the first serious investigation into the feelings of human subjects of medical investigation was made by a woman, Renée C. Fox, now professor of sociology at the University of Pennsylvania.

One of the disqualifications of women for professional status is that they are supposed to have great difficulty in taking the properly impersonal attitude toward the sufferings or feelings of the patient, client or subject. In one of the episodes of the television show "The Young Lawyers," a young woman lawyer has been dropped from the project because "she was trying to prove she loved the client instead of defending him," and is reprimanded by the judge for her inability to control her emotions. A real lawyer isn't supposed to care whether he wins or whether he loses, but only how well he plays the game.

Finally, of course, men in every profession construct the machinery of professional organization. Men administer school systems and make the rules, while women teach the children. No woman doctor has ever been a trustee of the American Medical Association, and no woman doctor is at present serving in the AMA House of Delegates which presides over the "rules" of medical practice in the United States.

3. *Competitive vs. Helping.* The talk of male professionals bristles with military language. Fields of inquiry are "invaded" and "defended" by rival disciplines and rival scholars. Problems are "attacked," "claimed" and "conquered." Truth itself is a prize to be "won," not because it will do any good, but because like the mountain to be climbed, it is "there." Difficulties are a "challenge." And while the male heads of departments in universities pursue the inter- and intradepartmental wars, women instructors and assistant professors teach, advise, coach, encourage and write letters of recommendation for students.

4. *Outside vs. Inside.* Men do what sociologist Jessie Bernard calls the "foreign relations" of the professions. They are the spokesman of an academic discipline with the public or with other professions, and they negotiate with the sources of funds, the clients, the customers, the government, the adversaries or the allies.

In law, men go to court and deal with clients, while women swot up briefs in the back room or become office managers. In many professions, women become the secretaries of the professional associations, or editors of professional news publications, which function to "integrate" the group, while men lobby for the profession with the "outside" authorities and represent it with the general public. The only across-the-board organization of professional bankers is the Women Bankers Association; men bankers are too busy joining civic organizations where business can be encouraged to support a group of their fellows.

Women are so essential as lubricants of male egos that it may be that some women are essential to keep any community from flying apart. American medicine may be flirting with this essential minimum. The most anti-women physicians, for instance, insist that the women already in the profession are all right. They cite useful work women are "better fitted" to do. It's *increasing* the percentage of "hen medics" that they oppose.

PROFESSIONAL TRAINING AS BOOT CAMP

Training for the traditional professions resembles the conditioning by which recruits in an old-fashioned boot camp became soldiers. The program is directed not so much to teaching them facts or skills as it is to inculcating a "professional" rather than a personal attitude to the suffering of a patient or the difficulties of a client; behavior to colleagues, respect for the established professional pecking order.

The ability to work without sleep figures in so many professional training programs that an anthropologist from Mars would compare them with the ordeals imposed on young males in many primitive cultures as the price of initiation into the adult "mysteries." These ordeals and rituals are always confined to males, and according to our anthropologists, expressly designed to exclude women. Even in our supposedly civilized culture, secret societies are male: women are notoriously unable to keep secrets, and would never have invented sororities if fraternities hadn't already existed.

Law clerks, internes, graduate students with teaching fellowships, junior accountants and other young professionals are put through a course of sprouts in an atmosphere as artificially authoritative, rank-conscious and competitive as West

Point. Hospital internes are worked around the clock. Architectural students are given design problems that can't be completed by deadline time unless the whole team works all night. The bigger, the richer, and the more prestigious the law firm, the harder it makes its junior lawyers swot. The ordeal is frankly intended to make "real" doctors, lawyers, architects or scholars out of them. And like primitive puberty ordeals, this training is also intended to prove that they are not women.

What does this do to the handful of women who get into the masculinist professions? In the minds of male professionals, it quite obviously desexes them. Here, in the mind, rather than in the logistics of the professions themselves, lies the well-publicized "conflict" which turns ambitious young women away from legal and medical careers. (The warnings sound a lot like the beating of drums and shouting many primitive men use to keep women away from their "secrets." Sir William Jenner, physician to Queen Victoria, once declared that he would rather follow the bier of his one "dear daughter" to her grave, than see her "go through such a course of study as medicine." She became a woman suffragist.)

Because this is mystiqueland, where hypotheses are self-confirming and premises unexamined, professional leaders assume they are being fair to women in treating them equally— "no special privileges on account of their sex, of course." In 1966, the dean of a leading law school admitted privately that he would admit more women if the big law firms would hire them. The story puzzled Seth Taft, who does recruiting at the important law schools for his firm in Cleveland. "I'd hate to think we're biased against women," he said. "It's just that we don't see many. Well-qualified ones seem to prefer welfare work to the type of practice we have." But after thinking it over a moment, he added, "Of course, our hiring practices do not fit in very well with their lives. We hire all our lawyers right out of law school, and we never hire any part-time. If you want to be a partner in our shop, you have to start young, work longer and harder than the other juniors, and you can't take time out to have babies." And that, of course, was that. Too bad for women. They could be lawyers if they wanted to be, but they'd have to choose between their careers or their sex.

The demand is more explicit in medicine. What American medical schools seem to be saying to women is, "Okay. You can be a doctor, but you have to prove to us that your sex— and the ultimate handicap, childbirth—isn't going to keep you from doing exactly what men do." Medical school deans queried by Harold Kaplan, professor of psychiatry at the New York Medical College, took unashamed pride in the lengths to which their women students went to carry on in spite of pregnancy and childbirth. The Medical School of the University of Texas at Galveston reported that pregnant students typically lost "as little as three days and as much as ten days as a result of childbirth. If this period coincides with scheduled quizzes or examinations, the faculty is invariably considerate in setting up an alternative schedule."

"One year we had three senior women give birth to children during the academic year," the State University of Iowa School of Medicine boasted. "Each of them cleverly arranged to be on the obstetrics service at the time of delivery and thus they claimed they did not miss a single day of school. We do not make any programmatic modification for women medical students with children in our medical school program. However, most of these students deposit their newborn in the metabolism research center where studies are being conducted on the metabolism of newborn infants."

What these deans seem to be saying is, "our women students are *doctors*, not women." By making a woman take an examination the day after she gives birth, they are simply applying to women the conditioning by ordeal which makes men doctors.

Concentrating training in the early twenties fits the life-cycle of men. It's the time when they are most vigorous, when they are marrying and taking on responsibility. Later on, after they've made it in their forties or fifties, they can take it easier, letting a younger generation of doctors, lawyers, accountants, professors do the dirty work which is regarded as character-building. Having been through intensive practice, the older professionals can contribute wisdom instead of sweat.

But does it have to be that way? If the professions were really demasculinized, and if training were really designed to fit the life cycle of women as well as men, provision for all sorts of career paths could be made. Young professionals of both sexes would start out easy and become heavily involved in their forties and fifties, when their children are grown. Since women hold up better physically in middle age than men, this scheme might favor women, whom present conventions leave underengaged during post-childrearing years, when their motivation for professional activity is highest. Experiment with many career pathways would liberate male professionals from the lock-step which prevents them from switching fields, taking time out for creative work or welfare projects, or merely investing less of their energy in the job that is now demanded of them. Men, too, can have the choices supposedly open to liberated women only if they are liberated from the need to prove their masculinity by surviving the ordeals of professional apprenticeship.

Would this lower professional standards? The answer, of course, depends on how you define professional standards. If professional standards are maintaining a stiff upper lip, "cool," devotion to the professional brotherhood, putting procedures ahead of immediate human need, then the answer is yes. But if service to the client or patient or customer, if the best interests of society as a whole, are the criterion, then the answer has to be that demasculinization is essential.

In medicine, at least, we have models. Countries which have a higher proportion of women physicians—and that includes just about all developed countries—offer women medical students at least as much time off for childbirth as we offer medical students of both sexes for illness or disability. Socialist countries safeguard paid maternity leave as a constitutional right. In the USSR, for instance, women doctors and medical students get eight weeks off with pay before the birth of a child and eight weeks after the birth, plus priority for their children in nursery schools and kindergartens. Similar provision for American women would undoubtedly increase the percentage of women in medicine. And as it seems necessary to remind some physicians, children in well-run day-care programs test no better or no worse than children from families with similar backgrounds who are kept at home.

DEMASCULINIZING POLICIES

Demasculinizing the professions would require many structural changes. Accounting firms still have rules against allowing women to travel to client firms with men if the trip requires the team to stay overnight. The presumption must be that women accountants are primarily women, and as such vulnerable to sexual exploitation. The rule appears to have something to do with conventions against drinking on the job or doing anything that could tempt an auditor to fudge the books.

Nepotism rules would have to go, too. The requirement that a woman quit when she marries a man in her work group implies that she does not exercise independent professional judgment or that if she does, disagreement about work will ruin her marriage. Actually, of course, the marital harmony of employees is no more an employer's business than the welfare of the children of woman employees. Policies intended to "protect" the private life of employees are suspect—especially when they are confined to "protecting" family arrangements which are incentive for men employees and disincentive for women. (Men with dependent families are, of course, much easier to manipulate than men with independent families.)

Real demasculinization would make it possible for social workers, research scientists, doctors, lawyers, teachers and other professionals to recognize the many unheralded ways in which they discriminate against the women on whom they practice their professions. Women's Liberation sessions have helped many women professionals to face the bias they have learned from their textbooks and, above all, their professional training. In psychiatry, the protests of women have effectively challenged the Freudian theory of "penis envy."

Women doctors cite unnecessarily rough pelvic examinations ("How is a man to know how the speculum feels in the vagina?"), refusal to perform abortions even where these are legal, and the sadism of inviting women abortion patients to watch the fetus being destroyed. According to Dr. Frances Norris, a Chevy Chase pathologist, male surgeons are so fascinated with the technical "triumph" of radical mastectomy that they prefer the dramatic operation to remedies less mutilating and disabling to women patients. At a cancer conference, one male surgeon admitted that the sex of most surgeons is the reason why "no ovary is good enough to leave in, and no testicle bad enough to take out." Only since Women's Liberation has serious thought been given to developing a *male* contraceptive pill.

Nowhere is the power of mystique more apparent than in the refusal of physicians, supposedly trained to be "objective," to look at evidence which fails to support the traditional nature of women on which their own masculinist professional status so squarely depends. Perceptive surgeons know, from their own experience, that women stand the strain of surgery better than men. Doctors know that women can stand more stress than men. Yet we have phenomena like the incautious public statement of Dr. Edgar F. Berman that women are unfitted to be president of the United States because of meno-pausal "hormonal storms." As one of the many physicians, male as well as female, who corrected him put it, "Anyone old enough to be president of the United States is old enough to have some judgment-impairing disability."

Demasculinizing professional practice is going to take a rough period of soul-searching on the part of women profes-sionals. Women's caucuses in most of the disciplines are work-ing at the job. Lawyers in Women's Liberation groups have launched projects in several law schools aimed at identifying the many different ways in which lawyers, judges, and espe-cially state legislatures assume that all women are family women and so discriminate against the many who are not. They cite laws of residence requiring that a woman follow her husband, state laws that make it hard for a wife to go into business for herself, longer prison sentences for women than men, state labor laws that still undertake to "protect" suppos-edly weak women out of good jobs. Other areas are the private regulations of insurance companies and pension plans. Until recently, for instance, a man could insure his car on the as-sumption that his wife would not drive it, but a woman with a husband whose disability carried premium liability insurance could not insure a car on the assumption that *he* would not drive it.

Many administrative practices are frankly—if uncon-sciously—discriminatory. In some states, for instance, a minor must have a signature of his father on an application for a driver's license; the presumption is that his mother is not financially responsible if she has a husband in residence. Most outrageous of all is the real estate practice of requiring evi-dence that an employed wife of childbearing age is unable to bear children before lending mortgage or purchase money to a couple.

Courses for the study of women in many colleges are under-taking to correct the textbooks. Women sociologists are demanding a change in the rule that the social class of a woman is always based on the social class assigned to her husband. This practice, incidentally, "loses" able women as a population for social research. Less is known about women than men because women of selected characteristics cannot be located directly, much as women have trouble locating their college classmates once they change their names in marriage. Women historians are resurrecting the achievements of women which male chauvinist historians have passed over or ascribed to the men in whose names many of them had to operate. School children do not realize from high-school textbooks that the abolition movement was spearheaded by women, and young women are woefully ignorant of the long, gallant and intelligent battle women suffragists waged to win the vote. Pioneer women are romanticized in television westerns, but the romances do not show the executive and business ability of the able "boss ladies" who rose to the responsibilities of managing sizable properties when widowed or left alone, a fate which was frequent on the frontier and in colonial days.

WHAT WOMEN CAN DO

The price of masculinism is getting too high for the professions to pay. No longer can we afford the ruthlessness, the violence, the withdrawal, the cruelty and the sheer ignorance of fact required to support the masculinist mystique. But how are we going to get rid of it?

It is tempting to suggest that the masculinist mystique will fade away when more women are admitted to the learned professions. But it is not so simple. Mystiques die hard, and the masculinist mystique is not confined to males. As people are fond of saying, "women are their own worst enemies."

The demasculinization of the professions cannot be done, at least singlehandedly, by successful women in them. To be successful in a profession, you have to be over forty, which means that successful professional women of 1971 entered the field at a time when the only avenue to advancement lay in finding some way to take advantage of the mystique. Successful women are sincere in reporting that being a woman helped. What is harder for them to see is that they have had to be "more royalist than the king" in order to avoid suspicion, and that demasculinization would destroy the ecological niche they created for themselves as editor of the *woman's* magazine, president of the *woman's* college, specialist in *women's* diseases, advisor on the *woman's* point of view, or dispenser of the "woman's touch" in the executive suite.

Even harder for successful women professionals to admit is what they have done to themselves. Like the "house niggers," successful women professionals are invariably "house women" who have to conceal from themselves the extent of their humiliation so that anger will not overwhelm them, and so they can escape notice as they slide through the side door of the men's club where the meeting is being held, or pretend not to notice that they weren't invited at all. Professional women are so full of defenses that the sociologist Peter Rossi once advised me to interview them by telephone, at odd moments, before they had time to worry about their public relations.

Many of these women professional leaders staunchly deny, as they must, that they have ever suffered any discrimination at all. I sympathize, because that was my own first reaction when I was asked to do a magazine article on the discrimination against women at work. Many are less than enthusiastic about the Women's Liberation Movement, as well they might be. Where they have succeeded as purveyors of the "woman's point of view," or as "women's women" selling to or supervising women, or as housekeepers keeping the office routines tidy, or as "gimmick women" attracting attention on a sales force, or "token women" representing women as a class in corporations or politics, there is room for only a few, and often only one—to say nothing of the pathetic satisfaction the victimized must take in being the only Jew on the block, or the only black in the office.

The ingenuity of professional women in exploiting the feminine mystique about the nature of women is a tribute to their inventiveness. As an architect for schools, Marion Yahn once told *The Detroit News,* that "it helps to look like just any other mother searching for a kid." A woman customs officer explained her success to another silly newspaper reporter by claiming that "woman's intuition" helped her to catch smugglers.

Women often feminize a job to get it. J. Klatil, the first woman designer assigned to passenger car exteriors at General Motors, confessed that although she signed her sketches with initials in order to get an unbiased judgment on them, she chose for a demonstration design the problem of making a car convenient for a woman shopper. Even Margaret Mead has said, on occasions, that being a woman made it easier for her to win the confidence of primitive women, and over her long career she has won credibility with the American public in family and child-rearing areas regarded as appropriate interests for women.

Successful professional women are full of anecdotes which illustrate how they have turned to masculinism to good account. Anna Rosenberg Hoffman, President Roosevelt's Assistant Secretary of Defense, says that she was able to report on the morale of the troops in World War II because men are more willing to express their feelings to a woman than to a man.

Only 1 percent of the presidents of California's junior colleges are women. One of them is Marie Mills, president of Mt. San Antonio College. She recalls, with amusement, the occasion on which she won a bout with a tough construction union leader noted for his exuberant profanity, because he was so inhibited by her feminine presence that he couldn't say a word.

Many women in journalism have turned the special freedom given to the "woman's angle" to good account. Because there is presumably a "woman's angle" to politics, or to sports, women are imported into these masculine strongholds to discern it. And because the "woman's angle" is regarded as not very important, and in any case opaque to male editors, these "woman's angle" women can often ask simple-minded questions the males are afraid to ask or even get informal interviews denied men. Gloria Steinem is a role model for young women journalists precisely because she has moved beyond the woman's angle toe hold into straight political reporting.

The danger of the advice "to find a woman's job to do" in the professions is that it requires a woman to pretend there is more difference between the sexes than she knows there really is, and so do violence to her own perceptions, if not her real nature. Women hired to sell insurance or airline tickets or automobiles to women know that women buy these products for the same reasons that men buy them. What men regard as the "woman's angle" is not a special feminine way of viewing things, but a freedom from the masculine mystique which condemns men in highly sexist occupations to deny a part of themselves which society erroneously labels "feminine."

The thinking of the automobile industry is a good example. Women imported into policy-making sessions of the automobile companies were expected to say that women were interested in the upholstery colors of cars. When these "woman's angle" women brought up car safety, reliability, and other mundane concerns, they were sometimes told that they weren't "typical" women (if they were, the implication ran, they wouldn't be at the meeting at all). The facts are, of course, that men are as interested as women in the "image" of the automobile, which psychoanalysts say they regard as an extension of their bodies, but they have been barred by masculine bravado from paying public attention to physical hazards. If automobile company executives had paid more attention to the women they hired to give them the "woman's angle," they would not have been so surprised at the widespread support for Ralph Nader's crusade against the automobile.

It is no accident that what Ralph Nader is bringing to the front pages of American newspapers used to appear, in blander form, on the women's page and in home economics courses designed for girls. "Doing good," empathy for the poor and unfortunate, is no longer relegated to the women folk, but is increasingly a concern of men. And the new environmentalists, the new poverty advocates, the new consumerists are not tame men, either. They are giving the lie to the notion that compassion and moral concern is somehow "soft."

The revolt against established authority, against what is increasingly recognized as the hypocrisy (or more objectively, the obsolescence) of the conventional wisdom, is inevitably a war against the sexism which supported it in exactly the same way that racism supported the plantation agricultural system of the nineteenth century South. This is the meaning of the unisex appearance and the unisex concerns of the young rebels. Young women are turning their backs on a family in the suburbs for the same reason that young men are turning their backs on a meaningless 9-to-5 job in a soundproofed executive suite. Sex roles are equally and oppositely coercive. Both are needed to support existing social arrangements.

More needed and just as interesting as the better publicized liberation of women is the liberation of young men from masculinist vocational roles. Welfare is big enough business, has been made big enough "business" by a welfare-oriented society to engage the services of men. Men are going into poverty law, into *pro bono publico* court campaigns. They are not ashamed to teach little children, or home economics courses, or refuse to serve in the armed forces, or admit they would rather make love than war. And by way of protest against the masculinist prods to conformity, they are growing their hair long.

TO A YOUNG WOMAN . . .

Young women entering the professions in the 1970's have some demographic trends going for them. The proportion of women in the professions has been declining since World War II, even as the proportion of women in the labor force has been rising. Women have been getting a raw deal, vocationally speaking: more of them working, fewer getting ahead.

This should change during the next decade. If present trends hold, women will marry later, have fewer children and later in their lives, and most important, an increasing proportion will take less time off for childbearing and child-rearing than in the past. Child care arrangements for all children, whatever their mothers do, are in the wave of the future. And the structure of work itself is changing to permit more part-time work, more off-hour work, varying lengths of work week, and sabbatical years of nonwork or study for professional and technical workers in every field.

Where does the revolt leave young women professionals? Better off, of course, but better off only because all of us are better off. For the short term, it means that a woman of twenty who wants to be a lawyer or a doctor or a college professor had better not follow in the footsteps of the sexist women professionals who are forever being held out as examples of women who made it in a man's world. It's no longer necessary —and hopefully some day it will no longer be possible—to get to the top by accentuating the stereotyped female role.

Changing demography which is putting more women into the labor force for longer periods of their lives means that it is no longer safe for young women to "wait and see" what kind of work they want to do. Sex desegregation of the professions will destroy the comfortable ecological niches created by a floating labor force of women with one foot in unpaid home work and one foot in paid employment. A girl who becomes a dietitian because it's so hard for a woman to become a doctor may find that all the head dietitians are men, too. A woman who ought to be a lawyer won't find it easier going in journalism; several newspapers have already rechristened the "Women's Page" and hired men to cover cooking, home furnishings, education and the areas some sexist newspapers still call the "Woman's World."

Young women in their twenties now need most of all to liberate themselves from vocational coercion. I would like to recommend to them a three-step program:

First: Liberate yourself. Join a consciousness-raising group if there is one handy, or just think about what you do because you're a woman. Undo your conditioning. This is always painful and it has to be done by taking thought and, I'm afraid, by rather compulsive, endless talk. People liberating themselves from conventions are humorous by definition, which is one reason why liberation comes easier in a small, loyal group.

Second: Prove your liberation by doing something about it. Join the National Organization for Women (there's a chapter in every big city). Or join any one of the hundreds of local groups that are working for day-care centers, for abortion reform, for enforcement of equal opportunity laws, for the Equal Rights Amendment that would remove sex differences from laws.

If you're not a joiner, then do something about it on your own. Ask for the better job in your office, reminding your employer that you cannot be denied consideration for promotion on the basis of sex. Help a woman make a complaint against a landlord or an employer who discriminates. If you are in doubt whether legal remedy exists, ask a woman lawyer. And don't get angry if she says she doesn't know. Respect her defenses and ask another woman lawyer.

Third: Choose the work you really want to do, and resist all attempts to sex type yourself in it or let teachers, employers or your clients carve out a feminine niche in it for you. Refuse special favors, but also refuse the demand that you be tried by fire to prove that you are twice as good as a man, or can "rise above" your sex.

This is, of course, easier said than done. It means reconsidering some very attractive job offers. In 1970, for instance, New York was full of schemes for making money on the Women's Liberation Movement. Avoid the "all-girl band" approach lest you be used as a gimmick. It might be better, for instance, to have a few men teaching courses on the status of women if only because that man might learn something new himself.

Ask the sharp question: Does a bank really need a "woman's department"? Does a company need a woman personnel worker in charge of the special problems of women? A special training course for women executives? If they want you to sell dynamos to power·companies, is it because you are knowledgeable about dynamos, or because they think that your sex will get you a hearing denied to most male salesmen? Be careful they don't use you as a gimmick.

Don't fall for a fancy title. It's customary now to call executive secretaries "administrative assistants." Perhaps not with intent to mislead, but simply because young women professionals really expect equal treatment and their bosses are sexist, many young women in finance, in law, are appalled that their job retitled "editor" on the magazine or book company, or "junior executive" is really the old girl Friday job—and sometimes at less than the old girl Friday pay.

When you are looking for a job, ask whether you are filling a job vacated by someone else. If so, what happened to him—or her? If a woman, why was she not promoted within the organization or did she leave, and why?

Don't let them use you as a rate buster. It is tempting to work twice as hard and "show up" the men or "prove" that you can climb the pipes. Don't do it. A great deal of exploitation of women is self-exploitation. Older women tell you how they took on extra work, how they quietly became indispensable. This succeeds, but it confirms sexism.

Don't accept a woman's "role." This may be hard because the men thrusting it upon you aren't necessarily hostile or deliberately trying to oppress you. They are the victims of the same conditioning from which you have liberated yourself. Still, *don't* start taking notes automatically when someone pushes a minute book at you because you are the only woman on the committee. *Don't* undertake to be the ministering angel to a member of the team who is in trouble. *Don't* undertake to go for things or you will become what in the theatrical trade is called a "go for." *Don't* do more than your fair share of the inside, paper-shuffling "homework." Nothing in female anatomy makes it easier for women to do "detail work."

Do insist that you get all the small perquisites that go with your status. Insist on the secretary, the office, the title that goes with the job. You aren't above status symbols.

Don't fall into the sexist language of your own profession. As a journalist, refuse to label the women you report as "beautiful, blond divorcée," or to designate the marital status of women but not men, or describe the clothing of women in the news when you wouldn't describe the clothing of a man.

Accord other women the courtesy of their gender. Speak of a member of Congress as a Congressman or a Congresswoman, whichever the case may be. Committees are headed either by a chairman or a chairwoman. There are spokeswomen as well as spokesmen.

Sex designations are useful but the designation "Ms." to match the male "Mr." is appropriate for the many professional situations in which the marital status of individuals is irrelevant.

Don't take a dead-end job. One smart woman agreed to take a job running the firm's first teletype machine if she were allowed to hire everyone who would be hired to use it. One of the best ways to demonstrate your own ambition is to suggest how a dead-end job offered you could be enlarged.

Don't be afraid to quit. Women have hung on to dead-end jobs for very practical reasons. As long as a woman gets ahead in an organization through some special situation, she has a harder time finding a comparable specialized niche in another organization and so fears to quit. Women also have less bargaining capacity when they are married and geographically limited. But these limitations are lifting. Young husbands have refused to move until or unless suitable jobs can be found in the new community for their wives, and some organizations have been willing to job hunt for the spouse of the person they want to move or hire.

Don't let an employer use childbirth to keep you down. Your private life and what you do with your children is none of his business. Females are subject to disabilities connected with childbearing, males are subject to disabilities connected with hernia, and both should be actuarial possibilities in health insurance coverage, not the basis of assigning work to individual men and women. Ask about maternity leave when you come to work in order to show that you *do* intend to return to work after having a baby, in case you do have a baby. And you might let drop the news that some unions, such as the Newspaper Guild, are negotiating contracts that provide for paternity leave as well as maternity leave, on the premise that the care of small children requires fathers to absent themselves from work as well as mothers.

Do make special efforts to keep in touch with professional colleagues if you plan a leave of absence to have a baby. Before leaving, talk over ways you might stay in touch or return to your field in future, ask for letters of recommendation which may be used in establishing contact elsewhere. If there are a lot of women in this situation in your occupation, college or town, you can organize a keep-in-touch group which will make it possible for women on "home leave" to have stimulating chats with colleagues on the firing line.

Don't overlook the possibilities of part-time work. The American Women's Medical Association has full information on the growing number of hospitals which arrange part-time work for women physicians. Universities often have work that can be farmed out to women professionals on a free-lance basis, even if it is no more than reading papers or taking over a laboratory class once a week. Wherever skills are hard to find, such as in data processing, part-time deals can be struck— even with thoroughly masculinist organizations.

Restructuring of professional career paths is not a concession to women. If it were, it probably wouldn't come as fast. Men need second careers, retraining periods, "lateral careers" (moving sideways to a nearby field instead of up) and recognition of other goals than power, prestige and income. A scientist put out of work by a change in the space program experiences the same difficulty in re-entering his profession that faces a woman who has taken four or five years out to have a baby. In order to retrain, remotivate and place him, you have to restructure work organizations in a way that will help her get back into things, too.

Does this mean that there are no important character differences between men and women? The answer has to be that we don't know what these differences are and, even if there are genetic, anatomical differences, they are subject, as are all other human endowments, to considerable modification.

A great deal of balderdash has been circulated over the past century about the noble qualities of women and the humanizing influence of putting women on committees, in government, and in other policy-making positions. Even today we have respectable social scientists like Erik Erikson who wax lyrical about the nurturing, supportive influence of the "mother instinct." Until women have as much opportunity for crime and misdeeds as men, it is safer to assume that they are not less cruel, but simply less able to practice wholesale cruelty than men.

Women can't humanize the professions by their physical presence in professional practice. As long as business and the professions are dominated by the masculine mystique, female as well as male professionals will be forced to behave in the competitive, "objective" and warlike way required of men. Even if deliberate barriers to women are dropped, more women than men will always refuse to do this violence to themselves, if only because women don't have to do it to prove their sex identification. President Margaret Mead would get us out of Vietnam faster than President Richard Nixon not because she is a compassionate woman, but because she is *not* a man. The difference is the difference between constraint and freedom. In our culture, men become men by doing something —usually something to somebody else—while women become women simply by not doing something. When they do act, as a woman president would be required to act, they are freer of cultural taboo. The fear of where this freedom could lead may be the real reason why many people, male and female, would be uneasy if we had a woman president.

The real question is whether it is useful now—as it may once have been in the hunting or agricultural past—to structure either human character or the division of labor on the basis of sex role. The answer to this has to be that the post-industrial technology offers individuals so many choices that it is no longer necessary to program men and women to specific roles. This means that an increasing proportion of men and women will successfully escape sex typing and many will be encouraged to experiment with new motivations, new professional attitudes, and new ways of being close to other human beings.

Sources of Further Information

Federally Employed Women (FEW). Ms. Daisy Fields, Suite 487, National Press Building, Washington, D.C. 20004

The Feminists; stressing group equality, pro-Lesbian, radical. Jo Ann Gardner, P. O. Box 10197, Pittsburgh, Pa. 15232

The National Organization for Women (NOW), the biggest organization securing political reforms through the power structure. National Office, NOW, 1952 East 73rd St., Chicago, Ill. 60649

The New York Radical Feminists; small, consciousness-raising brigades. Radical Feminists, P. O. Box 621, Old Chelsea Station, New York, N. Y. 10011

Older Women's Liberation (OWL); Marxist, interested in older women's problems. OWL Studio 29, 222 Central Park South, New York, N. Y. 10019

Professional Women's Caucus; enlists professional women to help in fight for women's rights. P. O. Box 1057, Radio City Station, New York, N. Y. 10019

Washington Opportunities for Women (WOW); nonradical and nonpolitical group aiming at finding women part-time work. Christine Nelson, Room 101, Vanguard Building, 1111 20th St. NW, Washington, D.C. 20036

Women's Equity Action League (WEAL); devoted to legal redress of sex inequality. Mrs. Elizabeth Boyer, 7657 Dines Road, Novelty, Ohio. 44072

Ronald Gross is a poet, teacher, editor and social critic best known for his books on school reform: *High School, Radical School Reform, The Arts and the Poor* and *The Teacher and the Taught: Education in Theory and Practice from Plato to Conant*. He is presently assistant professor of social thought at New York University, on leave of absence from his position as vice-president and editor-in-chief of the Academy for Educational Development. He coordinates The Free Learning Project.

Paul Osterman is a doctoral candidate in Urban Studies and City Planning at Massachusetts Institute of Technology. He was formerly special assistant to the president of Brooklyn College, program associate at the Academy for Educational Development, and a New York City school teacher. He is co-editor of *High School* and *Individualism*.